Romans is a mystery. Wright leads us on an exciting journey beyond the veil, into its inner sanctum. Discover how humans are being renewed in glory, creation refreshed, and God honored. As we gaze upon Jesus, our King and High Priest, we discover our true mission and human purposes.

MATTHEW W. BATES, professor of theology, Quincy University

Like a falcon in a dive, Tom Wright takes readers on a majestic and soaring flight through Romans 8, the heart of Paul's letter to the Roman house churches. There's so much to see on atonement, spirit versus flesh, adoption, love, and hope, and Tom does not disappoint with his amazing mix of explanatory insights and easy readability. For many readers, reading this book will be the first time Romans actually makes sense to them.

REV. DR. MICHAEL F. BIRD, deputy principal at
Ridley College, Melbourne, Australia

The greatest biblical theologian of our day offers his mature reflections on arguably the greatest chapter that the apostle Paul ever wrote—what more could we possibly ask for? This book is characteristically brilliant, its vision for the Christian life thoroughly compelling. Yet what sets *Into the Heart of Romans* apart is the care Wright takes, at every turn in his exposition of Paul's argument, to invite readers into the interpretive process. His is truly a summons to a better "Romans Road" than the parody of Paul with which many of us will be familiar. Read and be transformed!

MAX BOTNER, associate professor of biblical studies, Jessup University

Written in a similar tone as his For Everyone series, N. T. Wright's *Into the Heart of Romans* provides a commentary on Romans 8 that can function both as a hermeneutical primer and as an introduction to Paul's theology. From the vantage point of Romans 8, Wright invites readers to see that Paul's letter to the Romans is like a complex city, with intricate networks of districts and streets, being much more elaborate than a short commute down "Romans Road" can convey.

JOHN ANTHONY DUNNE, associate professor of
New Testament, Bethel Seminary

In his engaging, inimitable style, Tom Wright leads us into a profound encounter with one of the most profound chapters of Scripture. Challenging typical interpretations and offering new ones, he helps us see Romans 8 as a call for the church to enter the world's polyvalent pain in sync with the triune God. A much-needed challenge.

MICHAEL J. GORMAN, Raymond E. Brown Chair in Biblical and
Theological Studies, St. Mary's Seminary & University

Tom Wright models the Christian principle: "there's always more to learn from the Bible." Wright has written extensively on Romans, but now offers fresh insight by focusing on chapter 8, a central text bringing together key themes like new covenant, new creation, the love of God, and restored humanity. At first, you'll think you were studying Romans 8, but you'll end up better understanding the whole Bible. This is vintage Wright and will undoubtedly generate robust conversation about the heart of Romans.

NIJAY K. GUPTA, professor of New Testament, Northern Seminary

In *Into the Heart of Romans*, Tom Wright provides a master class in close reading of Scripture. In his fine-grained exposition, Romans 8 becomes a lens through which we can more clearly perceive the larger biblical story of God's design to overcome the power of death and redeem the broken world in and through a transformed people of God; conversely, Wright also shows how that larger story illuminates the logic of Paul's various affirmations within Romans 8. For those who assume that Romans is all about how individuals can have their sins forgiven and go to heaven, this book will come as a shock—and as a stimulus to a richer understanding of the gospel that Paul proclaimed.

RICHARD B. HAYS, George Washington Professor Emeritus of New Testament, Duke University

Vintage Tom Wright! Readers are enabled by Wright's careful guidance to glimpse both a compelling bird's-eye view of Romans 8 and to follow him in a deep dive that illumines the entire story of creation and salvation, highlighting key themes such as justification, glorification, fruitful suffering, and Christology. Especially helpful is Wright's newfound concentration on humanity as "image-bearers" (in continuity with the ancient fathers) and "temple-people" (in continuity with St. Paul himself!). Wright sings in harmony with St. Irenaeus, who also learned from the apostle Paul that "the glory of God is man fully alive."

EDITH HUMPHREY, William F. Orr Professor Emerita of New Testament, Pittsburgh Theological Seminary

This work is Paul's greatest living interpreter on the greatest chapter of Paul's greatest letter. Here Wright deftly elucidates Paul's grand biblical vision—creation, election, exile, new exodus, and new creation—all reworked around the Messiah and the Spirit. Paul's children (interpreters) are hereby liberated from venerable false antitheses and downright misunderstandings into the glory of the macro-theological vision of earliest Christianity's profoundest theologian.

CHRIS KUGLER, research associate, Keble College, Oxford

N. T. Wright has long made it clear that Romans 8 is a text that is dear to his own heart and understanding of Paul. In this book, we encounter Wright as pastor, professor, and scholar. He teaches us how to read a text (as professor), what he discovers in the text (as scholar), and why Paul's message in one of his most significant passages still matters for the church today (as pastor). It was also refreshing to witness Wright model the ability to grow as an exegete revising one's opinion when better readings present themselves. This book is an exemplar of a pastorally and exegetically rich analysis of a dense but rewarding section of Paul's most famous letter.

ESAU MCCAULLEY, associate professor of New Testament, Wheaton College

Having spent his life studying and living the writings of Paul, N. T. Wright offers *Into the Heart of Romans* with his hallmark exultant themes and dense yet conversational prose. With this fresh foray, he teaches readers not only how to understand this chapter but how to read Paul. Excellent for personal study, group discussion, or congregational preaching, he allows those who might feel nervous around such a vital theological chapter to gain their bearings. This book offers not just a detailed map but a personal guide through the intricate pathways of Paul's proclamation. I was led to gratitude for the clarity I gained, wonder at the brilliance of Paul, and praise for the grace of God in the victory of Jesus Christ.

AMY PEELER, Kenneth T. Wessner Chair of Biblical Studies, Wheaton College

Within the field of Pauline scholarship, one would be hard-pressed to name an interpreter more insightful, biblically integrative, or significant than Tom Wright. At the same time, he is also among the most prolific—a sometimes daunting reality for those unfamiliar with Wright and just don't know where to start. But now with this newest book, it's like having Wright as your own driver-guide, leading us through the heart of Paul's thought one manageable block at a time.

NICHOLAS PERRIN, president, Trinity International University

The so-called "Father of Pietism," Philipp Jakob Spener, is often credited for suggesting that if the Bible were a ring and Romans its precious stone, then Romans 8 would be the sparkling point of the jewel. This statement is on clear and brilliant display in this volume as Tom Wright treats Romans 8 with painstaking care and uncommon insight. In *Into the Heart of Romans*, you have a premier Pauline interpreter probing and plumbing the depths of one of the most meaningful and memorable passages the apostle ever composed. "What shall we say then to these things?"

TODD D. STILL, Charles J. and Eleanor McLerran DeLancey
Dean & William M. Hinson Professor of Christian
Scriptures, Baylor University, Truett Seminary

Tom Wright's new book *Into the Heart of Romans* is an exemplary display of scholarly rigor and Christian passion. Tom opens Romans 8 in a way that's both exhilarating and challenging. He shows us that Romans 8 is not a summary of how individuals get to heaven but is a stunning story of how the Father reconciles all creation to himself through the resurrection of His Son and by the power of His Spirit. Both the scholar and lay reader will find this book hard to put down.

PRESTON SPRINKLE, speaker, podcaster, and
New York Times bestselling author

Very few biblical scholars have the ability to distill the complex thought of Paul to any level of discourse so that all of us, including the novice, can begin to grasp the height and depth of Paul's rhetoric. But Tom Wright is that rare scholar who can do so, and in this little book that focuses on perhaps Paul's most moving and eloquent argument found in Romans 8, Tom is able to shed not merely fresh light but surprising light on this chapter. He argues that Paul is referring to the renewal of creation that will transpire at the same time the dead in Christ are raised, and that the believers will play a role when Christ returns in the restoration of all things—not somewhere out there in heaven, but right here on earth. In other words, God the environmentalist is not interested in letting his whole creation go to blazes (literally) in exchange for having some scrawny souls in heaven. No, God the creator wants it all renewed, restored, so there will be a new earth as well as a new heaven. The final destiny of faithful earthlings is not heaven but—wait for it—earth. This is must reading for all those who would know more about Paul's vision of the human future.

BEN WITHERINGTON III, Amos Professor of New Testament
for Doctoral Studies, Asbury Theological Seminary

INTO THE HEART OF ROMANS

A DEEP DIVE INTO PAUL'S GREATEST LETTER

N. T. WRIGHT

ZONDERVAN ACADEMIC

ZONDERVAN ACADEMIC

Into the Heart of Romans
Copyright © 2023 by The Society for Promoting Christian Knowledge. Text by Tom Wright.

Original edition published in English under the title *Into the Heart of Romans: A Deep Dive into Paul's Greatest Letter* by:

The Society for Promoting Christian Knowledge
36 Causton Street
London SW1P 4ST
www.spck.org.uk

Requests for information should be addressed to:
Zondervan, *3900 Sparks Dr. SE, Grand Rapids, Michigan 49546*

Zondervan titles may be purchased in bulk for educational, business, fundraising, or sales promotional use. For information, please email SpecialMarkets@Zondervan.com.

ISBN 978-0-310-15782-3 (audio)

Library of Congress Cataloging-in-Publication Data

Names: Wright, N. T. (Nicholas Thomas), author.
Title: Into the heart of Romans : a deep dive into Paul's greatest letter / N. T. Wright.
Description: Grand Rapids : Zondervan, 2023. | Includes bibliographical references and index.
Identifiers: LCCN 2023015847 (print) | LCCN 2023015848 (ebook) | ISBN 9780310157748 (paperback) | ISBN 9780310157816 (ebook)
Subjects: LCSH: Bible. Romans VIII—Criticism, interpretation, etc. | Bible. Romans—Criticism, interpretation, etc.
Classification: LCC BS2665.52 .W74 2023 (print) | LCC BS2665.52 (ebook) | DDC 227/.106—dc23/eng/20230516
LC record available at https://lccn.loc.gov/2023015847
LC ebook record available at https://lccn.loc.gov/2023015848

Scripture quotations from the New Testament are the author's own translation unless otherwise indicated.

Scripture quotations from the Old Testament are either the author's own translation or are adapted from the New Revised Standard Version of the Bible, Anglicized Edition, copyright © 1989, 1995 by the Division of Christian Education of the National Council of the Churches of Christ in the USA. Used by permission. All rights reserved.

Scripture quotations marked KJV are taken from the King James Version. Public domain.

Scripture quotations marked NIV are taken from The Holy Bible, New International Version®, NIV®. Copyright © 1973, 1978, 1984, 2011 by Biblica, Inc.® Used by permission of Zondervan. All rights reserved worldwide. www.Zondervan.com. The "NIV" and "New International Version" are trademarks registered in the United States Patent and Trademark Office by Biblica, Inc.®

Scripture quotations marked NRSV are taken from the New Revised Standard Version of the Bible, Anglicized Edition, copyright © 1989, 1995 by the Division of Christian Education of the National Council of the Churches of Christ in the USA. Used by permission. All rights reserved.

Scripture quotations marked RSV are taken from the Revised Standard Version of the Bible, copyright © 1946, 1952 and 1971 by the Division of Christian Education of the National Council of the Churches of Christ in the USA. Used by permission. All rights reserved.

Any internet addresses (websites, blogs, etc.) and telephone numbers in this book are offered as a resource. They are not intended in any way to be or imply an endorsement by Zondervan, nor does Zondervan vouch for the content of these sites and numbers for the life of this book.

Cover design: Micah Kandros Design
Cover photo: © Naoki Kim / Shutterstock

Printed in the United States of America
23 24 25 26 27 LBC 5 4 3 2 1

For the Revd Peter R. Rodgers

Contents

N. T. Wright is Research Professor Emeritus of New Testament and Early Christianity at the University of St Andrews, Scotland, and Senior Research Fellow at Wycliffe Hall, Oxford. Prior to that, he was Bishop of Durham (2003–10), Canon Theologian of Westminster (2000–3), Dean of Lichfield (1994–9), Fellow, Tutor and Chaplain of Worcester College, Oxford (1986–93), Assistant Professor of New Testament Language and Literature, McGill University, Montreal, and Honorary Professor, Montreal Diocesan Theological College (1981–6), Fellow and Chaplain of Downing College, Cambridge (1978–81), and Junior Research Fellow, Merton College, Oxford (1975–8).

Professor Wright is the author of more than eighty books, including *The New Testament and the People of God* (1992), *Jesus and the Victory of God* (1994), *The Challenge of Jesus* (2000, 2015), The New Testament for Everyone Commentary Library (18 volumes, 2002–14), *The Resurrection of the Son of God* (2003), *Paul: Fresh Perspectives* (2005), *Scripture and the Authority of God* (2005, 2013), *Evil and the Justice of God* (2006), *Simply Christian* (2006), *Surprised by Hope* (2007), *Justification: God's Plan and Paul's Vision* (2009), *Virtue Reborn* (2010), *Simply Jesus* (2011), *The New Testament for Everyone* (2011), *How God Became King* (2012), *Creation, Power and Truth* (2013), *Paul and the Faithfulness of God* (2013), *Pauline Perspectives* (2013), *Surprised by Scripture* (2014), *Paul and His Recent Interpreters* (2015), *The Paul Debate* (2015), *God in Public* (2016), *The Day the Revolution Began* (2016), *Spiritual and Religious* (2017), *Paul: A Biography* (2018), *The New Testament in Its World* (with Michael F. Bird, 2019), *History and Eschatology* (2019), *Broken Signposts* (2020), *On Earth as in Heaven* (2022), and *The New Testament for Everyone* (3rd edition, 2023).

Preface

The present book offers an in-depth study of what is arguably the greatest chapter in Paul's greatest letter. Romans chapter 8 is exciting and dramatic, but it is also dense and sometimes, to our minds at least, elusive. Some things that were obvious to his first audience are likely to be opaque to us. That is partly because we live a long time later in a different culture. But it's also because our various Christian traditions have conditioned us to expect Paul to say some things which he actually doesn't, and to screen out other themes which were vital for him but which haven't played much of a role in modern Christian thought. The only solution is to take a deeper dive into the detail of the chapter: to take the text apart piece by piece, study each element, and then put it back together again so that we are coming much closer, at least, to hearing what Paul was actually saying. That is what I have tried to do here.

This book owes its longer origin to my lifelong fascination with Romans, from my doctoral studies in the 1970s to several books and articles, notably my commentary in the *New Interpreter's Bible* (2003) and my popular account in *Paul for Everyone: Romans* (2004), and then to several substantial discussions in *Paul and the Faithfulness of God* and its companion volume *Pauline Perspectives* (both 2013). (A complete list of my relevant publications can be found at the back of the book.) But between 2010 and 2020, I found myself working on biblical themes I had not previously thought through, particularly to do with the Temple-theme and its retrieval by the early Christians, and also the early Christian emphasis on Jesus as the image-bearing human being, as in Genesis 1 and Psalm 8. In this, I was spurred on by some of my doctoral students, two of whom, Chris Kugler and Haley Goranson Jacob, worked specifically in these areas and challenged me to rethink some of my previous readings. So, too, did my old friends Brian Walsh and Sylvia Keesmaat, in private conversations and in their book *Romans Disarmed* (2019). All this, to my surprise, has nudged me into quite a different reading of Romans 8 from the one I grew up with, which is still reflected in the commentaries from twenty years or so ago. I hope the new points of view will commend themselves to readers, however much of a shift in mindset this may require for some.

The only way fully to engage with Paul is to read his original Greek. But since this will be out of reach for many readers, I have provided the transliterated Greek text, in parallel to my own English translation (*The New Testament for Everyone* (2011; revised edition, 2023). Those without any Greek should ideally have at least two or three English translations to hand so that they can sense how tricky it often is to catch Paul's nuances. No single English translation – certainly not my own! – can do justice to all his hints and allusions.

One feature of this book may make it a useful manual for further study of other passages in Paul and beyond. In each of the expository chapters, I have asked three questions. First, what does the paragraph itself, in its opening and closing, signal as its main theme? Second, how do Paul's small connecting words ('for', 'because', 'but' and so on) reveal his underlying train of thought? Paul's sentences are almost never just random ideas, one after another; they form logical arguments, indicating the deeper structure of his thought and of the gospel itself. Third, what contexts in Paul's wider world, either his Jewish world or the larger greco-roman world where he worked, would provide the natural resonances for what he says? This is a much bigger area than we can pursue in detail here, but some starting-points will be vital.

Here, as in some other work, I follow the practice of using a small 's' for 'spirit', including the holy spirit. The tradition of using capitals to signal divinity (which in any case only works in English!) was not an option for Paul. It is good to be reminded that what he said about the *pneuma* had to make its way in a world where many philosophers used the word in a variety of senses. I have followed the same practice with 'father' as referring to God, for similar reasons.

The present book began as a series of lectures in the autumn of 2021 at Wycliffe Hall, Oxford, which has become my academic home once more after a gap of fifty years. I am very grateful to the Principal, Dr Michael Lloyd, and to his colleagues and their students for their support, and also to the Friends of Wycliffe Hall whose help has enabled me to join in the congenial, prayerful, friendly and highly intelligent life of the Hall. I then enlarged and developed the material a bit for lectures in June 2022 at Truett Seminary in Waco, Texas, whose President, Dr Todd Still, created another wonderfully welcoming setting, while other old friends, Carey and Leanne Newman, looked after me magnificently in their home. The Truett lectures were also coordinated by the team from the Wisconsin Center for Christian Studies, led by Dr David Seemuth, who organize the courses at <www.ntwrightonline.org>, including the one which will provide an online version of the present book.

To my publishers, and particularly Philip Law at SPCK and Katya Covrett at Zondervan Academic, I owe the usual gratitude for advice and help in matters great and small. To my family, and especially my beloved wife Maggie, my debt increases with every passing year and with every further book. The dedication reflects another lifelong friendship. Peter Rodgers studied alongside me in Oxford in the 1970s and has remained, through the years and across the miles, encouraging and prayerful, a constant conversation partner, exegetically alert and pastorally wise.

Tom Wright
Wycliffe Hall, Oxford

1
Romans 8 in Context

In January 2000, my family and I moved to central London. I knew London slightly already. I knew the British Museum, St Paul's Cathedral and the Tower of London. I knew Buckingham Palace, the Houses of Parliament, Westminster Abbey. I could get from one mainline railway station to another. I could find my way to the really important places such as Lord's Cricket Ground. So I wasn't entirely clueless. But until I lived there, I didn't know how all these places joined up, or how to get to and fro between them. Travelling by the Underground, as I usually did, gives you no sense of geography. Underground trains are a bit like the wind in John chapter 3: you hear the sound they make, but you can't tell where they come from or where they go to.

But once we went to live there, I relished making the connections. I used to walk miles, discovering how it all fitted together. And I marvelled at how the London taxi-drivers knew their way in the vast and complex system. They scorn GPS systems. They become living, breathing maps. They train by spending two years walking round everywhere, memorizing, taking notes, figuring out the one-way systems and short cuts, until it becomes second nature. Brain scans have shown that taxi-drivers' brains actually change shape through that process. The hippocampus enlarges as spatial awareness is enhanced.

Many Christians feel about Paul's letter to the Romans like I used to feel about London. I suspect that most people who pick up a book such as the present one know at least a few

1

key passages. Obvious ones might include Romans 3.23 ('all sinned, and fell short of God's glory'); 5.1 (in the well-known King James Version, this reads 'being justified by faith, we have peace with God'); and 8.28, which is normally though wrongly translated as 'all things work together for good to those who love God'. Most, I hope, will know 8.39, which the late Queen Elizabeth II valued so highly that she commissioned a musical setting of it to be premiered at her own funeral: 'Nothing can separate us from the love of God in the Messiah Jesus our Lord.' I would like to think that many practising Christians know 12.2, Paul's command to 'be transformed by the renewing of your minds'. Many will be aware that Paul's doctrine of justification by faith is rooted in Romans 3. Many may recall that there is a centuries-old puzzle about whether Romans 7 refers to the Christian or the non-Christian, struggling with sin. And so on.

But how many, I wonder, know how these key passages join up? Or do we, as it were, travel by Underground, from one detached verse or passage to the next? How many of us could find our way to and fro above ground, on foot? If a younger Christian, perhaps a friend from church, came and said, 'I've been reading Romans, and I can't make head nor tail of it', how many would know where to begin?

Part of the reason for studying Romans intensively, as we will be doing in this book (focusing on its extraordinary central chapter), rather than just glancing at it and taking it for granted, is that the church as a whole needs, if I can put it this way, biblical taxi-drivers: people who have spent serious time walking around, street by street, learning key buildings and landmarks and knowing how to get to them, or past them to somewhere else. The church, not least for the sake of its mission to the world, urgently needs leaders, both clergy and lay, who fall in love with the great city we call scripture, and want to get to know it much better and to help others find their way wisely around it. We need people whose minds and hearts have been transformed by this amazing book. We need people whose biblical hippocampi have been enlarged, whose theological spatial awareness has been heightened. It's one thing to say, as many do, that we believe in 'the inspiration and authority of scripture'. That can be like saying, simply, 'Oh, I've got a city map in the car, so I'll find my way.' No self-respecting London taxi-driver would be content with that.

One of the fascinating things about Paul's letter to the Romans is that it is not only a vital part of scripture in its own right. It offers guidance on reading all the rest as well, Old and New Testaments alike. It doesn't cover everything, but it covers a lot. And, within Romans, chapter 8, by common consent, is one of the most spectacular pieces of early Christian writing. It is the very heart of Romans – and, with that, it has a claim to be near the heart of what the Bible, and Christianity itself, is all about.

The overall thrust of chapter 8 is clear, but its detailed argument is complex. It weaves a dense but wonderful tapestry of major biblical and theological themes. Romans 8 is about God the father; about Christology; about the spirit; about Jesus' Messiahship, cross, resurrection and ascension; it's about salvation, resurrection, redemption and adoption (which, by the way, are not just vague ways of saying the same thing); it's about suffering and glory and prayer and love. It's about holiness and hope. It's about the call to become genuine human beings through being filled with God's own life. It holds together the various categories theologians have sometimes sketched, such as 'covenant' and 'apocalyptic', or indeed 'justification' and 'being in Christ'. Romans 8 draws together Genesis and Exodus, the Psalms and Isaiah. And from the high peak of Romans 8 we can gaze ahead and glimpse the final chapters of Revelation as well.

Romans 8 is all these things because it is the climactic argument for what preachers call **assurance**: the conviction that 'nothing in all creation can separate us from God's love in Messiah Jesus our Lord'. But this assurance comes as the climax of the actual argument Paul has carefully constructed. It is not simply a detached aspirational dream. What's more, the argument Paul has constructed does not map well on to the normal topics that preachers, teachers and theologians have imagined since the Middle Ages, and especially since the Reformation of the sixteenth century. Rest assured: everything the Reformers were anxious to safeguard is here. But (as many devout scholars have recognized over the last generation or so) the argument belongs within a larger framework, somewhat different from the set of mediaeval questions that the Reformers were addressing. Recognizing this shift is, in fact, part of following the Reformers' own insights, that scripture itself must arbitrate over all traditions, our own included. (This is more complicated than it sounds; I have spelled out what I think it means in my book *Scripture and the Authority of God*.) Problems arise when one particular strand of church teaching or tradition labels itself as 'biblical', but without necessarily getting to the heart of what the Bible actually says. That, I fear, has often happened, not least in relation to the reading of Romans. The task of each generation of scripture students, I believe, ought to be to go deeper still into the God-given text itself and allow it to speak afresh.

All this means, as we shall see, that we need to pay special and careful attention to what precisely Paul is saying here. One way or another, this chapter is a city that every follower of Jesus ought to get to know. Those with whom you share in group Bible studies, or one-to-one fellowship sessions, those to whom you preach or with whom you minister, need you to get to know it. So my aim in this short but intensive study is to introduce the key landmarks, and the roads and footpaths that link them up.

For the moment, we're going to take a helicopter-view, getting an overall picture of the terrain. Once we've done that, we will be going down on the street, notebook in hand, walking verse by verse through Romans 8 until, please God, our spiritual and theological hippocampi have indeed grown to meet the challenge. My hope is that this will sharpen readers' taste for the detailed study of scripture which should be a lifelong delight, branching out from Romans 8 to the letter as a whole, and from there to the whole larger city of which Romans itself is one central part.

As we begin this journey, I need to issue three 'trigger warnings'. They are closely linked, but it may help to set them out as separate items.

First, Romans has regularly been read as a book whose primary, or even sole, topic is 'me and my salvation'. Many readers will be familiar with the old idea of the 'Romans Road', as used by many evangelists and counsellors to get people to follow a particular narrative through which they may be led to faith. The narrative in question goes like this:

1 I'm a sinner, deserving God's wrath;
2 Jesus died for my sins;
3 I believe in Jesus;
4 I will go to heaven.

Now let me be clear: I would much rather people believed that narrative than that they were atheists. But – rather as with the taxi-drivers who learn early on that the way across town is more complicated and interesting than they might at first have thought – the actual Romans Road is much bigger than, and significantly different from, that scheme.

The problem Paul is addressing, you see, is not just human sin and the danger of eternal punishment. The problem is the crisis of the whole cosmos, within which human beings were from the start designed to play a vital role. Here in chapter 8, at the climax of the letter so far, Paul says that the whole creation will be rescued from its groaning, sorrow and chaos when humans are raised from the dead to take proper charge of it. Salvation is not just God's gift *to* his people, it is God's gift *through* his people. That theme has regularly been ignored – with drastic results. So the first warning is that Romans tells a bigger story, a somewhat different story from the one many have been taught.

This leads to the second trigger warning, which makes a more specific point. For hundreds of years, Christians have told their story with a key element missing. The key element in question is the calling and subsequent story of Israel. Not long ago I saw a book in which the author made a great deal out of saying that we need to understand the *story* of scripture. Yes indeed, I thought – but when I looked inside the book the story I found there went like this:

1 God made the world;
2 humans sinned;
3 God sent Jesus;
4 that's OK then.

(This is, as you will see, quite like the 'Romans Road' narrative we just glanced at.) But telling the *biblical* story like that leaves a big hole in the middle: what about God's call of Israel? What about the long story from (if you like) Abraham to John the Baptist? What's happened to the Old Testament – which Paul insists is foundational for the gospel (Romans 1.2; 1 Corinthians 15.3–6)?

At that point, a great many Christians, through many generations and across many traditions, have said, in effect: 'Well, God had a first shot at rescuing people, giving them the law and all that – but it didn't work. So he had to scrap that plan and try quite a different way, pushing the Israel plan to one side and sending Jesus instead. Or, if you like, pushing the "law" plan to one side and looking for "faith" instead.' Some theologians still try to force through that kind of story. But this ends up reducing the Old Testament to a book of distant 'types', 'figures' and oblique detached prophecies. They then naturally have to distort the New Testament as well to fit – since the New Testament itself picks up the main Old Testament themes and celebrates their fulfilment, not their abrogation.

People do indeed sometimes imagine that if the New Testament were focused on the Jewish people and their hopes, its message would become irrelevant for gentiles from that day to this (including, of course, most Christians). Whole schemes of thought, of interpretation of Paul in particular, have been built up on that supposition. But if we want to understand Paul we can't be content with such an idea. The way Paul saw things (as we shall see more fully in a moment), God's purpose for Israel always was the focal point, and the intended means, of God's purpose for the whole world. God's plan to put the world right began with the call of Abraham, and focused on the covenant which God made with him. And when Abraham's people sinned, as God knew they would (since they were themselves children of Adam and Eve), God *did not scrap the plan*. He didn't change his mind. The covenant required a faithful Israelite, and that is what God provided in the person of Jesus, Israel's Messiah. This line of thought is, in fact, basic to the first four chapters of Romans, though you wouldn't know it from many expositions.

You see – and this will be important as we go forward into chapter 8 of Romans – the word *Christos* is not just a proper name. It means 'the anointed one', the Messiah who sums up Israel's vocation and destiny in himself. Jesus accomplishes, dramatically, shockingly, apocalyptically even, what the covenant with Israel has all along intended to achieve. So we mustn't be surprised that the story of Israel is woven into Paul's story of salvation all through, not least in Romans 8. This may make some things more complicated than many readers are used to. But that's like what happens when you walk the actual streets and lanes of London instead of avoiding them by using the Underground. Things become a lot more complicated, but you are much more likely to understand how the city actually works. When we factor the 'Israel' dimension back into Romans, we begin to grasp the larger story of salvation in its entirety. We get to see the plan of God from start to finish.

So, with a deep breath, to the third trigger warning, which is again linked with the previous two. We have got our story of salvation upside down. Ever since the early Middle Ages at least, most Christians have supposed that the point of the Christian gospel was to enable saved human 'souls' to go up to 'heaven'.[1] We've read Romans, not least Romans 8, in that way: when Paul says, at the climax of the chapter (verse 30), 'those he justified, them he also glorified', we have assumed that this means 'Justified sinners will go to heaven'.

But that isn't what 'glorified' meant for Paul. He never once mentions 'going to heaven', here or elsewhere.[2] The eternal security of God's people in the New Testament has

---

1 See Peter Brown, *The Ransom of the Soul: Afterlife and Wealth in Early Western Christianity* (Cambridge, MA: Harvard University Press, 2015).

2 On the meaning of 2 Cor. 5.1–5, Phil. 3.20 and similar texts, see my *RSG* and *SH* (acronyms used for my published works are listed in the Bibliography).

to do, not with their supposed disembodied post-mortem bliss, but with their resurrection from the dead into the rescued and renewed creation where they will have a truly human role to play. The story the Bible tells – Old and New Testaments alike – is about God creating a world in which he intends to come and live with his human creatures. The Bible ends, after all, not with saved souls going up to heaven but with the new Jerusalem coming down to earth, so that 'the dwelling of God is with humans' (Revelation 21.3). God's 'glory' comes to dwell in the Tabernacle in Exodus 40, in the Temple in 1 Kings 8, and now in Jesus himself and, by the spirit, in Jesus' followers. This gives them the 'glory' spoken of in Psalm 8, which is the restored human authority over the world. Paul says exactly that in, for instance, Romans 5.17, anticipating the larger exposition of chapter 8. The reason why God rescues humans from sin and death is so that they can take their proper place in the renewal of creation, the new world in which he will himself come to live, to be at home.

Thus, here in Romans 8, we see the incarnation of God's son, and the indwelling of God's spirit, dealing with sin and leading people to the promised inheritance. But the 'inheritance' of which Paul speaks here isn't 'heaven'. To repeat, 'heaven' is not mentioned in this chapter. The Messiah's 'inheritance', shared with all his people, is the whole redeemed creation, with forgiven sinners raised from the dead to share in ruling that new world.

This third point, in particular, will take some getting used to. But it makes much better sense of Romans 8 than the normal reading. And once you allow it to settle down in your reading of the whole Bible, it will make more sense overall than you could imagine. And with that, we need to begin our deep dive into the text of Romans 8.

Romans 8: The Shape and Theme

If, then, you flew slowly over Romans in a helicopter, what would you see as you passed above chapter 8? What are its main districts and buildings, and how do they link up?

It's comparatively easy to sketch the main divisions within the chapter – and that's always a good thing to start with, even if first impressions need to be modified later on. Verses 1 to 11 form a decisive and celebratory introduction. At the other end, verses 31 to 39 are, obviously, a decisive and celebratory conclusion. Those two great statements then frame the long middle passage, verses 12 to 30. Within that section, there is a clear transition at verse 17: verses 12 to 16 focus on the spirit and sonship, and verses 18 to 27 speak of suffering and glory. This all leads to the triumphant conclusion of verses 29 and 30, a conclusion not just to chapter 8 but to the whole of Romans so far: 'Those he foreordained, he also called; those he called he also justified; those he justified he also glorified.' This gives to verses 31 to 39 the feel of a musical coda, celebrating where we've now got to in high rhetorical style. So the main divisions are verses 1 to 11; verses 12 to 17; then, with 17 functioning as a bridge, verses 17 to 30; and then verses 31 to 39.

So what are these sections all about? As I said, Romans 8 is the chapter of *assurance*. From the dramatic opening ('there is therefore now no condemnation for those in Messiah Jesus') to the triumphant conclusion ('nothing in all creation can separate us from God's love in the Messiah Jesus') the chapter is designed to say to anxious Christians, and especially to Christians suffering and/or being persecuted, that their ultimate future salvation (rescue from death itself in the new creation) is rock-solid secure. It is guaranteed by the work of the Messiah himself (his death, resurrection, ascension and continuing intercession) and by the work of the holy spirit, leading Jesus' people in the path of holiness and enabling them to share in God's rescuing work through the prayer which, inspired by the spirit, arises from the midst of suffering.[3]

This all works at several levels. The little communities of Jesus-followers, not least in Rome itself, were regularly under threat. They often suffered violence or deprivation because they flouted social, cultural and not least religious norms. Within ten years of the Christians in Rome hearing this letter, Nero was making them scapegoats for the great fire of AD 64. Romans 8 is almost like a prophetic warning, coupled with the assurance: suffering is coming, but God's unbreakable love will hold you tight. But of course the argument functions at the broader, more general level. Followers of Jesus often find themselves becoming anxious that, even though they have believed in Jesus and been baptized, they still face the final judgment of which Paul had spoken in Romans chapter 2, and some might suppose that this could still go against them. Paul assures them that the verdict is already known in advance. 'It is God who justifies,' he writes; 'so who is to condemn?'

So the three main sections of the chapter balance out. Verses 1–11: there is no condemnation – because of the Messiah's death and the spirit's life-giving power. Verses 31–9: there is no condemnation – because nothing can separate us from God's love displayed in the death, resurrection and ascension of his son. In between, verses 12–30 explain that the spirit provides not only the assurance of sonship and inheritance, even when we are caught up in the groaning of all creation, but also the present mode of the God-given human vocation. By the spirit, redeemed humans have a decisive role to play

---

3 The reason why I write 'spirit' rather than 'Spirit' is explained in the Preface.

within God's purposes. Thus in verses 1 to 11, and 31 to 39, Paul appeals to the *objective reality* of the death, resurrection and ascension of the son and the gift of the spirit. And in verses 12 to 30 he displays the *subjective reality* of the work of the spirit, conforming believers to the image, and especially to the death, of the son, and thereby giving humans the dignity – the 'glory'! – of God's image-bearers, sharing in his project of new creation.

This is of course an oversimplification. That's inevitable at this stage. We will be filling in the details later on. But it gives us a sense of how the whole chapter works. God's salvation – that is, the ultimate rescue from death itself into new bodily life in the new creation – is assured because of the work of the son and the spirit, both *for* us and *in* us. And also, not least – though this is regularly forgotten – *through* us: through our sharing in the Messiah's sufferings and in the groaning of the spirit, which play a vital role in God's overall purposes. Romans 8 provides a dramatically Trinitarian view of salvation and the human calling.

That calling, then, is focused here on verses 12 to 30. Those who are 'in the Messiah', assured of God's unbreakable love, are called in the present time to be the place where, and the means by which, his glory is paradoxically revealed, in action, in the world. The assurance we are given in the whole chapter is needed not simply because we might worry about our final state, but because we are called specifically to go through the dark valley of suffering, one way or another, as part of the same overall divine purpose. As Paul says in verse 18, we share the sufferings of the Messiah in order that we may be glorified with him. We will explore that in considerably more detail later on. If Romans 8 is the heart of Romans, this passage about suffering and prayer is the dark but vital heart of the chapter.

Romans 8 within Romans as a Whole

Once we see how Romans 8 works as a whole, we can get at least an outline sense of how these themes draw together many strands of thought from the letter so far. Romans is like a symphony in four movements, each with its own integrity but also with multiple links to the other parts. It is full of interlocking lines of thought, not least through its complex invoking of scripture. The four movements are clear: chapters 1—4, then 5—8, then 9—11, then 12—16.

The argument is cumulative, so that our passage, chapter 8, is the conclusion to its own 'movement', chapters 5—8, and also to the whole first half of the letter, chapters 1—8. With that, it also forms the platform for the second half of the book. Our chapter is thus not a free-standing discussion of a detached topic. It means what it means within the larger flow of the letter. But it nevertheless has its own integrity, its own particular point to make, and that is what we are studying here.

Romans is above all a letter about *God*. That may sound obvious, but actually the Greek word for 'God', *theos*, occurs far more, in proportion to the letter as a whole, than anywhere else in Paul or indeed the rest of the New Testament. It would be well worth following this up in more detail, working through the different things Paul says here about God and how they all hang together – a task for which Romans 8 provides plenty of help. Paul then takes a deep breath before launching into the theme of God's faithfulness in chapters 9—11 and the God of hope in chapters 12—16, both of which are vital themes for the Roman church – and ourselves, to this day – to work through.

In particular, chapter 8 brings into sharp focus the theme Paul stated in 1.16–17: the gospel of God reveals God's **righteousness**. Here we face a well-known problem. The Greek word which used to be translated 'righteousness', *dikaiosynē*, carries a complex range of interlocking meanings, which the English term doesn't convey in today's world. Paul, as so often, follows scripture closely, and in his Greek Bible the word *dikaiosynē* and its cognates regularly translated the Hebrew *tsedaqah* and its cognates. The irony, for us, is that many people now assume that God's 'justice' and God's 'love' are radically different (supposing, for instance, that God's justice would make him punish us but that his love would find a way not to do so after all); whereas in the Old Testament the two go closely together. When the Bible speaks of God's justice, it is talking about the creator's utter determination, faced with his creation in a mess, to put it all right. When it speaks of God's love, it is talking about the creator entering into a 'covenant', a close personal relationship, with his people – *as the means by which he will put the world right.* Paul draws on this combined meaning, explaining throughout this letter how God has been faithful to his covenant and how that covenant faithfulness is the means by which he is putting the world right. That is what the divine love was bound to intend, and what, as Paul here explains, he has done in the central gospel events. We might sum this up in Johannine language: God so loved his world that he determined to put it right. And, again as in John, so in Paul: the way God has done and is doing this is through Jesus and the spirit – as the decisive accomplishment towards which, as we see in retrospect like the two disciples on the road to Emmaus, the whole story of Israel had been pointing.

All this enables us to understand the famous doctrine of justification, which Paul lays out in Romans. It isn't just about sinners discovering that they can be personally 'put right with God' and thus go to heaven. Personal reconciliation with God remains central, but it is itself part of the larger project which Romans 8 brings gloriously into focus in its picture of the renewal of all creation. Here's how it works.

God has promised in scripture (not least in Isaiah and the Psalms) to put the whole world right. Through the gospel (the events concerning Jesus, and their announcement in the power of the holy spirit) he puts humans right – *so that they can be part of his putting-right project for the world*. God always intended to work in his world *through* his image-bearing creatures, and this now comes into clear focus. That's why the assurance of ultimate salvation, which is what Romans 8 is all about, *contains within itself* that stunning passage of *vocation* in verses 12 to 30, which describes how, by the spirit, we are drawn into the suffering of the Messiah and, through that, into the paradoxically glorious task of praying to God the father at the place where the world is in pain.

So Romans 8, celebrating God's unshakeable love, at one level completes the whole letter so far, explaining more about how justification works out. But at another level it completes the more specific train of thought that began in chapter 5, which is about *the way in which justified humans are called to be shaped by, and to share in, God's ongoing work of new creation.* Paul's shorthand for this – to say it again – is 'glory'. Redeemed humans, like the Temple, are to be filled with the divine glory, and thereby to be set in authority over the world as the genuine humans they are becoming. Being 'glorified' means, simultaneously, being filled with God's own personal presence and power by the spirit, and being enabled to exercise the vocation of genuine, image-bearing human beings. 'Conformed to the image of the son' is how Paul sums this up in verse 29. This theme of 'glory', anticipated in Romans 2.7, 10, then stated firmly at 5.2, returns powerfully in chapter 8, binding the whole section together.

The call to be genuine human beings – to be 'glorified' in the two senses I just mentioned – has often been played down or even ignored. The powerful theme of God's saving and transforming grace, which sweeps through Romans like a rushing mighty wind, has sometimes led readers to suppose that we humans remain passive throughout the story of salvation. Romans 8 has often been read in that way: we are assured of salvation, the spirit enables us to live in God's way, and God will see us through any intermediate suffering. But that misses out the vital middle stage – that those who are declared to be in the right, to be God's people, are *the renewed humans*, the people God had in mind when creating his image-bearing creatures in the first place, the people who now, in the present age, have a decisive role to play in the coming to birth of the new creation. As we saw, God always intended to work in the world *through* human beings: that's part of the point of the 'image' in Genesis 1.26. That purpose, gloriously fulfilled in the ultimate Image, the man Jesus himself, is now shared with his people by the spirit.

This is all anticipated in the vocation of Israel itself. As I have explained elsewhere, and as many ancient Jewish readers of scripture had long realized, God called Abraham to undo the sin of Adam. Adam and Eve were told to be fruitful and multiply and look after God's garden; Abraham and Sarah are promised that God will make them fruitful (despite their old age) and give them a land (despite their presently being wandering nomads). This promise of the land had already been extended, in the Psalms and Isaiah particularly, to include the whole world – as Paul says in Romans 4.13. And the promises about the family had already been similarly extended to include all the other nations. Paul believed – and explained in detail in several places – that all these promises had come true in Israel's Messiah, the Jesus of Nazareth whose public declaration as 'son of God', through his resurrection, was the very heart of the gospel (Romans 1.3–5). Jesus is thus the rightful *kyrios*, 'lord', of the whole world. This remains a *Jewish* and *biblical* idea – that Israel's Messiah would be the rightful lord of the world. It didn't need 'translating' into non-Jewish terms to be relevant – uncomfortably relevant, of course! – to the world which already had other 'lords', Caesar in particular.

Those great biblical promises might have seemed, up to the time of Jesus, to have failed. Deuteronomy had warned that Israel would rebel against God and suffer the consequences, namely the decimation of the people and exile from the land. That is part of the point of Romans 7: Israel, left to itself, appears to have failed, and with that the promises themselves are called into question. But in Romans 8, Paul picks up what he had already said in 5.12–21: those who are 'in Christ', part of the Messiah's renewed people, will 'reign in life' (5.17). They will receive the 'inheritance' of the new creation. They will be the ones through whom God's purposes for his world, to be put into effect through obedient humans, will come true at last. *And that vocation begins here and now, albeit in the paradoxical form of sharing the Messiah's suffering and intercession.*

In order to prepare the way for our detailed study of Romans 8 itself, we need to stand back and look at these large themes, which draw together, in this remarkable chapter, a good deal of biblical theology as a whole. Reversing the move with which we began, we need to look back from the individual streets and lanes and remind ourselves of the larger city to which they belong.

New Creation, New Image, New Covenant

The city in question – the plan of the creator God as set out in Israel's scriptures and then by the early Christians – is **new creation**, with *renewed humans* looking after it. The whole chapter of Romans 8 offers, as we've said, the *assurance* of ultimate salvation. But salvation means rescue; the rescue in question is rescue from death and all that leads to it; rescue from death means *bodily resurrection*; and Paul declares that the resurrection of God's people is itself to be the means of the whole creation being saved from its slavery to decay. Humans were made to be God's agents within his world; that is part of what it means to be made in God's image. Until humans can take up this role, the world will remain unredeemed. Thus, the resurrection of God's people is what the whole world is waiting for (8.19–21). We are saved, not *from* the world but *for* the world.

This human vocation – to be the renewed people of God, through whom creation will be given its long-awaited freedom – has already become a reality through the work of the Messiah and the spirit. The 'glory' promised to humans in Psalm 8 ('crowned with glory and honour, with all things under their feet') has already been realized in Jesus. It now constitutes a key element in the present human vocation.

This theme comes as a surprise to people who have long been used to reading Romans 8 somewhat differently. As we saw, in the popular imagination Romans 8 is about God's people going safely to heaven at last. Correcting this oversimplification isn't simply a matter of adding a second stage to post-mortem existence, with the resurrection as 'life *after* "life after death"'. That is vital, but we need to fill in the picture by considering the *purpose* at which this rescue is aimed. We are to be rescued from sin, and from death itself, so that, as the book of Revelation insists, we can be the 'royal priesthood', God's image-bearing vicegerents, interceding for the world and ruling wisely over it as humans were always meant to do.[4] That will be the moment when, and the means by which, creation itself will be liberated from its slavery to decay, to gain the freedom that comes when God's children are glorified. And at the heart of Romans 8, we discover that this genuinely

---

4 See Rev. 1.6; 5.10; 20.6.

human vocation begins already in the present, manifesting itself paradoxically in the prayer that arises out of suffering.

To put it another way, God made humans in his own image so that they could reflect God's wisdom and life-giving rule into his creation. For that, they need to be raised from the dead to take up their ruling responsibilities in the new creation. The problem of sin isn't just that we become guilty and deserve God's wrath. It is that we fail to be effective God-reflectors, with the consequence that God's good creation falls into corruption and decay. Paul is not a Platonist. To leave this world and go to 'heaven' – the standard Platonic hope of his day, and of ours too! – would be to deny the ultimate goodness of creation itself. No. Creation itself is to be redeemed; and the means to that redemption is the rescue and re-embodiment of human beings. And if, as Paul has argued in Romans 6, baptized and believing Christians are already resurrection-people, enlivened by the holy spirit, then this work has already begun. What this means in practice takes us to the heart of Romans 8, particularly verses 18 to 30.

But if the major theme underlying Romans 8 is therefore God's promised new creation (with humans being rescued from sin and death to play a vital role within it), we should remind ourselves that in scripture new *creation* is always the result of the new *covenant*. Israel's scriptures, not least in the way some of Paul's contemporaries were understanding them, looked beyond the disaster of the exile in Babylon to a time of rescue and renewal. Classic texts such as Isaiah 40—55 pointed the way: God would return to Jerusalem (Isaiah chapters 40 and 52), dealing with the sins of his people (chapter 53), thereby renewing the covenant (chapter 54) and finally all creation (chapter 55). The back story and template for all such rescue and renewal remained the story of the exodus – the story which, ever since Jesus' own choice of Passover as the moment for his decisive kingdom-bringing work, remained central to early Christian understanding. Romans 8 is a central example of that 'new exodus' theme in early Christian reflection.

Here's how it works. The book of Exodus sets out dramatically God's rescue of Israel from slavery, his giving of the law (Torah) on Mount Sinai, and his coming to dwell gloriously in their midst in the newly constructed Tabernacle. As has sometimes been pointed out, the making, and divine filling, of the Tabernacle is really the climax of the whole Genesis–Exodus story. It's like a new creation: a micro-world where God wants to come and dwell. This is why God rescued his people from Egypt, because he could not come and dwell in that land of idols. And this is why he gave the people the law: not, as so often in Christian imagination, to give them a ladder of good works to climb up to heaven, but to make them into the people in whose midst he might indeed come and live.

This whole complex Exodus story answers, in principle, the two questions left hanging at the end of Genesis. Genesis tells the story of God's good and purposeful creation, entrusted to the image-bearing humans to manage; of how God's image-bearers went wrong, dragging the good creation back towards chaos; and of how God responded by establishing his covenant with Abraham. But, at the end of Genesis, Abraham's family are in exile in Egypt – an exile which will descend into slavery before God steps in to reverse it. Exodus answers the immediate covenantal question: God rescues Abraham's family from slavery and leads them towards the promised land. But the second, underlying question looks past the covenant to God's purposes for creation as a whole. *God will put right the problem of Genesis 3—11 by coming to dwell with his human creatures and thereby rescuing and renewing his whole creation.* When the Tabernacle is constructed, and God comes to dwell in it (Exodus 40), this is the sign and foretaste of the new creation itself, the world which God intends to fill with his glorious presence (Isaiah 11.9). The people of the renewed *covenant* are thus called to be, in their Torah-directed and Tabernacle-focused life, the small working model of new *creation*. God gives Israel the Torah to prepare for his coming to dwell in their midst. God then does indeed dwell in their midst as the sign of his intention to fill all creation with his glorious presence. These Exodus-based themes are vital for understanding Romans 8.

To see how this works, think in more detail through the earlier parts of Paul's letter to Rome. In Romans 3.21—4.25, Paul argued that God had been faithful to the covenant promises made to Abraham. He had fulfilled those promises by calling into being, through the Messiah, a worldwide family whose sins were forgiven. So he can now argue, in chapters 5—8 as a whole but particularly in chapter 8, that the new exodus is under way *as the means by which the new genesis is to be achieved.*

This shows where many readers have gone wrong. Much Christian tradition has assumed that the exodus-language is, at best, a distant pointer to the theme of rescuing humans *from* the world (by taking them to 'heaven'). That is not how the scriptural narrative works – the narrative that Paul is following through. Paul believed that Jesus had accomplished the true, ultimate exodus. God had come to dwell in the midst of his people, in and as a true image-bearing human, in order *both* to renew the covenant *and* thereby to renew the whole creation. And God was now dwelling, by his spirit, in the hearts and lives of his people, to implement exactly this project. God promised Abraham, says Paul, that he would inherit not just the promised land but the whole world (4.13). That promise is reinforced in scripture through the promises made to the Messiah, in Psalm 2 and elsewhere, promises of a worldwide rule. That is the basis for the church's mission, which is the purpose of its whole life. Thus through this new exodus, the work of Messiah and spirit, God renews the covenant, rescuing humans in order that creation itself may be rescued and restored. That is the logic of Romans 1—8.

After all, as I have said before and argued in detail elsewhere, in Genesis, and in much subsequent Jewish thought, the purpose of the covenant itself always was the renewal of creation. *God called Abraham to undo the sin of Adam and its effects.* God commanded Adam, 'Be fruitful and multiply, and look after the garden.' But he then promised Abraham, 'I will make you fruitful and multiply you, and give you the land of Canaan.' That's what is then accomplished through the exodus – God rescuing Israel from slavery, leading them to the promised inheritance by his indwelling presence. But Canaan was just a first stage, a forward-looking signpost. The whole world is now in view. That is then spelled out in Romans 8.18–28: creation itself will be redeemed. *And redeemed humans will be in charge of it.* That – and not 'going to heaven' – is the vocation of the Messiah's people.

Reflect for a moment on the role of human beings within this plan – something Christians today don't often talk much about, but which the early Christians took for granted. In Romans 5.17, and then in chapter 8, those who receive the gift of covenant membership *will reign in life.* That is the human vocation, the image-bearing vocation, highlighted then in Romans 8.18–30. We are, says Paul in 8.29, to be 'conformed to the image of God's son, so that he might be the firstborn among a large family'. Paul is resonating with Psalm 8, which celebrates the human vocation to be 'crowned with glory and honour' with all things put under their feet – the vocation fulfilled in Jesus *and now shared with Jesus' people.* To recapitulate what we said earlier about justification, God has promised to put the whole world right, and through the gospel he puts men and women right so that they can be, here and now and also hereafter, part of his putting-right project for the world. Justification and justice go closely together.

But the present 'reign' or 'rule' or 'glory' of God's rescued people is paradoxical. It involves suffering. The intercession which God's people offer in their capacity as the Royal Priesthood – the intercession that stands at the climax of chapter 8 – is prayer in the dark, where faithful and God-loving people are praying for they know not what. If we think of the present Christian life as being shaped by the eschatological principle of 'now and not yet' – something that is *already* true and something that is *not yet* true – then the prayer of which Paul speaks in 8.26–7 joins together the 'already' truth, that God is working his purpose in the world *through* his spirit-filled people, and the 'not yet' truth that we, filled with the spirit to pray 'Abba, father', *do not yet know how to pray as we ought*, and have to rely on the spirit deep within us to intercede with inarticulate groanings.

Let's probe a little further into this idea of new exodus in Romans 5—8. It's all too easy for us to 'hear' a passage like this, about the spirit, sonship, inheritance and so on, in terms simply of 'me and my salvation' or 'me and my spirituality'. But that's like walking round an art gallery wearing tinted spectacles so that you can only see one or two colours. You need the whole biblical picture – not simply as an 'illustration' of our salvation or spirituality, but as its necessary depth and meaning.

Think how the exodus story works, and watch how Paul retrieves it. Exodus, as we saw, has three moments: liberation from slavery, the giving of Torah on Sinai, and the coming of the divine glory to dwell in the Tabernacle, to lead the people to their inheritance. Paul follows this sequence. In Romans 6 the enslaved sinners come through the water of baptism into the Messiah and find freedom. Then the Israelites come to Sinai, where they are given the Torah – which promises life but warns of death. In Romans 7, Paul describes the coming of the law and its sad effects, all the way to exile. But then God deals with the people's sin, and comes in person to dwell within them in the Tabernacle. In Romans 8, Paul explains that what Torah could not do, God has done in the Messiah's death and the gift of the spirit. The spirit now dwells within Jesus' people, as in the wilderness Tabernacle, to give them the life the law had promised.

The glorious divine presence, given in Exodus 40, then leads the people of Israel to their promised inheritance, even though at various points they are tempted to go back to Egypt. In the same way, Paul declares (8.12–17) that the spirit is leading Jesus' followers to their inheritance, which (to say it again because it's so easy to flick back into 'normal' understandings!) is not 'heaven' but rather the whole renewed creation – and he therefore warns against any tendency to go back to slavery. The point is that *the whole world is now God's holy land.* Spirit-led Jesus-followers are to bring God's healing love to his world through their own sharing in the way of the cross, their suffering and their prayer. That is the dark heart of the passage, in 8.18–27, which we will get to in due course. This too echoes the exodus: the groaning of all creation, *and* of the church, *and then even* of the spirit, echoes the 'groaning' of the Israelites in their slavery, with God hearing, remembering the covenant and taking action.

Romans 8: True Humanity, True Divinity

Romans 8 thus holds out before us a rich vision of what it means to be human, and an even richer vision of who God himself really is. We will see this more fully as we go on, but it may be helpful to state it briefly here in advance.

Start with the astonishing double meaning of 'glorification'. 'Glory' here, as often in Paul, really means 'dignity' or 'worth' – the 'worth' being the vocation to be a genuine human being. But this glory is of course God's own glory. Just as the glorious divine presence indwelt the Tabernacle, to lead the people to their inheritance, so the spirit truly indwells God's people, making them already people of 'glory' even if (as Paul says in 2 Corinthians 3 and 4) this often seems deeply paradoxical. On the other hand, renewed humans receive the 'glory' of which Psalm 8 speaks: the human vocation is to be 'crowned with glory and honour' (the promise Paul had held out already in Romans 2.7–10) so as to rule God's renewed creation on his behalf. The 'glory' is therefore *both* the living presence of God within us *and* the genuine God-reflecting humanness that results. And of course this is no accident. This is what humans were made for, to find their own fulfilment in being God-reflectors. Irenaeus was right: the glory of God is a human fully alive, and truly human life consists in the vision of God.

The spirit thus constitutes Jesus' followers, corporately and individually, as *Temple-people*, places where God comes to dwell, points of overlap between heaven and earth. The wilderness Tabernacle and the Jerusalem Temple were signposts pointing ahead to the renewal of all creation. So now, because of Jesus and the spirit, Jesus' followers are called to be that kind of signpost, small working models of new creation, and hence active agents in the *present* renewal which anticipates God's ultimate new creation. In Romans 8, this means holiness and hope, suffering and prayer – not to undermine assurance and celebration, but to show how they work out in practice.

Within this framework of new creation and new covenant, then, in which humans are renewed to be genuine image-bearers within God's world, we find, looming up like a vast mountain out of the mist of exegetical detail, one of the greatest ever statements, from any period of theological history, of what became known as the doctrine of the Trinity. The father sends the son and the spirit to do 'what the law could not do', and to lead Jesus' followers to their inheritance. In the present time, the spirit groans within the inarticulate prayer of the church and of all creation – and God the father listens and knows the mind of the spirit. The church is thereby conformed to the image of the son. This is all about God's love, the Messiah's love, and – by the spirit – our love for God in return. That's what 'covenant' is all about. Paul does not, of course, use the word 'Trinity'. But this chapter embodies, in rich argument, appeal and celebration, the truth which later acquired that label.

Welcome, then, to the astonishing and multi-layered world of Romans 8. This is the very heart of the letter. New creation; new covenant; genuine humanness; the loving triune God. This is the city we are now going to explore, street by street. If studied prayerfully and carefully, this chapter will enlarge our minds and hearts, so that we can both enjoy the place for ourselves and, as and when we are called, become sure guides to lead others also into its life-giving secrets.

2

Romans 8.1–4: No Condemnation

So, therefore, there is now no condemnation for those in the Messiah, Jesus!
²Why not? Because the law of the spirit of life in the Messiah, Jesus, released you from the law of sin and death.

  ³For God has done what the law (being weak because of human flesh) was incapable of doing. God sent his own son in the likeness of sinful flesh, and as a sin-offering; and, right there in the flesh, he condemned sin.
⁴This was in order that the right and proper verdict of the law could be fulfilled in us, as we live not according to the flesh but according to the spirit.

Ouden ara nyn katakrima tois en Christō Iēsou.

²ho gar nomos tou pneumatos tēs zōēs en Christō Iēsou eleutherōsen se apo tou nomou tēs hamartias kai tou thanatou.
³to gar adynaton tou nomou en hō ēsthenei dia tēs sarkos, ho theos ton heautou hyion pempsas en homoiōmati sarkos hamartias kai peri hamartias katekrinen tēn hamartian en tē sarki,

⁴hina to dikaiōma tou nomou plērōthē en hēmin tois mē kata sarka peripatousin alla kata pneuma.

'So, therefore, there is now no condemnation for those in the Messiah, Jesus!' That splendid affirmation, launching us into the detail of the extraordinary chapter we call Romans 8, is right up there with the famous John 3.16, 'God so loved the world that he gave his only son.' Having surveyed the chapter from above, we are now down on the street, walking through the city district by district, getting to know the main buildings and the streets and lanes that link them up.

As we saw, the first main section of chapter 8 runs to verse 11, arriving at the ringing promise of bodily resurrection. We will delay the gratification of exploring that argument till the next chapter of the present book, because verses 5–11 stand firmly on top of verses 1–4; and those four vital opening verses, our present topic, demand more than a little care and concentration. Paul here holds together several central and living truths of the faith in a tight, dense bunch.

To help us as we plunge in, let me introduce the three basic rules for understanding any Pauline text. (As I said in the Preface, I assume that anyone reading this book is either able to read Paul's Greek or is willing to use at least two English translations. I have supplied opposite a transliterated Greek text and my own translation.)

The first rule for understanding any Pauline text – whether it's a verse, a paragraph, a chapter or a whole letter! – is this: **Take care to discover the main overall thrust.** Don't be distracted by important but secondary elements, however significant they appear in relation to all kinds of interesting theological discussions. Paul is well aware of what we might call the inner workings of his arguments, but he regularly draws together the threads of a paragraph or chapter in his opening and closing statements. That is where we should look first, to get our bearings. In the present case, as I just noted, we can look from verse 1 all the way down to verse 11: there is no condemnation . . . because God's indwelling spirit will accomplish our bodily resurrection. But the same principle works in shorter passages, too; and in the first four verses of the chapter, our present topic, we find that the affirmation of verse 1 ('no condemnation') is picked up in verse 4: there is no condemnation . . . because *the law's intention* (which was to give life, as Paul had said in 7.10) *is fulfilled through the Spirit*. That is in fact an initial statement of the same point that we find in 8.9–11: the spirit gives the life which the law could not. This is the main affirmation of these first four verses, anticipating that fuller statement: the spirit fulfils the law's life-giving intention and therefore there is no condemnation.

How has this come about? Clearly, through the work of the Messiah and the spirit. There is no condemnation for those 'in Messiah Jesus', because the spirit is doing law-fulfilling work (verse 2), and because sin itself has been condemned in the Messiah's death (verse 3). We thus have an initial sense of these four verses: 'no condemnation', because of the cross and the spirit.

That gives us a starting-point. But here, as usual with Paul, there are many other things going on as well. To get deeper, we need the other two rules.

The second rule for careful exegesis is more mechanical, but it works time and again. **Pay close attention to Paul's connecting words** – words such as *kai* ('and'), *de* ('but'), *gar* ('for'), *hina* ('in order that'), *ara* ('so then'), *oun* ('therefore') and so on. As with all translation, the Greek and English may not always match exactly. A word in one language – even a small conjunction! – may well not carry all the implications of its nearest equivalent in another language. But we have to do the best we can. Paul doesn't throw these little words around at random. Watch how he regularly argues: a string of *gars*, as in the present passage, means that he is digging more deeply into a particular truth (A happens *because of* B; B is so *because of* C and so on); then, when he's gone deep enough, he builds back up with a sequence of *de* ('but', in the logical sense of '*but if* that's so, then it follows that . . .'). That's how he gets to verse 11 with a triumphant *ei de* – 'but if that is the case, then it follows that . . .'. There then follows the QED of the whole paragraph.

Verses 1–4, and then 1–11 as a whole, thus offer classic examples of how Paul frequently structures his arguments. His sentences are not independent affirmations of distantly related points. They explore, with great precision, the logical inter-relation of the many-layered truth he is expounding. And it's the little connecting words that show us how that interrelation works.

The third rule is to **think into the first-century perspective**. People often say, 'Well, Paul may have written X, but what he *really* meant was Y', producing an anachronistic paraphrase – as though we have to help poor old Paul to articulate, a bit more clearly, what he really intended. (Some scholars have taken this pseudo-method to a wholly different level, suggesting that at times we can see what Paul *ought* to have said, if his argument was going to 'work' in the way we think it should, thus enabling us to correct – theologically! – what he actually says in the light of what (we think) he really meant. That kind of arrogance has no place in serious exegesis.[1]) No:

---

1 See the discussion of *Sachkritik* in *PRI*, p. 33.

the aim of all exegesis ought to be to get to the point where we can say, stand *here* (in the first-century world of a well-taught Jewish thinker); look at things like *this*; and then you'll see that he has in fact said exactly what he meant. *We* don't have to help *Paul* to get it right. We have to allow him to go on teasing us until *we* see *his* point, allowing the bits of the jigsaw to fall finally into place.

Of course, the question of 'What this means for us today' hasn't gone away. That is often what drives people to say 'What Paul *really* meant . . ?, hoping thereby to 'translate' what Paul actually wrote into something that preachers or teachers imagine will be meaningful for their audiences. This happens partly because Paul, quite often, is not actually addressing the questions with which contemporary readers come. When people reach too hastily for the 'so what?' question they will therefore often mishear what Paul is really saying. This puts the exegete, focused above all on Paul's original meaning, in a similar position to that of Jesus in the fourth gospel, constantly appearing to answer, not the question that had been asked, but the one that was hiding unrecognized behind it. Thus, in our present passage, Paul writes some very tightly packed sentences about the law: the law of the spirit of life, the law of sin and death, what the law could not do, the proper verdict of the law and so on. People today, unless they are thinking their way carefully into Paul's own world, will be puzzled. What does he mean by 'law'? How does that fit with our assumptions? Why is that so important for him? Most people today, hearing the word 'law', will think of the laws of their land; or, if they are familiar with older theological discussions, they may think of 'the law' as a strict God-given moral code (perhaps the one given on Sinai) by which all humans are to be judged – and which, many have supposed, was then abolished by Jesus. But when we get inside Paul's first-century Jewish world, things are significantly different. It is within that difference that we find the heart of his explanation of why 'there is now no condemnation for those in the Messiah, Jesus'.

This is one of those places, in fact, where what I said in the introductory chapter (about deficient ways of telling the biblical story) really comes home. If we have forgotten that the biblical story is focused for much of its journey on Abraham's physical family – in Paul's day, the Jewish people – we will be unprepared for the Israel-dimension, *and hence the Torah-dimension*, of Paul's key arguments. In Romans 7, we are clearly dealing with the law, the Torah – which was widely understood, not just as an abstract moral code, but as the covenant charter for God's people. It has been all too easy, from early days in the church, for people to sweep aside that Jewish perspective. Now we have the gospel, people have supposed, we don't need to bother about the law! But that was never Paul's view.

This plays back into the other question we raised earlier, the idea that, in order to make the gospel 'relevant' for non-Jews, Paul might have had to translate it into non-Jewish, that is, gentile, categories and terminology. Not so. The gospel was the news that the world was now under new lordship: a deeply Jewish message *for* the world, scandalous of course but (as Paul discovered) powerful. Thus, in order to understand the 'therefore' at the start of Romans 8, we need to do business with what Paul says about the law in chapter 7. That means understanding, in a brief form at least, the way he saw the whole story of Israel. Thus the point at which we might think, 'Why should I bother with all this complex stuff about the law?' is the point at which we are tempted to step off the narrow pathway of genuinely biblical thought and life, and settle for something less demanding, less biblical, less focused in fact on Israel's Messiah, Jesus.

Reading Romans 8.1–4: The Framework

With these warnings and encouragements to persevere with the details, let's read verses 1–4.

We apply the first rule of exegesis: the start and finish. Verse 1, 'there is now no condemnation'; verse 4a, 'the proper verdict of the law is fulfilled in us.' That is the real conclusion. The second half of verse 4 ('as we live not according to the flesh but according to the spirit') qualifies that statement, looking ahead to verses 5–8; but we should be clear that the concluding punchline of verses 1–4 is 'the law's verdict is fulfilled'. In other words, joining together the start with the finish: the law is *fulfilled* . . . so that is why there is no condemnation! Of course, we haven't yet enquired what precisely Paul means by this rather dense formulation, but we can already see that this is how verses 1–4 are meant to work.

One point, though, follows at once. Many Christians have supposed that Paul's line of thought runs like this: the law condemns us as law-breakers; but in Jesus' death God declared that the law was now wrong, irrelevant, demonic or otherwise redundant; therefore it is set aside, and there is no condemnation. This view owes much of its force to the sixteenth-century protestant reaction against the perceived heavy-handed and hell-threatening Roman Catholic moralism of the time. Sometimes Romans 10.4 (often translated as 'Christ is the end of the law') is quoted in support, though that is not at all what Paul meant there. This idea of the law as a moralist's charter now abolished by the gospel has little to do with what Paul is saying.[2]

So to the second rule of exegesis: pay attention to the little connecting words. Why is there no condemnation (verse 1)?

---

2 On Paul's view of the law, see the full treatment in *PFG*, ch. 10.

Because – *gar* – the law of the spirit of life has released you from the law of sin and death (verse 2). Why is *that* the case? How has that been accomplished? *For* – another *gar* – God has done what the law couldn't do (verse 3). He has done two things, the first being the basis for the second:

 1 the death of his son (verse 3)
 2 the work of the spirit (verse 4).

The *hina* ('in order that') at the start of verse 4 shows that the latter (the work of the spirit) is the *purpose* of the former (Jesus' death).

Now in a sense that is enough. There's plenty there, we might think, without all the fiddly stuff about the law in verse 2 in particular. We might rest content with the outline instructions: like a car driver knowing that you put petrol in here, you press a button there, and off you go. But we study Paul (to change my metaphors) partly to train as mechanics, to fix cars that have broken down, our own and those of others. And, sadly, western theology has regularly broken down at precisely this point. What Paul says here about the law is more complex than we have usually allowed. And in that complexity we will find further riches, often ignored, of his understanding of God's purposes.

A rather obvious clue comes in the opening of verse 1: *therefore!* The little word *ara* (properly, 'so then') tells us that there is a close logical connection in Paul's mind with what's just gone before. This brings us to one of the oldest clichés in the exegete's book: *when you see a 'therefore', ask what it's there for*. This 'therefore' at the start of Romans 8 is a well-known puzzle. In a sense, it's where we should have begun. It implies that Romans 8.1–11 is the *conclusion* to a longer argument, not the start of a completely new one.

But the 'therefore' here seems, at first sight, singularly misplaced. After all, Romans 7 ends in frustration or even apparent despair. The 'miserable person' cries out in 7.24, 'Who is going to rescue me from the body of this death?' Paul does indeed answer in 7.25a: 'Thank God, through Jesus our Messiah and Lord!' But the last half-verse of chapter 7 (7.25b), declares sorrowfully that 'left to my own self I am enslaved to God's law with my mind, but to sin's law with my human flesh'. So how can he go on at once to say that *therefore* there is no condemnation for those in the Messiah?

To answer this, we need to step back into Romans 7 itself. Only then will we see how the flow of Romans 8.1–4, and particularly Paul's dense statements about the law, actually work.

Interlude: Romans 7 as the Build-Up to Romans 8

Romans 7 has long puzzled readers. Who is this mysterious – and indeed miserable! – 'I'? The pre-Christian Saul? Paul as he now is? Or who? And – our particular question at this moment – how does the vivid and depressing description of this 'I', particularly at the end of chapter 7, enable Paul to say immediately afterwards that there is *therefore* now no condemnation for the Messiah's people?

We need to clarify four points. Each could be defended and explained at length, but we must be brief.

First, the whole chapter, Romans 7, is about the law – the Jewish law, the Mosaic Torah. The Greek word for 'law' is *nomos*. Don't be fooled by translations that lose their nerve and, in some verses, translate *nomos* as 'principle' or something like that. In the letter so far, Paul has said many striking and strange things about the law. This is where he explains how they all fit together, and how the larger picture then works.

After the opening illustration (7.1–3), Paul states concisely the point he makes in Galatians and elsewhere: that belonging to the crucified Messiah involves a break with Torah (7.4–6). But this, like several one-liners earlier in the letter, appears to cast Torah itself in a bad light. So Paul writes the next nineteen verses to clarify what's going on – as well as thereby advancing his overall argument. Those who have come to Romans 6—8 in search of a 'theology of the Christian life', and who have then struggled to understand who the subject of chapter 7 might be, have ignored what Paul is actually talking about. And, again, if people say (as they might), 'But questions about the Jewish law cannot be relevant to us today', they are simply revealing their unwillingness to follow Paul's own train of thought, and, with that, their unreadiness to engage with the fully biblical theology he will then expound.

The key passage (7.7–25) is framed by two questions: 'Is the law sin?' (7.7) and 'Was the good [law] responsible for my death?' (7.13). The answer to the first is: no, but 'Sin' *used* the good law to bring death. To the second the answer is: no, but Torah brought 'Sin' out in its full colours through the moral confusion of those who were wanting to follow it.

The first answer (7.8–12) is in the past tense: Paul is speaking of the past event of Torah's arrival in Israel. The second answer (7.13–19) is in the present tense, referring to the ongoing situation of 'Israel according to the flesh'. This then leads him to the conclusion (7.20–5): what he 'finds' about the law ('finds' in the sense of 'discovers as a result of this enquiry') is that it appears to split into two, just as he had said in 7.10. Torah promised life, but could only bring about death, because the material it was working on was the 'flesh' in which 'Sin' had taken up residence. This has had the effect of making Torah apparently do two opposite things (7.22–3). And that in turn anticipates the antithesis of 8.2, to which we shall presently come.

We should remind ourselves that for a Jew like Paul 'the law' – the *Torah* – was far more than just the Ten Commandments. It was the whole 'five books', the Pentateuch from Genesis to Deuteronomy. That was, and is, the bedrock of all Jewish life: its foundation, its covenant charter. If we imagine that 'law' simply means a moral code – as many readers of Romans have done – we will miss much of the point.

Second, 7.7–25 is telling the story of Israel in relation to the law. The character Paul refers to as 'I' is the whole people of Israel, from before the giving of the law, through that moment and on to Paul's own day. This rhetorical device of the 'I' enables Paul to tell this large, complex story as his own – which indeed it is, albeit seen now in retrospect – rather than distancing himself from the problem, and from the people of Israel, by saying 'they' or 'them'. One important result of this is that we would be mistaken to probe the chapter for elements of 'Paul's spiritual autobiography'. That's not the point. Paul is not describing 'his own experience' as such. It is his *present* analysis – from his position 'in the Messiah' – of his *previous* historical and theological position.

To ask about Torah is ultimately to ask about Israel as a whole. Torah was given to Israel; so if we want to see how it 'worked out in practice', Israel's story, in the Pentateuch and the subsequent historical and prophetic books, is the place to look. But there's a wrinkle here that we need to iron out. As we saw earlier, in Romans 6—8 as a whole, Paul is following the sequence of Exodus: crossing the Red Sea (chapter 6), arriving at Sinai (chapter 7), then, with God dwelling in the midst, being led to the inheritance (chapter 8). Within that, however, Paul knows that the Mosaic law itself contained, towards the end, a prophetic narrative for the whole of Israel's history. Among his favourite parts of the Pentateuch are the closing chapters of Deuteronomy, which focus particularly on the covenant blessings and curses of chapter 28, and which warn that Israel, faced with the choice of life and death, is going to choose the path of rebellion, idolatry and death. The ultimate curse – reflecting that of Adam and Eve in Genesis 3 – is exile. Adam and Eve were expelled from the garden near the start of the Pentateuch; Deuteronomy, near its end, mirrors this with the chilling warning that idolatry and injustice will bring about Israel's expulsion from the promised land.

So when Paul brings us, within the overall Exodus-story of Romans 6—8, to the giving of the law on Mount Sinai ('when the commandment arrived', 7.9), that allows him to display for a moment the full sweep of history which the law disclosed in the warnings and prophecies of Deuteronomy 28 and 32. Precisely by loyally clinging to the covenant charter, Paul finds himself (in his earlier life as a devout Pharisee) caught between the vocation to obey Torah and the fact that Jews, like everybody else, are 'in Adam' – in other words, that they share the 'sinful flesh' that is common to all humans. Torah insists upon, and highlights, both.

The result, then, is a dramatic *bifurcation* in Torah itself – which, again, will be vital for 8.1–4. Torah remains God's law, holy and just and good. It really does promise 'life' (7.10). *And in 8.1–11, Paul will show how this promise is dramatically fulfilled through the Messiah and the spirit.* But where Torah goes to work on 'sinful flesh' it is bound to produce death. And the 'death' takes precisely the form of 'exile' – exile from the garden (Adam), from the Land (Israel) and now from life itself. One regular word for 'exile' in the Greek version of Israel's scriptures was *aichmalōtos* and its cognates (as, for instance, in Deuteronomy 28.41; 32.42 and many passages in the Psalms and the Prophets).[3] This didn't simply mean 'captive' or even 'prisoner of war', as in most translations of 7.23. It meant actual exile, 'the Exile', as we call it, consisting of Israel living under pagan rule, a condition which most Jews of Paul's day, following the prophecy of Daniel 9, believed was still continuing.[4] Thus, *within* the overall story of 'new exodus' in Romans 6, 7 and 8, Paul has inserted the smaller but highly significant story of Israel-living-with-Torah, the Torah which promised life but which was bound to condemn Adamic Israel. *And in 8.3, Paul will show how, just as the Torah's promise of life is fulfilled through the spirit, this warning of condemnation likewise comes to its fulfilment, in God's action through the Messiah's death.*

Third, these verses are telling the story of Israel in such a way as to show how Israel has re-enacted the sin of Adam. This is exactly what we should expect from 5.20, where Paul had said (in his usual dense fashion) that 'the law came in alongside so that the trespass might abound'. The 'trespass' there was Adam's. Romans 5.20 insists that, when the Mosaic Torah arrived, it resulted in that primal transgression being amplified, filled out to its full extent.

This provides the answer to the question many non-Jewish readers, then and now, might well be asking at this point: but I'm a gentile! What has this complicated story of Israel got to do with me? That is where this third point comes in: *Paul is emphasizing that Israel's failure, foreseen in Torah itself, has re-enacted, and brought into sharp focus, the sin of Adam*; in other words, how the problem facing the whole human race, then and now, became focused, within God's strange purposes, on this one people. The Christian message must not bypass the

---

3 Obvious examples: Ezek. 40.1; Ps. 126.[LXX 125.]1, which begins, 'When YHWH turned again the captivity of Israel', where the LXX renders *shibat*, 'captivity', as *aichmalōsia*; also in v. 4.

4 See *PFG*, ch. 2.

story of Israel, though tragically that has often enough been done. This whole theme, actually (of Israel's story as the focal point of the larger human story), is woven into Romans at several points, emerging sharply as we noted at 5.20. We see this particularly in the way Paul's description of sin deceiving him and killing him (7.11) echoes the story of Adam, Eve and the serpent.

The problem of chapter 7, in fact, was that Israel was itself composed of Adamic humans; and all that Torah could do with Adamic humanity was to produce more sin and death. Thus it had been when Torah first arrived in Israel, with Moses coming down the mountain to behold Aaron and the people cavorting around the golden calf. Torah's only proper response to such pagan idolatry was to condemn it.

But in this passage, we begin to see the point. God's plan to rescue the human race (and thereby the whole creation) was focused on Israel; Israel found itself in the same plight as all other people; but, as Paul says in verse 13, all this happened in the divine purposes in order to draw 'sin' on to one place, and to show it up in its true colours. The repeated *hina* ('in order that') in verse 13 expresses the strange divine purpose in giving Torah: in other words, even the point about Torah appearing to make sin 'very sinful indeed' had the positive purpose of preparing for the climactic and decisive moment when God would condemn it once and for all (8.3). The Jewish reader of Romans 7 and 8 might reflect on how Israel's long struggles had been part of that strange vocation. The gentile reader, in Paul's day and today, might reflect that the moral impotence and frustration we see so vividly in chapter 7 does in fact correspond (and this may be part of Paul's clever point) to the frustration of so many pagan moralists, recognizing a high standard but knowing that they failed to attain it.

So, then, **fourth**, and especially vital for understanding 8.1–4: **the villains in the story are 'Sin' and 'flesh'.** The problem is not the law itself. Nor is the problem that of being human, or indeed of being Israel. Paul uses 'Sin' (*hamartia*) here to denote, not merely specific acts, but the dark power that lies behind all human idolatry, injustice and immorality. That's why I have given 'Sin' a capital letter here, to make this distinction. 'Sin' in this passage is thus almost the equivalent of 'the satan'. Similarly, Paul uses 'flesh' here to denote human beings, not simply as bodily (that, of course, was a good thing) but as physically and morally corruptible, and – a vital move – to align Israel 'according to the flesh', that is, ethnic Israel, with corruptible human nature as a whole, whether Jewish or gentile. All through, Paul is thinking as a creational and covenantal monotheist. God's creation is good, and will be reaffirmed despite corruption and death. Israel is God's people, and will be reaffirmed in the transformation that has been effected by Israel's own Messiah. God's law, the Torah, is itself holy, just and good – and will be vindicated through the gospel (as Paul insisted cryptically as far back as Romans 3.31!), even though, by itself, it cannot give the life it promised.

It is vital for Paul that, though of course the Messiah's people are still composed of 'flesh' in the sense of human physical bodies that will decay and die, they are not *determined by* 'the flesh'. The code he uses here for this 'being-determined-by-the-flesh' is to speak of being 'in the flesh', as in, for example, 7.5 or 8.9. This can be confusing, because in Galatians 2.20 he can speak of ordinary ongoing physical life in terms of 'the life I now life in the flesh'. Similarly, when he is faced with the prospect of imminent death in Philippians 1.24, he assures his readers that his remaining 'in the flesh' is more important for their sakes. Clearly he doesn't mean, in either of those passages, that he is 'determined by the flesh' in the negative sense. But here in Romans 7 and 8, building on what he'd said in Romans 6, Paul uses 'in the flesh' to indicate the pre-baptismal state of any human, and then particularly any Jew – though in the latter case Paul is aware of the heavy irony, found all through Israel's own scriptures: the Jew characteristically (and rightly!) delights in God's law, but finds its life-giving purpose all too elusive, because of Sin. It is the tension, if you like, between Psalm 105 ('look what splendid things God did for us in Egypt, all so we could be his people and obey his law') and Psalm 106 ('Yes, God rescued us, but we rebelled and sinned, and when God forgave us . . . we did it again. And again').

The transition between chapters 7 and 8, then, is matched by what we find in Galatians 2: those who are Jews by birth come to realize that belonging to the one whom the resurrection has identified as Israel's Messiah means *both* the fulfilment of their aspirations as loyal Jews *and* the radical redrawing of their identity as the people of God. When someone comes to be 'in the Messiah', by baptism and faith, the only identity that now matters is the new, messianic one. We are reminded of 2 Corinthians 5.17: if anyone is in the Messiah, there is a new creation: old things have gone, and everything has become new.

This, of course, is why the resurrection matters so much, whether in Romans 8 or in 2 Corinthians 5 or anywhere else. It is also why Paul is careful to speak of the resurrection of the *body*, not the flesh (compare 1 Corinthians 15.51). 'Flesh', for him, denotes the present corruptible, decaying world and humans; the new creation, and the new body, will be incorruptible. That is the somewhat technical sense in which 'flesh and blood cannot inherit God's kingdom', even though Luke, reporting in a less technical way the words of the risen Jesus in Luke 24, has him declare that a ghost doesn't have flesh and bones as he does. In Paul's sense, the present 'flesh' will decay and die, but God will raise his people from the dead into a new body like that of the risen Jesus. In the context of Romans 8, the main emphasis of all this lies upon the moral life, as in 8.5–8 and 8.12–16. In chapters 9—11, as in Galatians, Paul deals specifically, and in the same way, with 'Israel according to the flesh', the ethnically identifiable people of Israel. One of the fascinating features of Romans 7 is that it appears to lay the groundwork for that further argument.

But all that is for another occasion. Our present concern is with the transition between Romans 7 and 8. This brings us back at last, after a long but necessary detour, to the *ara*, 'so, then' or 'therefore', at the start of 8.1.

Romans 8.1–4: The Spirit and the Messiah's Death

So: there is *therefore* now no condemnation for those in Messiah Jesus! How does this work? *Because*, verse 2; *because*, verse 3; *because*, verse 5; *because*, verses 6 and 7; *well then*, verses 9 to 11! Whether or not the different translations of this passage use all those specific terms, that is how verses 1–11 work. Our task now is to look in detail at the first four verses in particular.

***

We begin with the initially problematic *therefore* of verse 1. This is how the argument runs:

1 here is the situation (chapter 7);
2 therefore there is no condemnation (8.1);
3 because here's how God has dealt with that situation (8.2–11).

The 'therefore' in verse 1 anticipates the 'because' in verse 2, which will explain what might otherwise have seemed illogical. It is as though I might say, 'My car has a flat battery, its tyres are ruined and its licence has run out; there is *therefore* no problem getting to my destination, *because* here is the mechanic who can fix the battery and tyres, and here is the government officer to issue me with a new licence.' Or, to use another illustration, it's as though someone might say, 'I am heavily in debt to the butcher, the baker and the candle-stick maker – I am *therefore* free of all financial obligations, *because* the bank has agreed to write off all my debts to local tradespeople.' Thus, to say it again, the *because* – in this case verses 2 to 4 and beyond, all the way to verse 11 – explains the otherwise puzzling 'therefore' in verse 1. Chapter 7 sets out the sorry state that 'I' am in; 8.1 declares that there is *therefore* now no condemnation; 8.2–11 explains this with *because*, *because* and *because*.

So to the detail of verses 2, 3 and 4. Here we find a typically Pauline sequence. Think of how a flower opens. Verse 1 is the bud – a tight little statement, so dense as to be cryptic, needing to uncurl a bit to be understood. No condemnation for Messiah's people! Verse 2 opens this out a little: the expla-nation of 'no condemnation' is *because* the Torah of the spirit of life in Messiah Jesus released you from the Torah of sin and death. Paul has taken the idea of the two-sided Torah from 7.21–3 and has turned it in a new direction. 'God's law' – the thing in which the devout Jew 'delights' in 7.21 – is now taken up within a whole new reality, enabling it at last to do what it was always meant to do. One might even say that if Torah 'came in alongside' the Adam–Messiah sequence in chapter 5, intensifying the 'trespass' (5.20), so here the spirit 'comes in alongside' the good and life-promising Torah and enables it to do at last what it really wanted. Paul thus picks up the double Torah (evoking the blessings and curses in Deuteronomy) resonating through Romans 7 and gives it a new direction:

Torah promised life, and it is now given in the Messiah.[5] Verse 2, however, is still quite cryptic. So the rosebud-like argument opens up still further in verses 3 and 4, announcing the double truth: sin is condemned at last, and therefore the spirit can and does give the promised life to the Messiah's people.

Verse 2, then, states the reason for verse 1 – but it does so in such a dense way that it itself needs considerable further explanation. This is typical of Paul: first to say something tightly packed, and then to allow it to unfold bit by bit. Here is the tightly packed version: 'The law of the spirit of life in the Messiah, Jesus, released you[6] from the law of sin and death.' Verses 3 and 4 then open this out further, pointing ahead to the longer argument of 8.1–11 as a whole.

The passage, then – as is fitting for the conclusion of chapter 7, which is what it really is – is still primarily about the law. Verses 2, 3 and 4 together insist, from three different angles, that the rescue operation effected through the Messiah and the spirit is the outworking, through God's fresh action, of the original intention of Torah. Verse 2: 'the law . . . released you.' Verse 3: 'God has done what the law [wanted to do but] was incapable of doing.' Verse 4: 'the right and proper verdict of the law [is] fulfilled in us.' The old idea, popular in much Protestantism, that Paul saw a basic antithesis between 'the law' (perhaps as a system of moralistic self-help) and the gospel, is clearly shallow and anachronistic. The problem, over against many misunderstandings, was not that Torah was a bad thing, needing to be pushed out of the way for God's purposes to go ahead. The problem, as Jesus says in Mark 10 and Paul in 2 Corinthians 3, was that the people to

---

5   It seems more natural to take the *en Christō Iēsou* here with the word *zōē*, 'life', which precedes it, not with *eleutherōsen*, 'released', which follows it.

6   Several manuscripts have 'me' at this point, probably reflecting an early scribe's assumption that Paul was simply continuing the first-person narrative of ch. 7.

whom Torah was given were hard-hearted. Thus, for Paul, that which God has done through the Messiah and the spirit is so exactly what the law had intended to do that he can speak, here in verse 2, of the law itself as the active agent in the work of release, of liberation. If that sounds paradoxical, it is the same paradox that he states in Galatians 2.19: 'through the law I died to the law, so that I might live to God.' It isn't enough to say merely 'I died to the law'; that might allow one to collapse back into the easy old antithesis, pitting (as it were) the old covenant against the new. No: this has itself happened 'through the law'. What God has done in the Messiah's death, and in the gift of the spirit, is to give the 'life' which Torah had promised all along.

Thus 'the law of God' in which the devout Jew 'delights' in 7.21 is now revealed in a whole new mode: through the gospel, it is transformed into 'the law of the spirit of life in the Messiah, Jesus'. And the 'release' is from the death which, though never the law's basic intention, was its necessary effect when applied to sinful, hard-hearted humanity, to the 'flesh' (both Jewish and gentile) that cannot please God.

That is why the same point continues – again to the surprise of many expositors – in verse 5–8, to which we shall come in our next chapter. Glancing ahead just to make the present point, we find in verse 7 Paul saying that 'the mind focused on the flesh . . . doesn't submit to God's law; in fact, it can't.' Here again the law is on the side of God's rescue operation. Verse 8 ('those who are determined by the flesh can't please God') repeats, in effect, what Paul had said in 7.22–3, with the implied antithesis, not of 'the law' and 'grace' (or whatever) but of 'the law of God' and 'the law of sin and death', the latter being the shadowy alternative-Torah of 7.23 and 7.25b, which, rightly if tragically, had to pronounce condemnation over the world of sin.

So, returning to verse 2: Paul is naming 'the law' – in a newly revealed sense! – as the active agent of liberation. What is this newly revealed sense? It is 'the law of the spirit of life in the Messiah, Jesus'. The rest of verses 1–11 explains what he means.

1 'Life' is the goal, as in 7.10 and 8.10–11;
2 this life is given by the spirit;
3 the spirit is actively at work within the Messiah's people;
4 giving life was Torah's original object; thus
5 Paul can telescope all this together by speaking of 'the law of the spirit of life in the Messiah, Jesus'.

This, of course, needs further unpacking, which is what he now offers – though his explanatory statements are themselves still quite dense and in need of careful handling.

***

The start of verse 3, literally translated, reads: 'For the impossible thing of the law, in that it was weak through the flesh, God [has done] . . .' Most English translations, like my own, have turned this round, starting the sentence with 'God'. But Paul's wording should force us to ask, what was it that Torah could not do? Many have supposed that the answer has something to do with the 'condemnation' of sin at the end of verse 3. But that ignores Paul's overall argument – not to mention the fact that Torah had no problem condemning sin! The answer, following once more from 7.10 and now from 8.2 as well, and looking ahead to 8.10–11, is that *Torah couldn't give life*. Granted that Israel too was 'in Adam' (as elsewhere in Paul), then however hard Torah tried – and however hard people such as Saul of Tarsus tried! – it couldn't give the life it promised.

Verses 3 and 4 form a single complex sentence, explaining how it can now be the case that the law's verdict of 'life' can be (not just 'pronounced', as though at a distance, but) *fulfilled* in those whom Paul is describing. Reduced to its basic terms, it goes like this: *God condemned 'sin', so that the law's life-giving verdict might be fulfilled in us.* Putting it like that sends echoes across the New Testament, for instance in John's comment about Jesus' promise of the spirit that 'the spirit wasn't available yet, because Jesus was not yet glorified' (John 7.39). Only after Jesus' 'glorification' on the cross can the spirit be breathed on the disciples (John 20.22). As will become clear in the rest of Romans 8, the spirit constitutes the new mode in which the living presence of God himself will dwell in and with his people, constituting them as the new 'Temple'. But for God to dwell in the Temple, the Temple must be cleansed of everything that pollutes it, everything that smells of death. How is that to be done?

With the Torah itself, it is impossible – not because there is anything wrong with Torah, but because Torah was given to the Adamic, 'fleshly' people of Israel. As Moses already warned (in Deuteronomy 32 and elsewhere), and as one prophet after another insisted, the people seemed incapable of keeping the holy, just and good law. The law was thus 'weak because of human flesh', unable to give the life it promised (7.10). And the problem with 'flesh', as Paul has analysed it in 7.7–25, is 'Sin', *hamartia*, which as we said is here more than just the sum total of human wrongdoing. It is the dark, quasi-demonic power that used even the holy law as a base of operations to whisper its seductions (7.8–11). What had to happen, therefore, is that *hamartia* itself needed to be 'condemned' – not just receiving the judicial verdict of condemnation, but having that sentence duly carried out. And that, declares Paul, is what God has done – in the death of his son. 'Right there in the flesh, [God] condemned sin.'

With this, we find ourselves gazing at one of the sharpest and most vital early Christian statements of the meaning of

Jesus' crucifixion. Every time Paul writes about the cross, he says something different, because in each passage he is expounding a particular line of thought, not constructing an abstract system. But what he says here sends a signal to all those who do want to construct such systems of theology. 'There is now no condemnation for those in the Messiah, Jesus' (verse 1), *because* on the Messiah's cross God 'condemned sin'. In the terms of much later debate, that is obviously 'penal'. The punishment deserved by 'Sin' has been meted out – on 'Sin' itself. It is likewise obviously 'substitutionary'. The death of the Messiah, as the means of sin's condemnation, results in there being 'no condemnation' for those 'in the Messiah'. He dies under the weight of sin; his people do not. Here, at the heart of Paul's vital argument, driving the larger analysis he will offer in the rest of the chapter, we have a clear and definite statement of what many later theologians will describe (in language which is actually vaguer than many of them realize) as 'atonement'.

But Paul is not constructing such an abstract scheme. What he says here is in the service of his actual argument, which is about the law's intention being fulfilled – the intention which had been thwarted by 'Sin' dwelling in the 'flesh' of the humans to whom the law had been given. So it is vital to observe, against the run of a great deal of popular preaching, that Paul does *not* say that God 'condemned Jesus', or even 'condemned the Messiah'. God condemned *Sin* – in the flesh of the Messiah! The same event – the horrid, bloody lynching of an innocent young man – carries this very specific meaning, relating directly to the problem as Paul had analysed it in chapter 7. This is how the story of ancient Israel, the scriptural narrative from Adam through Moses and on to the captivity of which Paul wrote in 7.23, is finally resolved. (To say it once more, if we try to snatch Paul's statement here out of that scriptural context we will inevitably misunderstand it.) The point, throughout, is on the *continuity* of God's overall purposes, despite all the failure of chapter 7, worked out through the radical *discontinuity* caused by the scandalous gospel events. Without that continuity we would never understand how it is that the picture of present and future redemption in the rest of chapter 8 remains deeply rooted in Israel's scriptures, bringing to surprising completion the narrative that, as the succeeding argument makes clear, stretches back to creation itself.

***

The second key point, dovetailing with this, is that, in giving Torah, God intended to deal with Sin, but not in the way we normally think. *This is the heart of Paul's theology of the cross*; it is important not to accept lesser alternatives. Recall again 5.20: the Torah came in (that is, into the historical sequence from Adam to the Messiah) *in order that the trespass might be filled out to full extent* – but where Sin increased, grace increased all the more. Imagine Sin as a small transparent photograph; Torah puts a bright light behind it and a large screen in front of it. Torah brings Adamic Sin to larger-than-life size, precisely and paradoxically in Israel, so that it could be dealt with there. The key link, as we mentioned before, is 7.13, and the key word is *hina*, 'in order that', picking up from the *hina* in 5.20. In 7.13, Paul declares that God's purpose in giving Torah – indicated with this repeated *hina* – was so that 'Sin might become very sinful indeed, through the commandment'. *The purpose of Torah*, Paul is saying, *was to lure Sin into one place, namely Israel, and there to let it do its worst, to become its full, horrid self* – so that in the person of Israel's representative, the Messiah, it might then be dealt with once and for all.

This is how the underlying narrative plays out. The exile of God's people, their subjugation at the hands of the pagan world, reached its final extreme in the execution of Israel's king outside his capital city. The Messiah represents Israel in himself; in his crucifixion, he draws Israel's whole vocation on to himself. Sin has done its worst, raising itself to its full height; and God, having planned this strategy, is able finally to condemn it right there. God's second self, his only son, has taken the heaped-up hatred, bitterness, sin and death of the world on to himself. This is not an abstract 'doctrine of atonement', a legal fiction somewhere up in the air. This is the historical story of God's people, Abraham's family, called to be God's partners in dealing with the problem of Adam. That purpose is finally complete when Torah's curse falls on Israel's anointed representative.[7] The fact that this way of reading Romans 8.3 and 4 leaves us precisely with the questions of Romans 9—11 is a strong argument in its favour.

Take these two points together – the promise of life and the luring of Sin on to one place – and what have we got? God, having drawn Sin on to one point and having condemned it right there, has done so in order to give, by the spirit, the resurrection life that Torah by itself could not. This brings us back to where we were before: God could not come to dwell where Sin was still powerful and polluting. Sin had to be dealt with once and for all, so that God's own life, his own spirit, could dwell in the Messiah's people.

People sometimes ask, what happens to Torah in New Testament theology? The present passage, together with other vital chapters such as Galatians 2 or 2 Corinthians 3, indicates that it is fulfilled, and transformed, in Messiah and spirit together. Paul would have been well aware that the Jewish festival of Pentecost celebrates the giving of Torah, consequent upon the victory over Egypt. So now, the Messiah wins the victory over sin so that the spirit can come to dwell and to

---

7   See Gal. 3.10–14, and my commentary on that passage.

give life. Paul, to repeat, is thinking *historically*. This is not an allegory for some otherworldly truth. God's plan of salvation has been worked out through Abraham's people, fulfilled in the Messiah, and now extended to the worldwide, Jesus-believing, spirit-filled family.

Any attempt, then, to tell the story of the cross while missing out this larger Israel-story is bound to introduce wrong emphases, as I stressed in the introductory chapter above. I have argued elsewhere that this passage is the clearest New Testament statement of what can be called 'penal substitution'.[8] But that phrase covers several different meanings, and some of the popular ones are at best sub-biblical and misleading. Paul elsewhere declares that the Messiah 'died for our sins *in accordance with the scriptures*'. This doesn't just mean a few proof-texts taken out of their larger contexts. It means the whole narrative of God's purposes with Israel, following through the Deuteronomic covenantal scheme of blessing then curse and thus requiring the apocalyptic fulfilment, the unveiling of God's covenant faithfulness, in Israel's representative Messiah. Without that narratival reading of scripture, you are left, as critics often point out, with God acting in an arbitrary and apparently unjust way, wanting to kill someone and taking it out on his own innocent son. But when we put the story back together again in Pauline fashion, we can see how it works. The Israel-dimension is vital and non-negotiable in the Christian narrative. I grieve that it is missing from many popular gospel presentations.

Here, then, we are at the heart of all Christian theology. God made humans to be his stewards, reflecting his wise image in the world, so that he might himself come into his world as the ultimate steward of creation. Following sin, God called

---

8 See *DRB*.

Abraham and his family to be the means of rescuing humans and thereby the whole creation – *so that he might himself come, as the anointed representative of Abraham's family, to rescue Israel and the whole world from sin.* Humans were made as appropriate vehicles for God's self-expression in his world. Israel was called as the vessel for the self-expression of God's rescuing love. Davidic Messiahship was called into being to bring Israel's task and destiny into focus on one figure, royal, rejected, resurrected, reigning. All this is here in Romans 8.1–4, dense and compact as only Paul could make it.

It is all, in fact, encapsulated in the phrase 'God's own son', which Paul introduces here without explanation. He uses this central title for Jesus at key moments (Romans 1.3; 5.10; Galatians 2.20). Paul is here picking up the ancient meanings of the phrase, namely Israel (Exodus 4.22) and the king (Psalm 2.7; 2 Samuel 7.14), and filling them with the breathtaking sense that these vocations were always designed, like the human vocation itself, for God's own use. They were, Paul seems to imply, the appropriate vehicle for God's ultimate saving self-revelation. The son as Israel; as Messiah; as God's own second self: a title designed – as Paul sees with hindsight! – for God's own personal use.

The 'sending' of God's son, like the 'sending' of wisdom in Wisdom of Solomon chapter 9, is thus the moment in which the creator's desire to come and dwell with his people, at the heart of creation, is radically fulfilled. He comes as the ultimate human: the phrase 'in the likeness of sinful flesh' echoes the 'image and likeness' of Genesis 1. God made his world so that it would 'work' properly *through the agency of his image-bearing creatures, humans.* Jesus does what he does, not simply because he is God's own second self, but because – precisely as in chapter 5! – he is the genuine human being. As we'll see later, in his incarnation, crucifixion, resurrection and ascended intercession, Jesus is doing what God made humans to do, reflecting God's love to the world and reflecting the world's worship and prayer back to the father.

Here then, as in chapter 5, the notion of Jesus as God's (unique) 'son' holds together Jesus' messianic status and vocation, as the one promised in 2 Samuel 7.14, Psalm 2.7 and elsewhere, with the mysterious intimacy not just of 'relationship' but of 'identity' between God the father himself and the man Jesus. That identity is clearly presupposed in Romans 5.10, since to say that the death of the 'son' demonstrates the love of God only makes sense if God himself is personally involved in, not merely distantly related to, that death. And, though Jesus is indeed publicly declared to be 'son of God' in the resurrection (1.4), our present passage (along with 5.10 and Galatians 2.20) makes it clear that Jesus is already 'son of God' in his human life and death.

Standing back from verses 3 and 4, then, we see more clearly how Paul's version of 'penal substitutionary atonement' actually works. 'There is no condemnation for those in the Messiah' – because God condemned sin in the flesh (thereby opening the way for the spirit to perform the life-giving work that Torah by itself could not). That is definitely penal; it is definitely substitutionary; but it doesn't work in the arbitrary fashion that theologians and preachers have often imagined. It works because of the vocation of Israel to be God's covenant partner, and because of God's sending his own son to be Messiah, bringing that vocation to its climax. We notice, once more, that Paul doesn't say that God condemned *Jesus*. He condemned *sin – in the flesh of Jesus*.

So Paul says that, on the cross, God condemned Sin itself. The word Sin, here and in Romans 7, appears to be a way of talking about the ultimate enemy, the sub-personal force we sometimes call 'the satan'. Here is the delicacy and inner complexity of Paul's atonement theology. On the cross, God wins the victory over evil, *through* penal substitution. And penal substitution itself works *through* the Messiah representing his people, and thence the whole world. And the sacrificial system, here represented by the sin-offering (see below), does the job, not of punishing an animal, but of cleansing the place where God will come to dwell; in the present case, making it possible for God's spirit then to fill his people. Subsequent thought has often played these ideas off against one another, with frustrating results. In Paul they are held tightly together.

This moment in Romans 8 therefore brings to its climax the doctrine of justification that Paul began in chapters 2, 3 and 4. In chapter 2, he looked ahead to the ultimate future, when God will judge the world justly, when he will rightly condemn evil. In chapters 3 and 4, he insists that the verdict 'in the right' is already declared over all Messiah-faith people. But that leaves open the question, how does that verdict in the *present* correspond to the verdict to be issued in the *future*, on the last day? Romans 8 gives the answer. 'There is therefore now no condemnation . . . because . . .'

The Greek word *nyn*, 'now', is important here.[9] There is therefore *now* no condemnation. This is both logical ('now therefore') and temporal ('in the present time'). The future verdict can be announced in the present, because the Messiah has dealt with his people's sins, and the spirit indwells them to bring them to resurrection. The word 'condemnation', *katakrima*, looks back to the final judgment (*krima*) in chapter 2, and particularly to chapter 5 where the *katakrima* is the condemnation of Adamic humanity. And Paul insists that those 'in the Messiah' will escape this.

---

9 For some reason, it had dropped out of the first edition of my translation, *The New Testament for Everyone*. It is back where it belongs in the new edition (2023).

So far in our exposition, we have taken for granted Paul's classic phrase *en Christō*, 'in the Messiah'. This has generated huge debates: in what sense are Jesus' followers 'in him'? I have long been convinced that this phrase depends upon the explicit messianic and Israel-focused meaning of *Christos*: the Messiah sums up his people in himself, so that what is true of him is true of them, and vice versa. We see that in various places, not least Romans 6 and Galatians 3. This is not the time to go into details.[10] But in the present passage, it is worth noting that the story of Israel, retold in dramatic fashion in chapter 7, reaches its culmination here with (as we shall see) the new exodus accomplished in the Messiah. In a similar way, the story of Israel as retold in Romans 9.6–29 points directly to 10.4 where the Messiah is the *telos nomou*, not 'the end of the law' in the sense of abolition, but the 'end' or 'goal' in the same sense as the present passage: what Torah could not do, but intended to do, God has now done in the Messiah. Even those first-century Jews who saw the messianic claims made about Jesus as a blasphemous nonsense would have agreed that, if indeed a Messiah were to appear, and somehow to receive divine validation, that would mean that the long story of Israel had arrived at the place that God had promised and intended all along.

***

Paul modifies the statement that 'God sent his son' in two parallel ways. In both cases, he uses a short phrase which he could, no doubt, have expanded into a whole chapter of exposition; but he is content, within his larger argument, to gesture to these points in ways that he must have hoped would be reasonably comprehensible.

---

10 See *PFG*, ch. 10.

First, God sent the son 'in the likeness of sinful flesh'. The word 'likeness' has produced much debate. Was Jesus' human make-up itself actually 'sinful', or was it some kind of pretence, a lookalike version without the reality? In the first case, we might seem to be denying what Paul himself says elsewhere about Jesus' sinlessness (2 Corinthians 5.21); in the second case, the 'condemnation' on the cross would not have hit the real culprit.

These questions ideally demand a much fuller study for which there is no space here. Suffice it to say that it looks as though Paul is still thinking in terms of Genesis 1 and 3 – as he was in 5.12–21 and 7.9–12, and as he will be again in 8.18–30. It is vital for his argument in chapter 5 that the Messiah, the truly human one, *came to the place where Adam had ended up*. He didn't (as it were) sweep aside the failure of Adam and start over with a clean slate. He came to the heart of the problem, in order to deal with it right there. That is part at least of the meaning of the very dense 5.15–17. And here again we see the point of 5.20, speaking of the law 'coming in alongside' – alongside, that is, the overall sequence of 'Adam and Messiah' – and of its effect of increasing sin at that very place. That, as we have seen, is what Paul then spells out in 7.7–25. Our present passage is then a shorthand way of saying what Paul insists in 5.20b: 'where sin increased, grace increased all the more.' What does that 'where' mean? It means that the Messiah did indeed come to the place – namely, Israel under Torah! – where, as in 7.13, Sin had done its worst. As Paul puts it starkly in 2 Corinthians 5.21: he (the Messiah) did not know sin, but God made him to be sin on our behalf.

The second modifying phrase is 'as a sin-offering'. The Greek phrase *peri hamartias* which Paul uses here is used frequently in the Greek Old Testament to refer specifically to the 'sin-offering', particularly within the sacrificial codes of

Leviticus and Numbers.[11] About this there are two important things to be said.

First, we remind ourselves (though many expositors of Romans have ignored this) that, in chapters 6—8, Paul is thinking in terms of the larger exodus story which is now fulfilled through the gospel. At this point, as we shall see when we get to verses 9–11, he is moving towards the vision of the spirit-filled church as the fresh equivalent of the wilderness Tabernacle, the shrine in which God himself would come to dwell in glory. But in the Pentateuch – as it now stands! – the establishment of the Tabernacle in Exodus 40 required the careful codes of Leviticus. If the glorious divine presence was to dwell in the midst of the people, their regular uncleanness and sin would somehow need to be dealt with, lest, by infecting the holy tent, they might make it impossible for God's presence to dwell there.

The 'sin-offering' is one of the key sacrificial means by which that problem is addressed. The blood of the sacrificial animals functions as the purifying agent to cleanse away any such pollution. So here Paul, preparing the way for the promise of the indwelling spirit (8.10–11), makes it clear (without, though, referring to the blood, as he had done at 3.25) that the death of the son will facilitate that indwelling and work of the spirit.

The second thing to say about the 'sin-offering' is that, in Leviticus and Numbers, this sacrifice relates specifically to sins of ignorance (when a person performed an action without knowing that it was forbidden) or to unintentional sins (they did know, but did not intend to commit the sin). It is fascinating to observe that in 7.13–20 Paul has analysed the ongoing sin of Israel in terms of just those two things: 7.15, 'I don't understand what I do; I don't do what I want'; 7.19, 'I

---

11 For details, see *CC*, ch. 11.

don't do the good thing I want to do, but I end up doing the evil thing I don't want to do.' The theme of 'ignorance' is then picked up elsewhere, for instance in 10.3 and passages such as Acts 3.17. Once again, this brief phrase seems to be gesturing towards the underlying theme of continuity. The Israel whose story Paul is telling in Romans 7 is not left behind – far from it! God has tailored the way of liberation precisely to the problem that Israel had experienced in the frustrations (as in Psalm 106, and so many prophetic passages) of living under Torah. By extension, as we hinted above, this therefore also includes the gentiles who, as the great moralists from Aristotle onwards regularly pointed out, were well aware that the good they glimpsed and intended regularly eluded them.

We can, therefore, draw together the threads of these remarkable four verses. The life that Torah promised but couldn't give is at last provided because of the Messiah and the spirit; there is therefore no condemnation for the Messiah's spirit-indwelt people. We shall say more about the end of verse 4 in our next chapter, since verses 5 to 8 are an expansion of the point. But verse 4a is vital: this was done 'in order that the right and proper verdict of the law [*to dikaiōma tou nomou*] could be fulfilled in us'. The Greek word *dikaiōma*, which I have translated 'the right and proper verdict', is in itself ambiguous. Without context, it could mean the *legal requirement* of Torah. But the larger context here makes it clear that Paul is using it in the same sense as in 1.32, where it is the 'decree' that *those who do certain things deserve to die*. Here the point, looking ahead to verse 11, is that 'those who do *these* things deserve to live'. Torah's *verdict of life*, that is, is now fulfilled in those who belong to the crucified and risen Messiah, those now indwelt and shaped by the spirit. When the spirit, poured out upon the Messiah's faithful people, produces in them the change that verses 5 to 8 will describe, then the right and proper verdict of Torah is what Paul had indicated in 7.10: life. In this case, resurrection life. That is how the larger unit, 8.1–11, works overall. And we have now seen how the dense, tightly packed opening statement of 8.1–4 serves as the foundation both for that argument and indeed for the rest of the chapter.

Conclusion

I suspect that all this will be both familiar and unfamiliar to most of my readers. The words and ideas are well known in themselves, but the way they fit together may feel strange, as indeed we may feel a strangeness as well as a familiarity when walking the actual streets of a city previously known only through maps or distant photographs. A serious deep dive into scripture often has that effect. My hope is that, as we continue with this intense and focused study of one of Paul's greatest chapters, his inner logic – how the whole 'city' works – will become increasingly familiar, exciting and life-giving. For now, we should celebrate, and cling fast to, that opening line: 'So, therefore, there is now no condemnation for those in the Messiah, Jesus!' Jesus' followers live in 'no-condemnation' land. Whenever we sense in our hearts the dark whisper of accusation, in whatever context, we should go back to Romans 8.1; we should pray through verses 2, 3 and 4; and we should praise God for the world-changing and life-giving work of the son and the spirit. Charles Wesley turned this passage into song: 'No condemnation now I dread; Jesus, and all in Him, is mine.'[12]

---

12 Wesley, 'And Can It Be That I Should Gain' (1738).

3
Romans 8.5–11: The Spirit Gives Life

5Look at it like this. People whose lives are determined by human flesh focus their minds on matters to do with the flesh, but people whose lives are determined by the spirit focus their minds on matters to do with the spirit.

6Focus the mind on the flesh, and you'll die; but focus it on the spirit, and you'll have life, and peace.

7The mind focused on the flesh, you see, is hostile to God. It doesn't submit to God's law; in fact, it can't.

8Those who are determined by the flesh can't please God.

9But you're not people of flesh; you're people of the spirit (if indeed God's spirit lives within you; note that anyone who doesn't have the spirit of the Messiah doesn't belong to him).

10But if the Messiah is in you, the body is indeed dead because of sin, but the spirit is life because of covenant justice.

11So, then, if the spirit of the

5hoi gar kata sarka ontes ta tēs sarkos phronousin, hoi de kata pneuma ta tou pneumatos.

6to gar phronēma tēs sarkos thanatos, to de phronēma tou pneumatos zōē kai eirēnē.

7dioti to phronēma tēs sarkos echthra eis theon, tō gar nomō tou theou ouch hypotassetai, oude gar dynatai.

8hoi de en sarki ontes theō aresai ou dynantai.

9hymeis de ouk este en sarki alla en pneumati, eiper pneuma theou oikei en hymin. ei de tis pneuma Christou ouk echei, houtos ouk estin autou.

10ei de Christos en hymin, to men sōma nekron dia hamartian to de pneuma zōē dia dikaiosynēn.

11ei de to pneuma tou egeirantos

one who raised Jesus from the dead lives within you, the one who raised the Messiah from the dead will give life to your mortal bodies, too, through his spirit who lives within you.	*ton Iēsoun ek nekrōn oikei en hymin, ho egeiras Christon ek nekrōn zōopoiēsei kai ta thnēta sōmata hymōn dia tou enoikountos autou pneumatos en hymin.*

The first four verses of Romans 8 have well and truly launched Paul's exposition of the work of the holy spirit. They form a platform for the rest of the chapter, and in particular for the rest of the longer opening paragraph, namely verses 5–11.

But as we pick up where we left off, there is one bit of unfinished business, namely the final clause of Romans 8.4. Verses 1–4 have as their main theme the claim that 'there is no condemnation for the Messiah's people' because 'the law's proper verdict, giving life, is now fulfilled in them'. But to that statement Paul added the line: 'as we live not according to the flesh but according to the spirit'. And with that, he points ahead to verses 5–8, which are the necessary preliminary to the climax of the single line of thought that reaches through to verse 11.

I stressed earlier, in providing general guidelines for reading any passage in Paul, that we must watch carefully for the little Greek words that link his sentences together, and which tell us how his train of thought was working. The word to watch here, linking verse 5 to what has gone before, is the little three-letter Greek word *gar*. This is often translated 'for', indicating that what follows is intended to explain what has just been said. A sentence linked to the previous one with *gar* is designed to drill down a bit deeper into the previous statement, to undergird it with further explanation. But sometimes – and I have a sense that this is one of those times – the English word 'for' seems a bit weak for the connection that Paul appears to be making.

That is why, on this occasion, I have unpacked the *gar* further by translating it as 'look at it like this'. As we said, the previous verses are in themselves very dense, like a rosebud which contains a much bigger flower than we might have imagined. Now the flower is opening up a bit more, disclosing what was, all along, hiding inside verses 1–4.

Verses 5–8 are therefore going deeper into the opening statement, in order to complete the foundations for the decisive statement in verses 9–11. These first eleven verses of the chapter perform a double role. They round off the argument about the law, the Torah, which began in chapter 7, while simultaneously introducing the theme of the spirit which then dominates most of chapter 8. In particular, as we saw, the Torah wanted to give life, but couldn't because of the 'weakness of the flesh', that is, because of the fact that Israel itself, the recipient of Torah, was still 'in Adam', still composed of weak human flesh. Now we see how God has done what Torah could not: God sent the son to take the weight of sin and death upon himself, and God sent the spirit to give the life which Torah promised but could not produce. So verses 1 to 11 as a whole are framed, as we saw, between 'no condemnation' in verse 1 and the promise of resurrection in verse 11. The verses in between explain how Paul can be so confident.

We should be quite clear, once again, that to say 'no condemnation' doesn't mean 'escaping this world, and hell, and going to heaven'. We hear the word 'condemnation' and we think 'hell', and because we are used to thinking of 'heaven and hell' as equal and opposite, as in much mediaeval and later theology, we assume that 'no condemnation' means 'going to heaven'. But it doesn't. Heaven is not mentioned in Romans 8. (Actually, the word only occurs twice in the whole letter, and on neither occasion is Paul referring to the destiny of God's people after their death.) Paul's focus, as we begin to see after verse 12, is on the *inheritance* of God's people, which, as with Abraham in chapter 4 verse 13, means the *world*, God's creation. God will renew his creation from top to bottom, will rescue it from its slavery to corruption, and will give us new bodily life, resurrection life, within that new world, and to assist in looking after it. That is the promise and the hope.

If there was still any 'condemnation' left over, that promise and hope would be null and void. But there isn't. It's been dealt with. Sin with a capital S has received its death-blow – and Sin in this sense, as we saw, is not just the accumulation of our own private sins, but the dark power that, luring us into idolatry, is bent on the distortion of our genuine humanness and the consequent dissolution of God's good creation, which we were supposed to be looking after. All of that – the dark power and its effects – was condemned in the death of Jesus the Messiah.

We see this graphically in John 12.31–2. Jesus declares, as he goes to the cross, that 'now is the judgment of this world; now is the ruler of this world cast out; and if I am lifted up from the earth I will draw all people to myself.' As he says a bit later, 'In the world you will have trouble; but cheer up – I have defeated the world!' (John 16.33). That victory, accomplished through his death on behalf of sinners and in their place, has opened the way for God's own life to be poured out afresh through his spirit. As in yet another passage in John, the spirit wasn't available yet, because Jesus was not yet glorified (that is, lifted up on the cross) (John 7.39). The victory of the cross clears the darkness out of the way so that, as in John 20.22, the spirit can come and indwell Jesus' followers, energizing them for their life of mission and holiness. This life is the active manifestation, in our present human existence, of the power, the energy, of God the creator. God now comes afresh into the world as the re-creator, giving life where there was none. That was the point which Paul had made about Abraham's faith, back in chapter 4: Abraham and Sarah had to believe that God would give them the new life of a child even though their bodies were, in reproductive terms, as good as dead (4.19–22).

So, following our first guideline for reading Paul, we note how the passage starts and ends. The second guideline is to note the connecting words. We saw the opening *gar* in verse 5. We then have another *gar* in verse 6, meaning that verse 6 in its turn unpacks and explains verse 5. Verse 7 then gives us *dioti*, which is often a slightly stronger version of the explanatory 'for'. I have here translated it as 'you see'. Verse 7a gives a further explanation of verses 5–6, offering a slightly new thought which is explained in turn, in the middle of verse 7, with another *gar*, and then at the end of the verse with yet another (*oude gar dynatai*, 'in fact, it can't'). So, to bring out these connections (in **bold** here), we could translate verses 5, 6 and 7 rather woodenly like this:

> ⁴ᵇ. . . we who behave not in accordance with the flesh but in accordance with the spirit. ⁵**Let me explain** [*gar*]. People of the flesh-determined sort set their minds on flesh-matters, but people of the spirit-determined sort set their minds on spirit-matters. ⁶**You see** [*gar*], the mindset of the flesh is death, but the mindset of the spirit is life and peace. ⁷**Because** [*dioti*] the mindset of the flesh is hostile to God; **for** [*gar*] it does not submit to God's law; **for** [*gar*] indeed it cannot do so. ⁸**What's more** [*de*], flesh-determined people cannot please God.

This shows us quite well the shape, the form, of this paragraph, before we get into the detailed meaning. Verses 5 to 8 constitute a little chain of reasoning, spelling out the difference between being 'in the flesh' and 'in the spirit', and thus filling in the significance of that final clause of verse 4, 'we [who] live not according to the flesh but according to the spirit'.

It is noticeable that here, as in verses 1–4, the Torah is still part of the subject – and is thoroughly vindicated against any suggestion that it was part of the problem in the first place. Granted what a bad press 'the law' has had in much Christian understanding, it is remarkable that Paul, completely consistently with what he had said in verses 2, 3 and 4, understands the Christian moral life as including 'submitting to God's law' (verse 7) and thereby 'pleasing God' (verse 8). Those brought up on the anti-legalist tradition of much Protestantism might find this difficult to comprehend, but the theme falls easily within Paul's wider statements such as in Romans 13.8–10, where love is the fulfilment of the law, and such (admittedly ironic) passages as 1 Corinthians 7.19, where neither circumcision nor uncircumcision matters because what matters is keeping God's commandments. But after verse 8 we hear no more of the law. As we might have guessed from verses 2, 3 and 4, its positive role has now been fully taken up by the spirit, and it is the spirit that will dominate the discussion from now on. We should, though, note that Paul, with the *dioti* of verse 7, thinks that the fact that 'the mindset of the flesh' is incapable of submitting to God's law is further evidence for why that mindset is heading for death. Once again, the ultimate point of Torah was to give life. And once this has been done through Messiah and spirit, with the people concerned not just 'submitting to God's law' but actually (verse 8) 'pleasing God' – another idea that has worried many anxious Protestants – the Torah can look on with satisfaction, its purpose fulfilled.

Having thus dug down to the foundations in verses 5–8, Paul can then build up again to his intended conclusion in verses 9–11. To get to the promised resurrection, to the ultimate verdict of 'no condemnation', one cannot go via the flesh, the *sarx*, the corruptible and sinful human self. But once someone is 'in the spirit' rather than 'in the flesh', all things are possible. This argument works through a chain of repeated *de*, a flexible Greek conjunction which mounts a logical argument going the other way. So far Paul has been saying 'A *because* B *because* C' and so on. Now he says 'But if . . .' In other words, there is no way to the promised destination through the flesh, *but if* the spirit of Jesus is at work, then 'no condemnation' is assured.

Thus, more specifically:

⁹ᵃBut [*de*] you are not flesh-determined people but spirit-determined people, ⁹ᵇif [*eiper*] the Messiah's spirit dwells in you; ⁹ᶜbut if [*ei de*] someone doesn't have the Messiah's spirit, they are not one of his people. ¹⁰But if [*ei de*] the Messiah really is in you, then, [though] the body is dead because of sin, the spirit is life because of covenant justice [*dikaiosynē*, often rendered 'righteousness']. ¹¹So then, if [*ei de*] the spirit of the one who raised Jesus from the dead dwells in you, the one who raised the Messiah from the dead will give life to your mortal bodies also, through his spirit who dwells in you.

Those three verses convey a sense of mounting excitement, as the goal is glimpsed in Jesus the Messiah (verse 10) and then, by the spirit, is guaranteed to the Messiah's people (verse 11). And this enables us to see how the whole passage is structured. Verses 5–11 start with a chain of repeated *gar*, digging down to the general point about people being either in the flesh or in the spirit and the results – death or life – of those two pathways. It then uses a chain of *de*, building up from there to what is true of the Messiah's spirit-indwelt people. The result is clear: there is no condemnation (verse 1), because of the sure and certain promise of the resurrection (verse 11). QED.

So: rules numbers 1 and 2 – the start and finish, and then the connecting words – clear the way for rule number 3: try to read with first-century meanings. Here there are two main points to spell out, with a third – perhaps surprising – hiding in between. These will take us right into the meat of the passage.

The first main point concerns the key terms 'flesh' and 'spirit'. The natural temptation of a modern western mind is to hear 'flesh' in terms of 'physicality' – solid material substance – and 'spirit' in terms of non-material reality. But that isn't how a first-century Jew would hear those words. The word *pneuma*, 'spirit', was in any case in widespread philosophical use at the time, with quite a range of possible meanings, by no means necessarily implying non-material reality. And the word *sarx*, 'flesh', likewise covered many things, as I shall shortly explain. A contrast of 'flesh and spirit', then, which to modern western minds sounds like the contrast between 'material' and 'non-material', was far more subtle.

For Paul, the rule of thumb is that *sarx*, which we translate 'flesh' for want of a better term, doesn't refer to materiality as such. Paul, as a good Jew, was a robust creational monotheist. At many points in his writings, it's clear that he celebrates the created goodness of the present physical world. Indeed, it is that which makes the early Christian rejection of idolatry and corruption so strong, driven by the sense that to *worship* any aspect of the created order is to miss the point, to distort the meaning and purpose of creation and, with that, to corrupt and distort our own God-given humanity and most likely that of those around us as well. Thus 'flesh' refers to the corruptible, decaying world; to corruptible, decaying human life within it; and then, very specifically, to Jews 'according to the flesh', highlighting the problem we saw in chapter 7 that the Jewish people, for all their great privilege of God's calling and the giving of Torah, are nevertheless still 'in Adam'.

But are we not all, Christian and non-Christian alike, still 'in the flesh'? Yes, in one sense. Paul allows in Galatians 2 that he still lives 'in the flesh'; but he insists that this is not the source and guiding power of his life. The fleshly life he still lives, he says, he 'lives in the faithfulness of the son of God who loved him and gave himself for him' (Galatians 2.20). Similarly, in 2 Corinthians 10.3 he says that though we are still fleshly people (*en sarki*) we don't conduct our campaign in a fleshly way (*kata sarka*): he may still, as a human heading for decay and death, be in that sense 'in the flesh' – but he is not living 'according to the flesh'. That is the key distinction, even though his phraseology is not always consistent. As here in verse 9, he can use *en sarki*, 'in flesh', to say what Christians are *not*, even though in those other passages he uses *en sarki* to designate continuing existence in the present corruptible physicality.

This basic meaning of *sarx* is why, for Paul, the resurrection body is not *sarx* but *soma*. *Soma*, which we normally render 'body', is for Paul the bridge term. Paul's anthropological terms are best approached as ways of referring to the whole human being but from one particular angle or with one particular aspect, rather than supposing they refer to different *parts* of the same human. Thus the Greek word *soma* denotes our whole public personal reality – the whole self, the body, in fact almost what we mean by the 'person'. This *soma* can still give in to sin. That is why, perhaps surprisingly, Paul can speak in verse 13 of the need to 'put to death the deeds of the body'. But it can also be the locus of our 'living sacrifice' as in Romans 12.1–2. The 'body', the whole self, is what we are to give in service to God and to our neighbour. And, decisively, the *body*, not the 'flesh', is what will finally be raised from the dead, as in verse 11.

By contrast, when Paul uses the phrase 'flesh and blood', he means 'humanity in its present corruptible state'. That's why, in 1 Corinthians 15.50, after talking about the resurrection *body*, he declares that 'flesh and blood cannot inherit the kingdom'. This has caused some confusion, because not all New Testament writers follow this distinction. Thus, in Luke 24, the risen Jesus tells the disciples that a ghost doesn't have 'flesh and bones', *sarka kai ostea*, as he obviously does. Paul is here using the word *sarx* in a tighter, more technical sense. Some of the early Fathers, in their determination to speak clearly of the resurrection of the physical body, used the word 'flesh' in that context as well, as when, for instance, Tertullian wrote of *resurrectio carnis*, the resurrection of the flesh. Tertullian didn't mean the corruptible flesh. That would have meant that resurrected people would have to die again, perhaps going round and round in an endless circle of being. That is certainly not what the early Fathers believed, any more than Paul did.[1]

Coming back to Romans 8.5–8, another vital parallel passage is Galatians 5.16–26, where Paul places in contrast 'the works of the flesh' and 'the fruit of the spirit'. How easy it would be, again, to suppose that 'the flesh' here has to do with what we would call *physical* sin and misbehaviour, and that the 'fruit of the spirit' is to do with what we call 'spiritual' things such as prayer, love, wisdom and so forth. But, in fact, as many have pointed out, the 'works of the flesh' in Galatians 5 could mostly be practised by 'a disembodied spirit' – jealousy, malice, sorcery, ambition, party spirit and the like. And the 'fruit of the spirit' includes various things expressed in bodily action, such as kindness, generosity, gentleness and so on. So clearly the distinction Paul is making between 'flesh' and 'spirit' does not map easily on to the way we, in the largely Platonic modern west, have come to use those words.

So what is Paul talking about here, once we've got ourselves unstuck from those tricky issues? Paul is making a sharp

---

1 On Tertullian and the other early Fathers on the meaning of resurrection, see *RSG*, ch. 11.

contrast between those 'in the flesh' and those 'in the spirit'. He is talking about the *basic orientation* of someone's life. In particular, he's talking about the *basic mindset*, the *focus* of the mind and its *habitual patterns*. He clearly doesn't imagine that Christians are now sinless, or that they never suffer from wandering thoughts or wayward actions. Had they been sinless, he wouldn't have had to give such frequent moral exhortation.

Paul is obviously very concerned, in this letter and elsewhere, about outward bodily behaviour. But here he is thinking particularly of the mind, the thoughts. Verse 5: those in the flesh – I've cashed it out in my translation as 'people whose lives are determined by human flesh' – *think about*, focus their minds on, matters to do with the flesh. They focus attention, in other words, on the things he lists in Galatians 5 as 'works of the flesh', things such as factionalism and party spirit, jealousy and envy, as well as drunkenness, sexual immorality and so on. In today's world, our news media make sure that we do indeed focus our attention on such things – the factionalism, the party spirit, the jealousy and envy particularly of well-known people, and then of course the immorality that becomes a source of endless (and delighted) gossip. It takes a constant effort to drag the mind away from such things and to focus instead on 'the things of the spirit' (kindness, generosity and so on) and how to bring them about. Part of Paul's point, here as constantly in the letter to the Philippians, is that Christian living doesn't just happen. It takes what we call a *mental effort*, a concentrated exercise of the mind to focus on God's way of being human. That is all right there in summary form in verse 5.

Then in verse 6, Paul refers back, by way of explanation, to this whole way of learning how to think and what to think about with the abstract term *phronēma*, 'mindset', which I have cashed out in my translation in terms of the regular *focus* of the mind. Of course, he doesn't mean that, as long as your mind is focused in the right place, you can do what you like with your body! On the contrary: as in the start of chapter 12, the way you present your whole selves, your *bodies*, is precisely by being, as he says, 'transformed by the renewing of your minds'. What you learn, by regular and disciplined practice, to think about will show up in your outward behaviour.

This brings us to the further explanation in verse 6. Here is the great either/or from Deuteronomy and Joshua, coming into sharp focus: choose life, not death![2] Here, specifically, he urges his readers to choose the *phronēma tou pneumatos*, the 'mindset of the spirit', rather than the *phronēma tes sarkos*, 'the mindset of the flesh'.

Now of course this isn't easy. It requires the effort of choice, a choice to be made again and again. Your *phronēma*, your mindset, is a deeply engrained habit. Christian virtue includes retraining the habits of heart and mind. It requires the thousand regular and difficult choices of focusing on kindness, gentleness, love, peace, rather than envy, malice, factional spirit or bodily licentiousness. We have to go on making those choices until they become, as we say, 'second nature', the well-formed, spirit-led *phronēma*. Even then, there will be fresh challenges. The reward for climbing one moral mountain is to be given a steeper one next time. Those in Christian leadership particularly need to be clear on that.

Paul offers yet further explanation of all this in verse 6. Here the *phronēma tou pneumatos* is not just life, verse 6b; it is life *and peace*. That has a covenantal, indeed priestly, echo. In Malachi 2.5, God's covenant with Levi was for 'life and peace', going perhaps with the new-Temple theology we will discover in a moment.[3] But before we can get to that, verses 7 and 8 link the contrast of flesh and spirit back to the question of

2 Deut. 30.15–20; Josh. 24.15.
3 See too the 'covenant of peace' in Num. 25.12; Isa. 54.10; Ezek. 34.25; 37.26.

Torah, which Paul has still had in mind ever since the start of chapter 7, even though by now the work of the spirit is taking over, fulfilling what Torah by itself could not. The *phronēma tēs sarkos*, the mindset of the flesh, he says, is 'hostile to God'. God is the God of *life*. Death is an affront, a slap in the face, for God the good creator. And the flesh, heading for death, is thus a small version of that affront. That's why the whole sacrificial system in Leviticus and elsewhere is designed to keep the holy place clean of any reminder of death, so that God may dwell there. Torah, however, promised life, as we saw from 7.10 and 8.4: the right and proper verdict of the law is fulfilled in the spirit-people. So the flesh-mind cannot submit to Torah! That was the point of 7.7–25. This is the last mention of Torah in the present long argument. Its work is done. It has handed on the baton to the Messiah and his spirit, and they are giving the life that Torah could not.

The negative result of this (verse 8) is that those who are, in this sense, *en sarki* cannot please God. That is a remarkable statement, implying as it does its converse: that those who are in the spirit *can and do* please God, as Paul says in various other places.[4] There is a strand of post-Reformation spirituality that is so anxious to avoid any appearance of 'works-righteousness' that it shies away from any suggestion that anything we can do might actually please God. The best we can hope for on that score is to avoid getting into trouble. But if God's spirit is at work within us, then of course we ought to please God! Of course, we will be caught up in his love and his purposes, as we shall see later in the chapter. To all this we shall return.

So, as previously mentioned, the first main thing we must recognize – which will require some retraining in our thinking as we try to live in the minds of first-century Jews rather than

---

4 E.g. Rom. 12.1–2; 1 Cor. 7.32; Col. 1.10; 1 Thess. 4.1.

the mindset of western late modernity – is that 'flesh', *sarx*, doesn't just mean 'material physicality', and spirit, *pneuma*, doesn't mean 'non-material reality'. That Platonic misunderstanding has often been invoked. The same mistake is regularly made today, sometimes under the guise of retrieving 'spirituality' in the midst of secularity. But Plato is a delusion. He and the later Platonists had no desire for bodily resurrection. We have to learn to think Jewishly – granted that quite a few Jews of the time, such as Philo of Alexandria, were looking to Plato for help. Paul does not. For him, resurrection is vital; and the moral choices implied in verses 5 to 8 are themselves *part of the promise of resurrection itself*. They are about the new way of life that is God's advance gift from the ultimate future. Ethics isn't just a matter of learning how to behave, though it is that too. It is primarily a matter of inaugurated eschatology. The spirit comes to us from God's future, enabling us to live as already-renewed humans even in the midst of a world of sin and death.

The second main theme for which we need to think as second-Temple Jews – reshaped around the crucified and risen Messiah – is the underlying Temple-theology of verses 9 to 11. We easily miss this because we neither catch the echoes nor follow the underlying narrative flow. We have to bring both into focus.

First, the echoes. Look for the word 'dwells', though in my translation it is simply 'lives'. First, in verse 9: you are not *en sarki* but *en pneumati*, not in the flesh but in the spirit, if the spirit of God *dwells* in you, lives in you (*oikei en hymin*). That vital little clause is repeated in verse 11, speaking of the spirit of the one who raised Jesus from the dead *dwelling* in you, *oikei en hymin*. Then, more fully at the end of verse 11, bodily resurrection results from the spirit *dwelling* (literally, 'indwelling') *in you* (*dia tou enoikountos autou pneumatos en hymin*). Now, of course, the words 'dwell' and 'indwell' are relatively common.

But one of their regular biblical uses is in relation to YHWH himself 'dwelling' in the wilderness Tabernacle and then in the Jerusalem Temple.[5] But why would Paul want his readers to hear *that* echo here?

The answer, second, is in Paul's larger implicit exodus-narrative. Think how the original exodus worked. God rescued his people from Egypt so that they could leave the land full of idols and worship him in the desert. The idea was that, after coming through the Red Sea and being given Torah on Mount Sinai, God could establish his Tabernacle in their midst and then come to *dwell* there in person, living alongside his people, leading them to their inheritance. Exodus–Torah–Tabernacle–inheritance. To repeat what I said before, Romans 6 speaks of the exodus: the slaves come through the water to freedom. Romans 7 brings them to Sinai, with all its puzzles and problems but with its continuing promise of life for those who actually keep Torah. But how (granted that, as in 7.17, 'Sin' dwells within them)? Paul's answer is the spirit – and now the spirit coming to *dwell* actually within humans themselves, not just in a tent outside the gate of the camp. This is the new Tabernacle. And then, as we will discover in the subsequent passage, the spirit *leads* God's redeemed people to their *inheritance* – which is not 'heaven' but the entire renewed creation.

Paul, like several of his contemporaries, is rereading the exodus-story in the light of all that had gone wrong with the people of Israel in the meantime. Jesus had chosen Passover – the exodus-moment – to do what had to be done. He had given his followers a new version of the exodus-meal, the Passover.

---

5 The LXX regularly uses the root *katoikein* (e.g. Ps. 132[LXX 131].14, *hōde katoikēsō*, 'here will I dwell'; 135[LXX 134].21 (YHWH *katoikōn Ierousalem*, 'dwells in Jerusalem'). Paul echoes this root in e.g. Eph. 2.22 (*katoikētērion*, cf. e.g. Ps. 76[LXX 75].2; cf. Matt. 23.21). By Paul's day, the difference between *katoikein*, *enoikein* and simply *oikein* seems to have been flattened out; but the more precise meaning of the *kata-* prefix, that of someone *coming to dwell* in a place as perhaps for the first time, was less suitable for his meaning.

The early Christians quite naturally saw themselves as the new-exodus people. And part of the Judaean expectation of the second exodus was the longing that Israel's God, YHWH, would come back in person, as he'd always promised. The Judaeans had rebuilt the Temple after the return of some of them from Babylon. They had restarted the sacrifices. But the indwelling divine glory had not returned. Isaiah 52 had promised the visible return of God. That hadn't happened. Nor had the similar promises of Zechariah or Malachi been fulfilled. But *Paul, like all the other early Christians, believed that with Jesus and the spirit the promise had in fact been finally fulfilled.* Jesus himself was the living embodiment of Israel's God, come to be and do at last what the Temple was and did. And now – exactly as with the Pentecost-scene in Acts 2 – the spirit comes to constitute Jesus' followers as the new-Temple people, those in whom the glorious divine presence genuinely dwells. The Temple was the joining-place of heaven and earth. In Acts 1, Jesus' ascension means that part of 'earth' is now firmly established in 'heaven'; in Acts 2, the breath of heaven begins the work of new covenant and new creation on 'earth'. Paul expounds all this elsewhere, particularly in the Corinthian correspondence and then, dramatically, in Ephesians. But it's there all the time, underneath so much of his thought. As often in Paul's writings, the conclusion of one section of a larger argument is repeated, having been further explained, in the next section: verse 11 corresponds to Romans 8.30: 'those he justified, them he also glorified.' The glorious divine presence already dwells in all Jesus' people.

As with the Temple destroyed by the Babylonians, so with the Temple of our bodies. God had promised that the Temple would be rebuilt. Well, if God has dwelled already in our present bodies, he will certainly rebuild that Temple. Verse 11: he will give life to your mortal bodies also, through his spirit who indwells you. The promise of our final resurrection, within the eventual new creation, is rooted in the ancient Passover-story, and in the Temple-shaped hopes of the second-Temple Jews. It's all there in the closing chapters of Ezekiel, which – unsurprisingly – follow the dramatic 'resurrection' prophecy in chapter 37. Much food for thought there.

All this then enables us to read these dense verses, 9 to 11, with their three-dimensional meaning. Verse 9a is the starting-point. If God's spirit dwells in you, then your basic identity is not 'in the flesh' but 'in the spirit'. There is the danger of an initial confusion here, because Paul can talk almost in the same breath of us being 'in the spirit' and also of the spirit being 'in us'. Which does he mean? The answer seems to be: both! Partly, perhaps, because Paul may have formulated the phrase *en pneumati* on the analogy of *en sarki*; but also because God's spirit is of course not confined to the interior lives of believers, but is living and active all around us, so that when the spirit dwells within us we are in tune with the new-creational purposes of God which are going ahead in a thousand ways we don't normally see. That too is a theme deserving of more attention than we can spare at the moment.

To this basic statement in verse 9a, Paul adds a warning note: if someone doesn't have the Messiah's spirit, they do not belong to him. That goes with other warnings, particularly in 1 Corinthians, against presuming that, because we associate with other Jesus-people, we must be doing all right. Paul doesn't stop here to deal with the pastoral questions that arise, or the worries that some may have about their own state or condition. But note the fascinating way in which he refers in a variety of different ways to the work of the spirit. Verse 9a speaks of the spirit of God. Verse 9b speaks of the spirit of the Messiah. Then in verse 10 he simply says that the Messiah, *Christos*, is dwelling in you. This corresponds to various passages, such as Galatians

2.19–20, where, having said that he has been crucified with the Messiah, he says that he is nevertheless alive – but it isn't him, it's the Messiah living in him. Or think of Philippians 1.21 – 'for me to live means the Messiah'. Or Colossians 1.27: 'the Messiah, living within you as the hope of glory'.

In each of these passages, Paul is talking of the remarkable phenomenon at the heart of Christian experience: a new life, a new energy, bubbling up inside us, leading us to praise, urging us to prayer, warning us against complacency or sin, nudging us to acts of love and gentleness, providing fresh glimpses of previously unimagined wisdom and illumination, leading us to places and tasks that might seem crazy but that might just be our true vocation. This indwelling life, this new-Temple existence, is what matters. To speak personally for a moment: when I was confirmed, on my fifteenth birthday, and began regular attendance at Communion, I used to pray that old chorus:

Cleanse me from my sin, Lord;
put your power within, Lord;
take me as I am, Lord,
and make me all your own.
Keep me day by day, Lord,
walking in your way, Lord;
make my heart your palace
and your royal throne.[6]

(The only thing wrong with that chorus, by the way, is the use of the word 'Lord' as a semi-colon. That's a habit to avoid if possible, especially in extempore prayer.) The point was and is the humble invitation to Jesus himself to come and dwell within us by his spirit. That is a Temple-prayer.

---

6 Ascribed to R. Hudson Pope (1879–1967).

Now we see at last how the larger passage works. Part of the point of the Temple in Jerusalem was that it was an advance signpost to the eventual new creation. It was a heaven-and-earth structure, pointing forward to the promise of new heavens and new earth. In the same way, we human 'temples', individually and together, are meant to be signposts pointing forwards to the final new creation of which Paul speaks in verse 18 and onwards. Thus Romans 8.1–11 establishes the base of operations – the promise of bodily resurrection – so that Paul can then move on from verse 12 onwards and explain that what God promises to do in and for his people he will do in and for the whole creation in the end.

But we are not just mute signposts to that coming fulfilment. We are given an active role in working towards it. In fact, as he will shortly explain, we are caught up, often painfully, in the middle of the process, as active, prayerful, suffering agents. That, actually, turns out to be part of what Paul will mean by 'glorification'. God had promised that his divine glory would come back to dwell in the Temple. Well, as with Jesus' own 'glorification', this is what it looks like.

Notice how Paul puts it in verse 10. If the Messiah is in you – well, the body is dead because of sin, but the spirit is life because of *dikaiosynē*. I have translated this dense term here as 'covenant justice', partly because (to be frank) the normal translation 'righteousness' means anything and nothing these days. But this theme of life because of *dikaiosynē* goes back to 5.1–11, and behind that to 1.17: *ho dikaios ek pisteōs zēsetai*, 'the *righteous* shall *live* by faith.' Life and righteousness. If we were to stand back from the present passage and quickly read through the whole of Romans (a great thing to do, by the way), it would become clear that 'justification by faith' depends for its own inner logic on the work of the spirit through the gospel. That should have been clear from Galatians, where Paul weaves the work of the spirit into his whole discussion of justification; but the rhetorical demands of his larger argument in Romans mean that he has delayed bringing the spirit on stage (so to speak) until 5.1–5, 7.4–6 and now chapter 8 itself, to which those earlier passages look forward.[7]

This, then, is what Paul means in Philippians 1 when he speaks of the 'good work' that God has begun, with the converts' initial coming to faith, and then of the certain fact that God will bring this 'good work' to completion at the Day of the Messiah. The point is that the present body is heading for death because it has been the locus of idolatry and injustice, missing the mark of genuine humanness, the word for this being *hamartia*, sin. We have all taken part in that, colluding with the anti-creational forces of death. But the spirit – and at this point, with further potential confusion, Paul seems to be referring to the *human* spirit, as he will again in verse 16 – the spirit *is already* 'life' because of God's verdict of 'in the right', the verdict of covenant justice. God has justified this person, declared them to be 'in the right'; so those who are righteous by faith will have life. (I will say more about the interplay between the human spirit and God's spirit when we get to verse 16.) There is thus a sense in which Romans 8.9–11 provides a kind of QED to the opening statement of Romans 1.16–17.

Just in case we might have thought that the passage was getting too straightforward (if Paul can on occasion use irony, perhaps we can as well?), we have in addition here a remarkable small window on Paul's view of what we often call 'life after death'. Once we abandon Platonism, with its view of an immortal soul – something never mentioned in the New Testament – we are left with the question, where are we, who are we, what are we in between our bodily death and

---

7 Another anticipation of this argument is found in 2.25–9.

our bodily resurrection? How can we talk wisely and humbly about this intermediate state, this apparent reality which, again, is hardly ever mentioned in scripture? Part of the answer seems to be that, as God's spirit has come to dwell within us, enlivening our own spirits, so God's own spirit will hold on to us hereafter until the time of resurrection. I note that, at key points, from Jesus himself and elsewhere, it is the human *spirit* that is commended to God upon the death of the person.[8] Thus, insofar as God's spirit has as it were *become* us, taking on our identity to live and work in and through us, so after death we remain in the multi-track life-giving memory of God's own spirit, until the time of resurrection. I think we need to reflect more on the place and work of the holy spirit in grounding what has been called the 'intermediate state'. That is again a topic for another time; but that is where verse 10 seems to be pointing.

So to verse 11, the climax of the chapter so far and the ultimate answer to the questions of Romans 7. Notice how Paul oscillates deliberately between 'Jesus' at the start of the verse and 'Messiah', *Christos*, in the second half. The name 'Jesus' refers specifically to the human Jesus, the man from Nazareth; the word *Christos* refers to the same person, but *seen as the representative of God's people*, the anointed one who sums up his people in himself. Paul, as usual, is writing with great precision. Think of how, at the end of Romans 4, he speaks of Christian faith as 'faith in the-God-who-raised-Jesus-from-the-dead'. Well, he now says, if the spirit-of-the-God-who-raised-Jesus-from-the-dead indwells you – the phrasing is very close to 4.24 – then the one who raised *the representative Messiah*, the *Christos*, from the dead will give life to the mortal bodies of the

---

8 See Luke 23.46 (quoting Ps. 31.5); Acts 7.59; John 19.30; compare (for various nuances) Num. 16.22; Eccles. 3.21; 12.7; Job 34.14.

Messiah's people, too, *through* that spirit, his own spirit, who dwells in you.

We may well find ourselves marvelling at the way Paul has woven all the threads together to reach this dramatic conclusion. This is where God's purpose for Torah has ended up. Through the Messiah and the spirit, God has given the life that Torah promised, the resurrection life which, beginning already through the spirit, is to be anticipated (as in verses 5–8) in the moral mindset and actions of God's people.

We might also, to be frank, marvel at the fact that these first eleven verses of chapter 8, complex and dense though they are, are simply the first part of the larger argument of the chapter as a whole. But above all, we ought to marvel at the reality of which Paul is speaking: the reality of the living God coming to dwell not just among us but within us. The ancient promises of YHWH's return to Zion, and the rebuilding of the Temple, are coming true not 'in heaven', as the older allegorical exegesis would have it, but in the new creation. And the new creation, which will involve as we shall presently see the renewal of the entire creation, and also the personal bodily resurrection which we are promised, includes also the anticipation of that resurrection in the present moral life, the mindset of the spirit. This paves the way for 8.12–16, which, again using exodus-language, focuses on the bracing challenge of learning to think and live in the spirit rather than in the flesh.

Coming back in conclusion to one of the vital – and often ignored – elements of this passage, we think again of verse 8, where Paul declares that those in the flesh 'can't please God'. As I noted earlier, the idea of 'pleasing God' has almost been banned from some circles. We have been long schooled to recognize, and reject, any sense of works-righteousness, of the pride which imagines that we are, as we stand, morally capable of doing what God wants, perhaps even of putting him in our debt. The earlier chapters of Romans should have made it clear how foolish and impossible such an idea would be. But the traditions that have rightly rejected any pride in our own achievements have sometimes failed to complete the narrative, Paul's larger story in which God's spirit does what the Torah could not do, enabling the Messiah's people, even in the present time, to become already part of his ultimate new creation, and therefore to give God real delight. But here, and in the other passages we referred to before, Paul really does indicate that those who are living by the spirit will actually please God. Not to recognize this would be to fall into the trap of Jesus' critics in Luke 15, to whom the answer was that the angels were having a celebration in heaven because of sinners being rescued and that therefore a similar celebration on earth was thoroughly appropriate.

We shouldn't be shy about this. Some of our trouble, I sometimes suspect, comes from an upbringing where parents or teachers were hard to please. We have then transposed that, tragically, on to God himself. Perhaps that's why certain Christian sub-cultures are so anxious about the whole idea. But think of Eric Liddell in *Chariots of Fire*. 'God made me fast,' he said, 'and when I run, I feel his pleasure.' It is worth pausing to ask, what has God made you? What is it which, when you do it in the power and joy of the spirit, enables you to feel God's pleasure? Might that perhaps be part of God's ultimate new creation, breaking in to the present?

4

Romans 8.12–17: Led by the Spirit

¹²So then, my dear family, we are in debt – but not to human flesh, to live our life in that way.
¹³If you live in accordance with the flesh, you will die; but if, by the spirit, you put to death the deeds of the body, you will live.
¹⁴All who are led by the spirit of God, you see, are God's children.
¹⁵You didn't receive a spirit of slavery, did you, to go back again into a state of fear? But you received the spirit of sonship, in whom we call out 'Abba, father!'
¹⁶When that happens, it is the spirit itself giving supporting witness to what our own spirit is saying, that we are God's children.
¹⁷And if we're children, we are also heirs: heirs of God, and fellow heirs with the

¹²*ara oun, adelphoi, opheiletai esmen ou tē sarki tou kata sarka zēn.*

¹³*ei gar kata sarka zēte, mellete apothnēskein. ei de pneumati tas praxeis tou sōmatos thanatoute, zēsesthe.*

¹⁴*hosoi gar pneumati theou agontai, houtoi hyioi theou eisin.*

¹⁵*ou gar elabete pneuma douleias palin eis phobon alla elabete pneuma hyiothesias, en hō krazomen Abba ho patēr,*

¹⁶*auto to pneuma symmarturei tō pneumati hēmōn hoti esmen tekna theou.*

¹⁷*ei de tekna, kai klēronomoi: klēronomoi men theou, synklēronomoi de Christou,*

Messiah, as long as we suffer with him so that we may also be glorified with him.	*eiper sympaschomen hina kai syndoxasthōmen.*

With the first eleven verses of Romans 8, Paul has simultaneously finished his long argument about the Torah, which began in chapter 7, and launched his exposition of the spirit's work, which continues through most of chapter 8. And with this, we arrive at the great central section, verses 12 to 30.

We recall how the chapter is shaped. Verses 1–11 and 31–9 form obvious sections in their own right, leaving verses 12–30 as the substantial central section. This looks like a characteristically Pauline outline; another example would be 1 Corinthians 15, which also has an eleven-verse opening and a nine-verse conclusion, with a long middle section. I have the sense (over against any idea that Paul was just 'making it up as he went along' in dictating this letter) that he had long planned and shaped all this, through many a lecture or informal discussion, and with much prayerful consideration of how to say what had to be said within the practical limits of a letter.

Here in verse 12, Paul seems to take a deep breath: 'So then, my dear family . . .' We have now arrived at the heart of what he wants to say, from this point all the way through to the great conclusion in 8.29–30 in which, rooted in Christology, justification leads directly to glorification.

All that is well known. But we now run into a problem that is becoming familiar. The meaning Paul himself gives to these themes, justification, glorification and, indeed, the work of the spirit and the call to holiness, is subtly different from the meanings that the western church has often read into them.

We have assumed that we knew what questions Paul was addressing, and what he meant by the themes and categories he develops. But as so often, we have to proceed carefully to see what Paul himself *actually* says, as opposed to what our traditions have wanted him to say. Thus, this chapter is all about the ultimate Christian hope, the Christian inheritance. But if you speak of 'hope' and 'inheritance' to most western Christians they will think of heaven, or of 'waiting to be called home', or of 'going to be with Jesus, way beyond the blue'. But Romans 8 never mentions heaven, or going up to the sky as opposed to living on earth, or waiting to be called home, or anything like that. Nor is there any mention of a 'soul' waiting to be saved. This chapter is about new creation, not about escaping the present creation and going somewhere else. I have said this already, but it needs to be repeated, because our minds can easily flick back into 'ordinary' mode, particularly when many songs used today in worship express Platonic versions of the faith. As we in our generation face the groaning of all creation rather obviously, whether in climate change or the increasingly unstable world of wars and rumours of wars, let alone in our personal lives and those of people for whom we share a pastoral concern, we urgently need to recover the genuine biblical message.

Within the long section of verses 12 to 30, the first sub-section, which we're looking at in our present chapter, is verses 12 to 17. Actually verse 17 itself is a kind of bridge, a transition, between verses 12 to 16 and verses 18 to the end, so we will include it both in the present paragraph (starting with verse 12) and also within the paragraph that continues with verses 18 onwards.

So, taking verses 12 to 17, we need to ask our basic question, the question you can put to virtually any passage in Paul: look at the start and the finish, and see what he himself thinks he's talking about. In what way does verse 17 round off at least the first part of the train of thought begun in verse 12?

Asking that question is tricky in this case, because Paul appears to skip over what he might have said at the end of verse 12. (He does this fairly frequently, not least in Romans, with his thought racing ahead to the next main point and omitting to fill in the gaps in the first one.) 'We are in debt,' he says – 'but not to human flesh, to live our life in that way . . .'. But if that's the negative, telling us what we are *not* in debt to, we expect him to go on to the positive, to tell us who or what we *are* then in debt to. He appears to leave the thought hanging in the air.

Some have thought Paul means that we are indebted to the spirit. Since he regularly pairs spirit and flesh, as indeed in verse 13, that's quite sensible. But as the paragraph develops and reaches its goal, it becomes clear that he is thinking of our debt to God himself, to God the father. From verse 14, this theme builds up: we are God's sons; we've received the spirit of sonship; we cry out to God as Abba, father; the spirit testifies that we are indeed God's children and – here in verse 17 is the conclusion to this specific argument, linking back to verse 12 – we are indebted to God in quite a strict sense because we are his *heirs*, 'fellow heirs with the Messiah'. God has made a wonderful creation, and he is bequeathing it to his children. The promise of resurrection within God's new creation, as set out in verses 9 to 11, brings Paul to this point: we have been left a glorious legacy, namely to be God's heirs and also co-workers in his new world, sharing his wise and healing rule.

Normally, you only receive an inheritance after the giver has died. Though you may be, in that sense, in debt to the person who has left you the bequest, they are by definition no longer around to receive your thanks. But when it's a matter of inheriting, from God himself, our stewardship of the whole new creation, we are (Paul strongly implies) in a perpetual state of happy indebtedness to him. As the chapter goes on this turns out to be, as my teacher George B. Caird used to say, a debt of love that only love can repay.

At this point, we face rather directly the challenge to think with Paul over against the whole of the western Christian tradition, both Roman Catholic and protestant. You see, the shape of western theology for many centuries, dominated by the prospect of 'going to heaven' and/or the 'beatific vision' where the 'soul' is finally allowed to see God himself, has pulled us towards dividing our theological topics into 'salvation' on the one hand and 'ethics' on the other. That, I think, is the inevitable result of thinking of salvation in terms of 'going to heaven', leaving us with the question not only of how we are supposed to behave in our present earthly life but of what the relationship is between that behaviour and the ultimate destiny.

Thus, as I argued in my book *The Day the Revolution Began*, we have *Platonized* our eschatology, thinking in terms of a disembodied 'heaven', and that has resulted in our *moralizing* our anthropology, thinking that the only thing that matters is whether we've kept some moral code or not, and that, when we discover that God has saved us despite our moral failures, we then simply have to learn how to live properly in the interim. But once we think in Pauline terms about the new creation, and about the way in which the spirit has made us already new-creation people, standing on the threshold between the present age and the age to come, we discover a quite different category: the category of **vocation**. And that is what this whole passage is about. Who are we called to be, standing perhaps uncomfortably at the overlap of the ages? This passage gives the start of Paul's answer: we are already part of the new creation which, having come to birth with Jesus' resurrection, is on the way to the final rescue of the present creation from its slavery to corruption. By the spirit, we find ourselves part of the active pilot project for that ultimate new creation, both new-creation people in ourselves and called to be agents of new creation in the present. We are therefore already called to live gladly and gratefully as God's free children, God's new-exodus people, and to be caught up in the present work of God's spirit who enables us to pray 'Abba, father', even when – particularly when! – the world is dark all around us. That then points on to the great climax of the chapter a dozen verses later.

That gives us the outline framework for 12–17: we are *in debt to God* because, being his heirs, we are to live in the present time as his sons and daughters, the people at whom the world looks to get an impression of who the father must be.

Thus being God's sons and heirs (in the Exodus 4.22 sense of 'Israel is my firstborn son') is not just a matter of ethical obligation ('so now you must behave like *this*', though that is true as well). It is a matter of calling, of vocation. In Exodus 19.6, Israel is called to be God's royal priesthood, standing between him and the whole world. That is part of the preamble to the Sinai covenant. So Paul is going to expound in verses 18–30 what it means for us, as God's inheriting children, to be faithful to that larger vocation in the present time, in relation to the suffering and groaning creation.

That answers our first exegetical question, the outline framework. The second question is then, what about the little connecting words? Here again, as in 8.1–11, we have from verse 12 to 15 a string of *gar* clauses, digging their way down to the basic point in verse 16; and then in verse 17 we have a *de* clause building up from that point. This is the case *because* this *because* this *because* this – and then, 'but if', or if you like 'well then, if *that* is so then *this* is going to follow'.

Here's how a literal translation might read, emphasizing the connecting words albeit in a rather wooden fashion:

¹²So then, my family, we are debtors: but not to the flesh, to live in accordance with the flesh. ¹³**For** [*gar*] if you live according to the flesh, you are heading for death; but if by the spirit you put to death the deeds of the body, you will live. ¹⁴**For** [*gar*] those who are led by God's spirit are God's sons. ¹⁵**For** [*gar*] you didn't receive a spirit of slavery, leading back again to fear, but you received the spirit of sonship, in whom we cry, 'Abba, father'. ¹⁶[When that happens], the spirit is bearing witness with our spirit that we are God's children. ¹⁷**But if** [*ei de*] [we are] children, then [we are] heirs: heirs (on the one hand) of God, but (on the other hand) fellow heirs of the Messiah, assuming we suffer with him so that we may also be glorified with him.

Translation, as always, is tricky, partly because in today's English the word 'for' sounds quite stilted, which Paul's Greek is not. That's why sometimes the more fluent English is to make the causal connection simply by juxtaposition, as I've done in verse 13. Technically I could there have written, '*For* if you live in accordance with the flesh you will die.' But in English we often just put two things side by side and leave the reader to infer the connection, whereas first-century Greek rather enjoys adding the little words that make the link explicit. Or, as in verse 14, where once again the Greek word is *gar*, which students learn to translate as 'for', we in modern English might say 'you see'. But the meaning is the same.

(As an aside: this highlights the dilemma of all translation. Strict word-for-word accuracy is great, but sometimes it results in the new text feeling very stilted and awkward, which means it is *not* accurate because Paul is seldom, if ever, stilted or awkward. The translator is always compromising between words and moods, trying to get both right but realizing it's often impossible.)

Here, then, is how this little passage works. Verse 12: We are debtors, but not to the flesh; *because* (*gar*), verse 13, the flesh leads to death but the spirit to life; *because* (*gar*, verse 14, translated here as 'you see') the spirit-led people are God's sons; *because* (*gar* again, verse 15, translated here by the idiomatic 'did you') you didn't receive the spirit of slavery (did you?) but of sonship. This is further explained in the tricky but vital second half of verse 15 and then the whole of 16. That's the heart of this little passage: our present vocation as God's children and heirs is to be the people in whom God's spirit, bearing witness with our own spirit, prays the prayer that Jesus prayed in Gethsemane. Then, having reached that deep point, Paul builds up to the new conclusion, here in verse 17, with the *de*, as we watched him do in verses 9 to 11: But ('well then', as we might say) if *that* is true, then *this* is also true. This is where the whole paragraph was going: if we are children, we are heirs. And *that* is why we are 'debtors', not in the sense of owing God a grudging or uncomfortable obedience, but in the sense of discovering our vocation to be God's agents, his prayerful stewards, in the present task, within the groaning of the old creation, of witnessing to the promise of the new.

So, putting the paragraph together, we see why we are in debt, and to whom. Paul, to be sure, writes allusively. Sometimes he skips over bits of argument he assumes he can take for granted. But the sequence of connecting words helps us to find our way through.

So, moving to the third vital question, what happens when we try to read this passage with first-century eyes?

Let's imagine we are in one of the Roman house-churches, listening to Phoebe, who has been entrusted by Paul with taking this letter from Greece to Rome, reading out what he's written. What would his hearers be thinking? The great theme of sonship – being sons of God – would undoubtedly resonate with some of the listeners. Inheriting a great empire was a well-known theme. A hundred years before, Julius Caesar had adopted Octavian, subsequently known as Augustus; when Julius was deified after his death, Augustus styled himself 'son of the deified Julius'. He was the adopted son, inheriting the empire and being loyal to the memory of Julius Caesar himself. So it continued with Tiberius and the others. In fact, the first five emperors (Augustus, Tiberius, Caligula, Claudius, Nero) weren't related as father to son; they were chosen and adopted, groomed for the job. Then, when the old emperor died and was divinized, the new one would be 'son of the deified one', inheriting the empire.

So now Paul is claiming here, as he did right at the start of this letter, that Jesus is the true son of the true God – and that all Jesus' people *share that sonship*. Jesus' people are God's adopted royal family. The sons are what they are, not simply so that they can feel good about their relationship with the father, but in order *to carry out the father's project*. To rule wisely over God's empire, which is the whole world – the inheritance he promised to Abraham, as we saw before in a backward glance to Romans 4.13. So, as in 5.17, those who receive God's gift will *reign in life*. This is indeed a counter-imperial claim, if ever there was one – though, of course, for a very different kind of empire, with a very different modus operandi. As we will see later, this is part of what Paul means by 'glorified': set in authority over God's world.

The other obvious echo of 'being sons of God' is in the Exodus-narrative. This may help to explain why I have followed Paul in speaking in some places of 'sons', not just of 'children', despite the (to us) uncomfortable gender specificity. Thus, on the one hand, Paul is echoing 'Israel is my firstborn son' in Exodus 4.22. On the other hand, he is confronting the emperor's claim to be 'son of God'. He broadens it out into 'children', because

94

of course he has in mind females equally with males, but those resonances matter as well.

I therefore suspect that Paul's reference here to the key theme of sonship, *hyiothesia*, is deliberately designed to hold together in characteristic fashion two specific things. First, there are the Jewish roots of the idea, in the Exodus-story where the slave people of Israel are given this amazing royal dignity. Then there are the pagan targets, in this case Caesar's arrogant claim to some kind of worldwide empire. New Testament theology regularly has that dual focus (Jewish roots and pagan targets), exactly in line with the Psalms, Isaiah and the rest. What often happens in the New Testament is that we notice a theme growing out of Israel's scriptures; the theme then gets reworked around Jesus and the spirit; and then, in line with the intention of Israel's scriptures themselves, it turns out to confront rather sharply the claims and pretensions of the pagan world, not least of pagan empire. That is so, actually, with the powerful word 'gospel' itself: *euangelion* is an Isaiah-word that confronts a Caesar-word.[1] And it's so in this instance of 'sonship'. That word here seems to refer to *the status of being sons* rather than to the process by which someone might arrive at that status, that is, 'adoption' or some equivalent. Thus we find that in verse 15 the 'spirit of slavery' refers to the status of being a slave and the 'spirit' that goes with that, not the process by which someone becomes a slave.

This gives us at least a start towards a larger historical framework within which to glimpse the meaning of 'adoption' and/or 'sonship' in Paul's world. Scholars continue to debate the details, but the biblical and Roman contexts, which I've briefly sketched, seem to me decisive.

---

1 See the discussion in *PFG*, ch. 12, with details.

So how does that biblical context work? What is Paul affirming in this passage?

We have already noted that, throughout Romans 5—8, Paul is working with a kind of large-scale exodus-story. In Romans chapter 6, the slaves come through the water to freedom. In Romans 7, they arrive at Mount Sinai, where Israel recapitulates Adam's sin, resulting in exile and death. But the gospel events provide the necessary rescue, and as Torah is strangely fulfilled through the work of the spirit, so the spirit is to be seen as God's own glorious presence coming to dwell amid the people, as in the wilderness Tabernacle. That's in verses 9 to 11. But now the story continues. In verses 12 and 13, Paul is echoing Moses' stark challenge to the people on the verge of their crossing over Jordan: here is death, here is life – so choose life.[2]

The rhetorical force of all this is that Paul is saying to his hearers: fancy getting within sight of the promised inheritance and then deciding to quit, or even to go back to slavery! Fancy preferring slavery in Egypt to the land flowing with milk and honey! Yes, there will be challenges ahead, but they will lead to the inheritance. After all (following his underlying train of thought), you are here in the first place because, as Moses said to Pharaoh in Exodus 4.22–3, 'Israel is my firstborn son . . . so let my son go *that he may serve me*.' Israel is to worship God, in other words, to be God's priest; and, as God's son, also God's *royal* priest, to be set in authority over the world. That had been Israel's vocation. It is now supremely fulfilled in Israel's representative, Jesus the Messiah. And it is now shared, by the spirit, with all his people, Jew and gentile alike. This is central to all that Paul is now saying.

It should by now be clear that this vocation, to be the royal priesthood, is itself actually the fleshing out of the vocation

---

2 Deut. 30.15.

to be God's image-bearers. Humans were designed, created and called to reflect the praises of creation back to God, and to reflect God's wise rule into the world. That is why Paul's argument ends up in verse 29 with Jesus' people being conformed to the *image* of the son. The status of sonship is not simply a generalized sense of close familial relationship, in this case of the filial relationship with the world's creator – though it certainly is that. It is the status given to Abraham's people as they are brought out of Egypt, called to worship the true God and to be his agents within the world. The gospel then focuses this vocation on the Messiah himself, and then through him on his larger family. As such, they constitute the true royal family, even though Caesar will naturally regard them as an irritating nuisance.

The exodus-narrative is clearly visible in verse 15, where Paul contrasts sonship and slavery. You *were* slaves; you *are now* called to be sons; so don't even think of going back to Egypt! Recall how, as early as Exodus 16.3, the Israelites lamented the loss of all the good food in Egypt. They did the same, when they were thirsty, in Numbers 20.3–5. In between those two, in Numbers 14, the spies saw what they would be up against in trying to take possession of the promised land, and most of them were all for choosing a leader and – yes! – going back voluntarily to slavery in Egypt. That repeated theme is what Paul is here picking up. No, he says: that would imply that you were possessed, not by the spirit of sonship, but by a spirit of slavery (perhaps Romans 7.13–25 is still in mind here). He is, in other words, still thinking in terms of 'sons of God' as an exodus-shaped Israel-designation: we are the people of the new exodus. When today's Bible readers forget the rich scriptural heritage on which Paul was drawing, it is all too easy for the present passage and others like it to be interpreted simply in terms of 'our relationship with God' – which is itself important; but the force of what he's saying comes directly from the eschatological challenge, to recognize *where one is standing in God's great story of redemption*, and to embrace the consequent vocation.

God's response to the cowardly spies in Numbers 14, who want to turn back from going on to the inheritance, looks all the way forward to Romans 8 itself: As I live, says YHWH, and *as all the earth shall be filled with the glory of YHWH*, none of the cowards will see the inheritance.[3] God is not simply able to bring them into the promised land; that is only the first stage of what he intends. The land is itself a signpost to the far greater reality, the entire creation which will in the end be flooded with God's knowledge and glory.[4] The journey that follows, with the people being led by the presence of God himself, is pointing on to God's intention to fill the whole creation, not just one small tent, with his glorious presence.

All this enables Paul to change gear swiftly in verse 17 and link up Israel as God's 'son' with the Messiah as God's 'son' – the firstborn son as he will say in 8.29. That phrase 'son of God' is a messianic designation, all the way from Psalm 89.27 to Colossians 1.13. The deep structure of Paul's thought brings together Israel as God's people with the Messiah as the embodiment of Israel: the corporate 'son' and the messianic 'son'.

So if we are indwelt by God's spirit, as in 8.9–11, on the model of the wilderness Tabernacle where the divine glory came to reside, it's no surprise that in verse 14 Paul speaks of being *led* by the spirit. This picks up another aspect of exodus-language, where the people of God are *led* through the wilderness to the promised land. That's the language Deuteronomy uses about their journeys, which is picked up

---

3 Num 14.20–2.
4 Isa. 11.9; Hab. 2.14; Ps. 72.19.

later by Isaiah and Jeremiah. The prophets were looking back to the original exodus in order to point on to the new one, the return from exile. That is where Paul is positioning himself and his hearers.

When Israel's scriptures speak of God's presence with his people in the wilderness, they sometimes envisage this in terms of God's spirit. Haggai 2.5 explains that when God says 'I am with you', this corresponds to his indwelling at the exodus: 'my spirit abides among you; do not fear'. Isaiah 63.7–14 likewise looks back to the exodus, when Israel was designated as God's children, and when God put his holy spirit within them (63.11, 14) even though they then grieved that spirit (verse 10). Nehemiah, in the great prayer in chapter 9, refers back to God's leading the people in the wilderness, giving his good spirit to instruct them (9.20). These references were picked up in various second-Temple writings, including the Dead Sea Scrolls. This is classic new-exodus language. It grounds both the hope of the inheritance and the holiness required to attain it in the ancient promises of God which are now fulfilled in Messiah and spirit. And, as I've said, it confronts the pretensions of Caesar's empire with the reality of a new people, those who hail not Caesar but Jesus as *kyrios*, Lord and 'son of God'.

So, in verse 16, the indwelling divine spirit provides the assurance that 'we' – the Messiah's people – are indeed 'God's children'. The 'we' here is clearly the whole messianic people, extended not just to Jews but also, in line with the original Abrahamic promise, to believing gentiles. The 'we' here, in fact, means all those who are *en Christō*, all baptized and believing Jesus-followers. There was, in Rome, a tricky and delicate relationship between Jewish and gentile Jesus-believers, and Paul addresses that in chapters 14 and 15. Here, he assumes that he is talking to *all* the Messiah-people. If there is any doubt about the status of gentile Jesus-followers, any possible challenge which, as in Galatia, might have demoted them to second-class status, it is the presence and work of the spirit that provides the necessary assurance that they are all 'children of God'. They all, together, form the one new-exodus family.

One other exodus-motif that doesn't appear here but comes later in the passage is the *groaning* of the people as they await their redemption. We'll come back to this when we're looking at verses 22 to 25. But this completes the set of exodus-references, encouraging us to see the whole passage in this light.

So to the 'inheritance' – which, to say it one more time, is not 'heaven'. It is the entire creation. Here the key text, lying not far beneath the surface of verse 17, is Psalm 2, one of the most popular psalms in the early Christian writings. Remember how that psalm works: the nations rant and rage against God the creator, but God installs his king in Zion and addresses him as his son. 'Ask of me,' he says to the king, 'and I will give you *the nations* for your inheritance, and *the uttermost parts of the world* for your possession' (see Psalm 2.8). This is in line with those other great messianic psalms, 72 and 89.

Psalm 2 encapsulates a vital move in biblical eschatology. Just as the promises to Adam in Genesis 1 become commands to Abraham in Genesis 12 onwards, so the small-scale promises to Abraham – one family, one particular land – become worldwide promises to the Messiah. The 'inheritance', from Psalm 2 through to Romans 8, is no longer one strip of territory in the Middle East. *The whole world is now God's holy land.* What God does in and for Israel is what God is going to do *through* Israel, specifically through Israel's anointed king and his spirit-filled followers, *for the whole world.* Paul doesn't use the word 'kingdom' (*basileia*) at this point, but he is none the less picking up the kingdom-of-God language which he had set out in Romans 5.12–21, retrieving the relevant themes from Isaiah, Daniel and of course the Psalms. And now this 'kingdom', this messianic inheritance, is to be shared with all the Messiah's people. If we are God's heirs, and thus indebted to God (picking up verse 12, as we saw), then we are *fellow heirs* with the Messiah.

Once we see this, we find verse 17 turning in an unexpected direction. Psalm 2, left to itself, implies that the Messiah will inherit the world through military conquest. But the other scriptures to which Jesus himself was obedient made it clear that the way to that 'glory' – the glory of worldwide rule – is through the hard pilgrim road of suffering. That is the point that Jesus explained to the two puzzled disciples on the road to Emmaus in Luke 24. And it goes back all the way to passages such as Mark 8, the challenge to follow Jesus along the path of true kingly power – by taking up the cross. And, of course, this theme comes to a particular focus in the Gethsemane scene in Matthew and Mark, the one place where Jesus himself is recorded as addressing the father as 'Abba'. Jesus on that terrible night was wrestling with his vocation, knowing from the scriptures – even though his whole self recoiled from the idea – that the way to the kingdom lay through the cross.[5]

And all this enables us to understand verses 12 and 13 more fully. Paul there makes it clear that the road to life is the road of *mortification*, of the active putting-to-death of things that the body would otherwise want to do. This isn't just pragmatic, as though Paul were simply reflecting ruefully on his missionary experience, on what it costs to live and preach the message of the crucified Jesus. It is deeply theological: Paul has learned, at the foot of the cross, that this is how Israel's God reclaimed his kingship over the world; *and* – though the church has by no means always figured this one out – that this is how Jesus'

---

5 Matt. 26.36–46; Mark 14.32–42.

followers will make that kingship a reality in the present and the future.

All this comes together, then, in the three interlocking emphases of these dense verses, 12 to 17. Let's walk through it one more time and see. First, we have a spirituality of holiness and hope, verses 12 and 13. Second, undergirding this, we have the vocation of being God's children, verses 15 and 16. Third, resulting from this, we are called to share the Messiah's cross-shaped path to his kingly rule over the world. A word or two about each.

First, the spirituality of holiness and hope. We here pick up the regular biblical theme of pilgrimage: the Israelites' pilgrimage through the wilderness, but also the regular pilgrimages to Jerusalem, evoked in psalms such as 84 (the people going through the vale of misery on the way to the holy city and finding that valley to be a well of water) and the Psalms of Ascents (120—34). Once more, we must be careful not to slide into thinking of these pilgrim psalms, celebrating the journey up to Zion, in terms of a Platonic 'heaven', as was customary in the Middle Ages. Zion wasn't meant to point away to 'heaven'; it was the place *where heaven and earth came together*. That is the promise for whose fulfilment Paul is hoping in verses 18–30. And that's why holiness is important, not because God is a killjoy, but because we are called to be fully human in a way most of us have scarcely begun to imagine. *We ourselves are to be places where heaven and earth come together*, which means that, as we pray for God's rule to become a reality 'on earth as in heaven', we must daily seek to live out that reality in our own recalcitrant bodies. Platonic escapism and the asceticism that goes with it is a philosophical attempt to avoid that moral challenge by saying that the body is bad; the biblical vision is that the body is good and is to be raised – but only if it learns to die. 'If, by the spirit, you put to death the deeds of the body, you will live' (verse 13).

Paul is here highlighting something he says frequently in various ways. In Galatians 5, he insists that the Messiah's people have crucified the flesh with its passions and desires. In Colossians 3, he stresses that you must 'put to death all that is earthly in you'. And in 1 Corinthians 9 he likens himself to an expert boxer, one who doesn't just flail around in mid-air but one rather who lands his punches – on his own body, to bring it into submission.[6] He does this, he says – and if Paul says this to himself we can be sure we should be saying it to ourselves – in case, having preached to others, we ourselves might end up being disqualified. Our generation has seen too many such cases, in churches of all sorts.

The danger today is that we all too easily slide into would-be 'Christian' versions of the easy-going moralisms of the world around. We think of 'authenticity' or 'spontaneity', 'doing what comes naturally', 'going with your heart' and so on as the primary imperatives, often failing to realize that the heart is deceitful and, as Jesus warns, full of all kinds of things that would make us unclean.[7] Christian ethics means going with the *renewed* heart, bringing the life of heaven to birth in a new earthly lifestyle. That new lifestyle, if we embrace it and learn to live into it, will indeed become spontaneous, and in that sense authentic. But that will only happen through hard-won and spirit-driven Christian virtue.

Again, we must note that this holiness is part of *hope*. I don't mean simply that people who learn to live in God's way can thereby be assured of the ultimate hope; there is some truth there, provided we recognize that this learning and living is the result of the spirit's work within us. No: what I am saying is that holiness means drawing down, from God's promised future, the life we are to live in the present. As in Romans 6, we are

---

6 Gal. 5.24; Col. 3.5; 1 Cor. 9.26–7.
7 Mark 7.17–23.

to be resurrection-people – already in the present time. And, to repeat, this happens *by the spirit* (verse 13). The spirit is not only the guarantee of our ultimate future. The spirit brings that ultimate future into present reality.

So: first, the vision of holiness and hope. Then, second, the vocation to be God's children. Verse 15: 'you received the spirit of sonship, in whom we call out "Abba, father!"' – and, when we do that, 'it is the spirit itself giving supporting witness to what our own spirit is saying, that we are God's children'.

There are two problems here, one in the sentence structure and the other in the meaning. The punctuation of the sentence is the first problem (see Table 1).

Does *en hō krazomen Abba ho patēr* go with what precedes it, or with what follows it? In other words, should we be putting a break after 'sonship', or after 'Abba, father'? The first way of reading it is to say, 'we have received the spirit of sonship *in whom* we call Abba, father', and then to begin a new sentence – without any characteristic Pauline connecting word – with 'the spirit bears witness with our spirit'. The second way is to say, 'we have received the spirit of sonship', full stop, and then to start the new sentence with 'When we call Abba, father, the spirit is bearing witness with our spirit'. You will see in my translation that I have tried to get the best of both worlds by rendering it: 'You received the spirit of sonship, *in whom* we

Table 1 The Sentence Structure of Romans 8.15–16

Option 1	We have received the spirit of sonship in whom we call Abba, father. The spirit bears witness with our spirit.
Option 2	We have received the spirit of sonship. When we call Abba, father, the spirit is bearing witness with our spirit.

call out, "Abba, father!" *When that happens*, it is the spirit itself giving supporting witness . . .", and so on. I think that probably catches Paul's complex meaning. He wants to say *both* that the cry of 'Abba, father' is the sure sign that we have received the spirit of sonship – otherwise why would we find ourselves calling God father in this familiar way? *And* he wants to say that this is the sign, more specifically, that the holy spirit is getting together with our spirit, fusing with our own deepest inwardness, to say, Yes, we really are God's children.

So much for the sentence structure. What about the meaning? Here Paul refers to the *human* spirit of the believer. He has done this already in verse 10, and he does it as well in 1 Corinthians 2.11–12, which is quite close to the present passage. Please note, again, that Paul doesn't talk here about the *soul*. When he refers to the deepest human interiority – we quickly run out of language at this point and have to use cumbersome phrases like that – he speaks of the human spirit. And here he declares that the holy spirit as it were gets together with our own spirit to tell us the same thing, that we really are God's children.

We have to be careful here at a pastoral level. People's 'experience' varies widely according to personality. It's easy to be fooled either way: either into imagining something is the case when it isn't, or into imagining something isn't the case when it is. There are many casual or 'occasional' church attenders who have a vague sense of God being around the place somewhere and so assume they are 'all right'; and there are many devout, prayerful folk with sensitive consciences who agonize over whether they are genuine Christians. And there are many other possibilities too. Pastoral experience suggests that the only way through is by prayer and gentle active listening as we seek to help one another discern, as we say, 'where we really are with God'.

But at the heart of it here is this strange Aramaic word 'Abba', as in Galatians 4.5–6 and Mark 14.36.[8] Granted that most of Paul's hearers will not have been Aramaic speakers, why does he assume that they all use this word in prayer? I don't think Paul can mean that they all speak in tongues and that, when they do, this is one of the things they say. Nor do I think it refers to the church praying an Aramaic version of the Lord's Prayer, though that is not impossible. I think it must go back to the early catechesis, the teaching of converts, when people would come to faith and discover that the God who made the world was neither an impersonal force nor a distant faceless bureaucrat, nor yet a capricious and possibly malevolent personality, but was both deeply personal, deeply loving and deeply – in the best sense – paternal. And when the teachers in the early church recognized this new awareness in converts, they would guide and encourage them to address God in the way that Jesus himself had done in that memorable scene.

But this then projects us forwards to verse 17, which we will pick up in our next chapter. This is where we discover that the vocational pathway for those who pray the Abba-prayer is the same as it was for Jesus himself: the path of suffering. If Paul assumes that all Christians will address God as 'Abba', perhaps this is partly because he also assumes that all Christians will suffer – and it was as Jesus faced the sharpest suffering that he addressed God in that way.

But this suffering is not (as we shall see later) a question of 'something unpleasant we just have to get through'. Like the sufferings of Jesus himself, Paul seems to envisage this suffering as an active quality. Strange as it may seem, this is one of the ways in which Paul understands Jesus' followers to be exercising their vocation as the royal priesthood, as the

8   The parallel in Matt. 26.39 has translated this into Greek: *ho patēr mou.*

image-bearers, the true humans, the true children of God. This is how, in fact, we are 'conformed to the image of the firstborn son', as in verse 29. This doesn't simply mean that we are to be like Jesus, awaiting the resurrection in which we will at last resemble his glorious body (Philippians 3.21). It means that, through our life, and especially through our needing to pray the strange and dark prayer of verses 26–7, God's purposes may be worked out, not only in and for us but (as befits the royal family, the family of whom Caesar's family are a trivial parody) actually *through* us. This is how, as in 5.17, those who receive the gift of righteousness begin their glorious vocation of *reigning in life* through the one man Jesus the Messiah. And that is part – though only one part – of what Paul means by our being 'glorified'.

But to take this further we need to look at verses 17 to 21.

5
Romans 8.17–21: The Liberation of Creation

¹⁷And if we're children, we are also heirs: heirs of God, and fellow heirs with the Messiah, as long as we suffer with him so that we may also be glorified with him.
¹⁸This is how I work it out. The sufferings we go through in the present time are not worth putting in the scale alongside the glory that is going to be unveiled for us.
¹⁹Yes: creation itself is on tiptoe with expectation, eagerly awaiting the moment when God's children will be revealed.
²⁰Creation, you see, was subjected to pointless futility, not of its own volition, but because of the one who placed it in this subjection, in the hope
²¹that creation itself would be freed from its slavery to

¹⁷*ei de tekna, kai klēronomoi: klēronomoi men theou, synklēronomoi de Christou, eiper sympaschomen hina kai syndoxasthōmen.*

¹⁸*logizomai gar hoti ouk axia ta pathēmata tou nyn kairou pros tēn mellousan doxan apokalyphthēnai eis hēmas.*

¹⁹*hē gar apokaradokia tēs ktiseōs tēn apokalypsin tōn hyiōn tou theou apekdechetai.*

²⁰*tē gar mataiotēti hē ktisis hypetagē, ouch hekousa alla dia ton hypotaxanti, eph' helpidi*

²¹*hoti kai hautē hē ktisis eleutherōthēsetai apo tēs*

decay, to enjoy the freedom that comes when God's children are glorified.	*douleias tēs phthoras eis tēn n eleutherian tēs doxēs tōteknōn tou theou.*

We ended our previous chapter with Romans 8.17. As we saw, verse 17 functions as a kind of bridge, drawing together the line of thought in verses 12 to 16 and forming the foundation for what is to come. Paul has declared that we suffer with the Messiah so that we may also be glorified in him. But what does 'glory' actually mean? Today's passage will tell us; but the church has been surprisingly slow to pay heed.

The deliberately slow pace at which we are moving through the chapter gives us the chance to look simply at this short passage, verses 17–21, rather than dashing on at once to the remarkable material that follows. Verses 22–30 are indeed fascinating, but they mean what they mean because of what we find here in 17–21. Paul has announced, in verse 17, the theme of suffering and glory. He will come to the suffering presently. These verses, through to 21, are simply about the glory, what it means and how it is to be attained.

Glory, of course, is where verses 18–30 are going, all the way to the climactic last clause of verse 30: those he justified, *them he also glorified.* So what does *that* mean? The church has usually understood Paul to be affirming that those who come to faith in Jesus, and so are 'justified', are assured of going to heaven. But if our present passage, verses 17–21, shows us what Paul means by 'glory' and 'being glorified', then we have to revise that view quite radically. Verse 30 is the conclusion to *this* passage, and to *this* point, not to something else. To say it again, Romans 8 is simply not about 'going to heaven'. Heaven is never mentioned in this chapter; indeed, 'heaven' in the sense of 'where Christians will go after death' is missing from this whole letter and indeed Paul's whole correspondence. The common contemporary Christian usage of the word 'glory' to mean 'heaven' as normally conceived (as when someone who has died is spoken of as having 'gone to glory') misses Paul's point. So what is he saying?

The primary meanings of 'glory' in this passage are, simultaneously, **the glorious presence of God himself dwelling within us by the spirit**, and **the wise, healing, reconciling rule of God's people over the whole creation**. These two – God's presence and human rule – are made for each other. They fit together.

We have already seen, in verses 9–11 and then in verses 12–17, that Paul is retrieving the exodus-story at the point where God comes in person to dwell in the Tabernacle. That is the implication of all that Paul says about God's spirit dwelling within believers to lead them to the 'inheritance'. Those 'in the Messiah' are 'new-Temple' people. Paul insists in 2 Corinthians 3 and 4 that the divine glory really does dwell within Jesus' people, even though, as cracked clay jars, they know themselves to be deeply unworthy. That is the first meaning of 'glory', and it suffuses this whole passage. But all that we will now say about the second meaning of 'glory' – the human vocation and destiny to be set in authority over the world – is not to be played off against this Temple-idea of the divine glory dwelling within Jesus' people. One of the spectacular features of this whole chapter is that the two meanings converge – as they did, and do, in Jesus himself. In technical theological terms, we are at this point near the heart of both Christology and pneumatology. In terms of what Paul is now going to say, we are reaching the point of convergence between God's ultimate purposes for creation and his challenging vocation to his spirit-filled people.

The primary meaning of the many-sided word 'glory' (*doxa* in Greek, looking back regularly to *kabod* in Hebrew) is 'dignity', 'worth' or 'status'. The Hebrew carries the notion of 'weight', as we might speak about the 'weighty presence' of a powerful or influential figure or the 'weighty words' of an important speech or sermon. This idea of dignity, worth and status goes with both sides of Paul's meaning.

Before we get further with the exegesis, there are two preliminary remarks, one about our present global context and the other about the incomprehensibility at this point of the well-known King James Version of the Bible.

First, today's context. We are more aware now than ever before of the crisis in ecology and climate change. That is of course controversial. Some of the rhetoric about it – on both sides of the debate! – is clearly driven by political and ideological agendas from which some of us would want to hold back. But, like the arguments a generation ago about the ill effects of smoking tobacco, the evidence is massive and mounting daily. From greenhouse gases to bad farming practices, not to mention nuclear accidents and 'dirty bombs', the post-Enlightenment world has twisted the vocation to be image-bearing stewards of creation into the chance to exploit creation to serve our pride, or greed, or both. This, alas, is scarcely new. Ancient empires, not least the Romans, routinely used a 'scorched earth' policy, literally or metaphorically, when it suited them. A rebel country or city might not only be defeated in battle. It might be rendered uninhabitable, with its wells poisoned and its fields sown with salt. That, we grant, wouldn't have threatened the whole planet. But it was the smaller-scale equivalent of what we now face. If we, called to be wise stewards of creation in the twenty-first century, are to be true to that calling, this present passage will be one of our primary resources for a theological response to the crisis.

Of course, the western church has regularly ignored this theme. This is partly because concern with creation has seemed 'unspiritual', being earthly minded rather than heavenly. If Romans is read as a book about 'how to go to heaven', then why would we bother with looking after the present space–time world? Well, thank you, Plato, enjoy your philosophical detachment – while the poorest of the poor face rising sea levels and acid rain. And sometimes, particularly in America, this Platonism has been reinforced by the caricature of biblical eschatology we find in the so-called 'rapture' doctrine, which actually welcomes signs of the imminent destruction of Planet Earth, or of a coming Armageddon, or whatever. Romans 8 stands firmly over against any such nonsense.

But Romans 8 has often not been well understood. This is partly because what Paul is saying doesn't fit with what the theologians have wanted to emphasize, from the Middle Ages through to our own day. That is why the best-loved English translation from the last four hundred years, the King James or Authorized Version, makes such a mess of it: this simply wasn't a theme that the learned translators of the early seventeenth century thought important. The result is that, if you want to avoid the challenge of the present passage, then read it in the King James Version, where you will find it as clear as mud. That will encourage you to read on quickly out the other side to the climactic verses 28–30 which you will be able to read in the way the tradition wants you to.

Actually, when I was in pastoral ministry I sometimes used this passage, cheekily, for this purpose. I had one or two regular readers – people who would volunteer to read scripture during worship – who liked to insist on using the King James Version.

So I would give them passages such as this one to read. Here are verses 19–21 in the King James:

> For the earnest expectation of the creature waiteth for the manifestation of the sons of God. For the creature was made subject to vanity, not willingly, but by reason of him who hath subjected the same in hope, because the creature itself also shall be delivered from the bondage of corruption into the glorious liberty of the children of God.

Best of luck with that, out loud at 10.30 on a Sunday morning or any other time. You see, once you translate *ktisis* as 'creature' the meaning has already become unclear. For us, the word 'creature' doesn't mean 'creation' as a whole. It means a small animal. By the time the text then says that the 'creature' became subject to 'vanity', we will be imagining that same small animal admiring itself in a mirror. As to who 'subjected' this creature to 'vanity', or how or why this was done, and as to what deliverance from that plight might consist in, the theological tradition both of the Middle Ages and the Reformation offers little or no help. And the ordinary reader hurries on to a few verses later, which appear to teach what we normally expect to hear.

Let us then do what we've been doing up to this point. Let us stand back a bit, to apply our normal questions to the passage and see what happens.

First, look at the start and the finish of the passage. Obviously, the verses we are concerned with here (17–21) are part of a longer train of thought, with verse 30 as the real 'ending'. There, sure enough, Paul lands where he began, with the promise of glory, emerging out of suffering. But our present short section, as a sub-set of that, reflects the same point. We begin and end with glory. Verse 17: 'we suffer with him so that we may also be glorified'; verse 21: 'the freedom that comes when God's children are glorified'. This is the controlling theme of these verses. They expand and explain the last line of verse 17, and they set the context for verses 22–30. This is the framework within which we must understand verses 19–20. *But this 'glorification', clearly, is not about faithful Christians going to heaven.* It is about creation being rescued from corruption! What has that to do with 'the glory that is going to be unveiled for us'? The answer is in the biblical background. We will come to that presently.

The second thing about reading Paul, we recall, is to look at the little words that tie together his clauses and sentences. Here, once again, we have three sentences linked to what precedes with *gar*, 'for'. In my own translation, since a repeated 'for' sounds quite stilted in regular English, I have used other joining phrases but, if we render *gar* as 'for', the logical links become clear. Thus:

> [17] . . . we suffer with him so that we may also be glorified with him. [18]For [*gar*] the present sufferings are not worth comparing with the glory that is to be unveiled for us. [19]For [*gar*] creation is on tiptoe, waiting for God's children to be revealed; [20]For [*gar*] creation was subjected to futility . . . in the hope [21]that [*hoti*] creation itself would be freed from slavery, to enjoy the freedom that comes when God's children are glorified.

Now if we assume the 'normal' reading of this passage, verse 19 doesn't look as if it explains verse 18 at all. It looks like a non sequitur, moving from the coming glory (which the normal reading would assume to be 'heaven') to the longing of the present space–time–matter creation. But Paul links it with *gar*, 'for' or 'because'. In my own translation, I have expanded this into 'this is how I work it out', partly because, at the start of verse 18, Paul uses the verb *logizomai*, which means 'I work it out' or 'I reckon it up'; it's a *calculating* word. So if Paul has just said that the present sufferings don't compare with the coming glory, why would he *explain* that by talking, in verse 19, about creation longing for God's children to be revealed? And why would he then explain *that* (with the *gar* at the start of verse 20) by digging down, not to the human problem of sin and death, but to the cosmic problem of futility and corruption? Answering these questions will give us a steer on where the whole larger passage is going.

We can approach these matters best by asking our third regular question: what happens when we try to read this text within the world of Paul's day, within the worldview, narratives and assumptions that his contemporaries would have in mind?

The world into which Paul went as a missionary was the world dominated by Rome, by Caesar. For the previous century, the Roman propaganda machine had been churning out one particular myth (see Appendix 1). Many ancient pagans saw the great sweep of history in terms of a succession of ages – a golden age, then silver, then bronze, then iron. There were several variations on this theme, but they always pointed to a final return to the golden age, the age (as they thought) of Saturn. And in 41 BC, three years after Julius Caesar's assassination, a brilliant young poet, Virgil, penned an eclogue declaring that the golden age had indeed come round again, bringing peace and harmony to the world of nature. Virgil said much the same in the *Aeneid*, tying this now explicitly to the rule of Julius Caesar's adopted son, Augustus. The earlier poem was later taken up by Christians as a pagan prophecy of the incarnation of Jesus. (That is why, in some Christian circles, particularly in the Middle Ages, Virgil becomes a kind of honorary semi-saint, as in Dante's great poem.)

Augustus solidified his imperial rule by engaging in a massive publicity programme, not just through his court poets and historians but in symbolic statues. The *Ara pacis*, the altar of peace, which you can still visit in Rome, declares symbolically that with Augustus as emperor there is now a time of peace, harmony and fruitfulness. The ground is bringing forth all that humans could desire. This scene of peaceful life and plentiful harvests was copied on coins, and carved in marble, right across the empire. Nature herself was seen as a placid matriarch, resting at peace, surrounded by abundant provision. The message was: you've never had it so good – and it's all because Caesar's heir is on the throne, bringing peace and justice to the world! And of course, the subtext of this, the message to the far-flung inhabitants of the empire, was: so please settle down and get used to Roman rule. Don't even think about rebellion. Why would you? You are in the best of all possible worlds.

That line of propaganda was continued by later emperors, not least Nero, as in the third extract in Appendix 1. In the days before mass media, the way the message got out was through coins, statues, inscriptions and particularly poems. Rome, like all empires before and since, went on pushing this line. That was true throughout Paul's lifetime, and in towns and cities more or less everywhere he went. Indeed, he seems to have made a point of visiting key centres of Roman influence, such as Ephesus and Corinth, intending then to go on to Rome itself and to Spain, the important western outpost of Roman rule. His strategy seems to have been to announce Jesus as the true *Kyrios*, the world's true Lord, in places where that word, and the claims that went with it, had been firmly linked to Caesar.

So in this letter, sent to Rome itself, Paul is declaring powerfully that, like all pagan claims, the Roman claim is at best a parody of the truth. Everybody knew, of course, that in its own terms it was a lie. Rome's supposed glory was built on ruthless military conquest, often backed up by crucifixions. Rome's rule was always as precarious as the next provincial rebellion, or the next riot over food shortages if the grain ships failed to arrive on time. And for Paul, in any case, 'nature' was not an independent peaceful matriarch. The wider world, from his biblical and Jewish perspective, was not a self-supporting 'nature'. It was 'creation', the good world made by the good creator God, but now groaning in labour pains, longing to give birth to the real new age as opposed to the glossy fake one imagined by the Roman court poets.

Paul, in other words, was thinking with the Bible rather than with imperial propaganda. He believed in the ancient Hebrew promise of new creation (see Appendix 2). The Old Testament regularly points ahead, even in the midst of Israel's rebellion and failure, to the promise that the God who made the world would one day remake it. There would come a time of cosmic harmony.

Two features of this stand out. On the one hand, this would come about through the work of the Davidic Messiah, as in Isaiah 11 or Psalm 72. On the other hand, it would reveal the divine glory, as in Isaiah 35 or 40. Actually, Isaiah 11 and Psalm 72 say that as well: the whole earth will be full of God's glory, rather as the wilderness Tabernacle, or Solomon's Temple, had been filled with the glorious divine presence. These promises were variously retrieved, developed, expanded and celebrated in second-Temple Jewish writings. We sometimes call these writings 'apocalyptic', which means 'revelatory', because they speak of God the creator suddenly revealing his new creation as the shocking fulfilment of his age-old plan. Again we note the contrast with the Roman vision of a present imperial utopia. The Roman dream is built on violent military conquest. The Hebraic and Jewish vision regularly emerges through a time of intense suffering.

The early Christians quite naturally retrieved and restated this biblical theme of new creation for the obvious reason that it had begun to be fulfilled in the resurrection of Jesus. They believed that, by the spirit, this new creation was powerfully at work both *in* faithful human beings and *through* them in the wider world.

It is of course strange, from our much later perspective, that the two stories, the biblical and Jewish one on the one hand and the Roman one on the other, developed in unintended parallel. The Jewish texts go back long before the rise of Rome; and the Roman texts were certainly not borrowing ideas from Isaiah or the Psalms. However, many Jews of Paul's day, calculating the future on the basis of 'seventy weeks of years' in Daniel 9.24, concluded that the new age was about to dawn in what we call the first century.[1] And that, for quite different reasons, was the very moment when the Roman empire was trumpeting the arrival of its own new age through the Caesars. The great story of the gospel – the good news that the creator had rescued his creation through his son, and was bringing justice, salvation, peace and glory to all – was born into a world where there was already a powerful and well-publicized story about the good news of a son of god who had brought justice, salvation, peace and glory to the world.

So here, at the climax of the letter precisely to the church in Rome, we see the implicit clash of controlling narratives. Of course, we can't simply look back at ancient parodies of the truth and feel smug that we are not subject to similar distortions ourselves. We ought to ponder carefully the ways in which the vast and socially powerful narratives of both modernity and postmodernity have offered the world things that look a bit like the Christian gospel but are in fact deadly parodies.

---

1 On the retrieval of Dan. 9 in this period, see *PFG*, ch. 2 (pp. 96, 133 and 142).

Thus modernity has tried to steal Christianity's clothes with its talk of progress and enlightenment, offering an eschatology without God and a would-be wisdom without God. Postmodernity, in reaction, has given us a harsh doctrine of original sin – the hermeneutic of suspicion is the secular version of that dogma – but without any hope of redemption or forgiveness. There are not, after all, that many great truths in the world. The Christian gospel has them all, and in proper balance. But powerful sub-Christian movements regularly snatch bits and pieces of them and try to put them together in new ways which never actually do what they promise. Modernism already showed its true colours with the guillotine, and followed that up with the Holocaust. Postmodernity does to cultural icons what tyrannical empires have always done and are still doing, demolishing everything but with no plans for rebuilding.

But the parodies of the truth are not just to be seen in the secular world. They crop up with sad regularity in the people of God themselves – ourselves, I should say. This sorry story goes all the way back to Aaron making the golden calf, at the very moment when God was giving Moses the pattern for the Tabernacle. It comes all the way forwards to what happens when God's people today, individually or corporately, are seduced into grasping after something that looks like a good gift, but which in fact, like Caesar's promises, is all smoke and mirrors, dust and ashes. Where the biblical meaning of creation and new creation has been long obscured through semi- or sub-Christian teaching, it is fatally easy for toxic mixtures of faith and politics to push themselves in and take over.

But this brings us back, above all, to the biblical meaning of 'glory'. To go back to the key words: the Hebrew word *kabod*, and the Greek word *doxa*, do indeed come to include things such as radiance and brilliant light. That is what many readers imagine Paul is talking about. But this isn't their basic meaning, and it isn't what Paul normally means. In the Hebrew scriptures, 'glory' regularly comes to refer specifically to *rule* or *power*. That is why 'glory' is regularly a royal term, symbolized visually in crowns, sometimes with rays of bright light streaming in all directions. The bright light isn't the glory itself. The light *tells you about* the glory, the weighty dignity and power. The honour of the person is *symbolized by* that bright light. So when scripture promises that God's glory will flood the whole creation, that doesn't mean that the whole world will become luminous, as though it had a powerful light bulb somewhere deep inside. It means that God's creative power and wisdom will, as we say, shine out visibly all around.

This promise about the coming glory – the glory of human beings put in charge of the world – is a major theme for Paul. It goes closely with the promise of resurrection, which is built on the foundation of Jesus' own resurrection. Paul retrieves these biblical promises in other related passages, particularly 1 Corinthians 15.20–8 and Philippians 3.19–21. Both of those passages make explicit what here is said densely and allusively. (That often happens with Paul: he spells out a point in one place and summarizes it in a puzzling aphorism somewhere else. You need to check the spelling-out to be sure you've understood the aphorism.)

In particular, in those passages in 1 Corinthians and Philippians, Paul evokes three psalms and a chapter of Daniel. The passages in question, worth studying carefully at leisure, are Psalm 2, where the Davidic Messiah is set in authority over the world; Psalm 110, where the Messiah is installed at God's right hand to be over all enemies, a point strongly echoed in Daniel 7; and especially Psalm 8, the vocation of human beings to be God's stewards in looking after his world: crowned with *glory* and honour, with all things put in subjection under their feet.

That's 'glory' for Paul in these passages. Psalm 8, in particular, is vital. It picks up and focuses the promise of Genesis 1, of humans made in God's image and given responsibility for God's creation. That is one way in which the two meanings – the presence of God and the authority of humans – converge.

These pictures go together not least because some Jewish readers understood Psalm 8 in terms of the Messiah, making the coming king to be the ultimate, true human being. This aligns with a regular ancient view of kings as being made in the divine image. Genesis 1, of course, insists that actually all humans are image-bearers; all humans possess royal dignity. But many ancient Jews continued to read Psalm 8 messianically; and that opens the way for Paul to link it, in the passages just referred to, with other messianic texts.

Paul too saw Psalm 8 fulfilled in Jesus, the one to whom all things are put in subjection. For Paul, as we would expect after the famous Adam-and-Messiah passage in Romans 5, this is then about Jesus as *the ultimate true human*, just as in 1 Corinthians 15. Modern Christians have often assumed that our main task as apologists is to persuade people of Jesus' divinity; but Paul, without in any way denying or undermining that, insists in these passages that Jesus is the truly human being. And his regular point, in line with the biblical democratization of the Davidic promise, is that Jesus, as Messiah, *shares this role with all his people*. Verse 29: we are to be *conformed to the image of the son*, 'so that he might be the firstborn of a large family'. Psalm 8 picks up Genesis 1 and 2, insisting that the human vocation remains on the agenda, even though it wasn't clear – until the coming of the gospel – how it would all work out. Those who belong to Jesus, who are indwelt by his spirit, share his vocation, shaped by Genesis 1 and Psalm 8.

Romans 8 contains much more. But this is a start. It's enough to help us through these four vital verses. What then emerges into view, as perhaps the most mind-blowing feature of this whole passage, is the double meaning, to which I already alluded, of 'glory', of the 'hope of glory', and of 'glorification'. We need to take a moment and ponder this two-sided reality, and what its two-sidedness means.

If you had asked a first-century Jew, 'What is "the hope of glory"?', they would probably have answered, 'We are hoping that our God will return in power and majesty, to dwell in the Temple and establish his kingdom over Israel and the world.' But they might also have said, 'The hope of glory is that God's people will be set in authority under him and over the world.' The Dead Sea Scrolls, referring to their own community, say that to them 'all the glory of Adam shall be given', which means that they will be installed as world rulers, reflecting God's wise order into his creation. That is a classic reading of Daniel 7, one indeed validated by the passage itself, which explains the exaltation and world rulership of the 'one like a son of man' in terms of *the people of the saints of the Most High* who receive the kingdom and rule over it for ever.

This double hope – the divine glory and the human glory – then comes astonishingly together. The *divine* glory, promised in Isaiah 40 and 52 and in Ezekiel, returns to the Temple in the person of the Messiah, and also, as in Romans 8.9–11, in the spirit. And those who are thus declared 'sons of God' are thereby given the *human* glory, dignity and authority of being, like the Danielic son of man, set under God and over the world. Think of Psalm 8 once again, where the humans, 'the (corporate) son of man' in fact, is or are 'crowned with glory and honour'. Paul had used that phrase already in Romans 2.10, when speaking of the ultimate state of God's people. So you could say that Isaiah 40 (the return of the divine glory) is fulfilled through the fulfilment of Psalm 8 (the exaltation of the true human or humans) – and vice versa. This is a huge and vital vision. It is nothing short of a Trinitarian theology of glory, which includes at its heart the original divine intention for human beings.

Paul's point in verse 18 – which appears obvious once you see the whole picture! – is that this glory bears no comparison with the present suffering.

With all this in mind, we turn at last to the detail of these five vital verses, 17–21. Verse 17: 'we are . . . fellow heirs with the Messiah,' Paul declares, 'as long as we suffer with him so that we may be glorified with him.' 'Glorified' here is thus another way of saying 'receiving the inheritance', which is the human rule over creation. In and with the Messiah, we are to be set in restorative authority over God's world. This is then explained in verse 18 with the solemn word 'reckon', *logizomai*; Paul has 'worked it out'. He has, as people say, done the maths. What he says here goes closely with 2 Corinthians 4, where Paul declares that the present troubles are a slight momentary affliction that cannot begin to compare with the eternal weight of glory.

So in verse 18 he contrasts the 'present time' with the 'coming age'. In the present time, since the resurrection of Jesus, the old age and the new age overlap. They run in parallel. In the final 'coming age', the glory will be fully revealed; but it is already at work. At the end of the verse, he insists that the glory will indeed be unveiled *for us* or *upon us* (*apokalyphthēnai eis hēmas*). This *eis hēmas* is unexpected. We might have thought that the glory would be revealed *to* us, in the sense that we would be spectators, looking on, when the divine glory returned in all its fullness. That would have required just the dative, *hēmin*. But no. The divine glory is going to be unveiled *upon us*. We will discover that we are clothed in it, invested (as we say) with it. This requires, and in Romans 8 is given, a full, dense theological understanding of the holy spirit, as simultaneously the glorious divine presence in the Messiah's people and the one who enables them to be the true humans within God's present purposes. Thus in the coming sudden unveiling, the 'apocalypse' whose centrepiece will be the return of Jesus himself, we redeemed humans will be invested, equipped, with that divine authority over the world that already belongs to Jesus himself. As he says at the end of Matthew 28, all authority is given to him. Even there, already, his followers are commissioned to go into the world to make that authority a reality. In the end that work will be complete.

It's important to get our minds round how all this fits together. For Paul and all the early Christians, the coming apocalypse would unveil Jesus himself. When Jesus returns, or when he 'reappears' (as Paul and John put it in Colossians 3.4 and 1 John 3.2), the twin halves of the good creation, heaven and earth – at present mutually opaque – will become fully and visibly one. Paul speaks of this moment in 1 Corinthians 15, Philippians 3 and elsewhere. But in the present passage, it is *Jesus' people themselves* who are the subject of the 'apocalypse'. They are themselves to be 'unveiled'. As he says in Colossians 3.4, when the Messiah appears, '*you too will be revealed* with him in glory'. We normally think of *Christians* waiting for the *Messiah* to be revealed; but here it is the *cosmos* waiting for the *Christians* to be revealed! And that leads us straight into verse 19.

Look closely at how verse 19 works in the Greek. Paul has already used the word *apokalyphthēnai* in verse 18. Now he seems deliberately to exploit the poetic potential of the word with the repeated *apo*, the 'k' sound and also the 'd': *hē gar apokaradokia tēs ktiseōs tēn apokalypsin tōn hyiōn tou theou apekdechetai*. Those words starting with *ap-* (*apokaradokia, apokalypsin, apekdechetai*) created an explosion of consonants, highlighting the explosive nature of the moment when God will finally complete his work with Jesus' return and the transformation of all things.

It may seem odd, at first sight, to have *apokaradokia* as the subject of the sentence. That word properly means 'eager longing'. It gives the sense of someone straining their head forward to see what's coming round the corner. This makes translation difficult, of course, since literally it means 'the straining forward of the creation is eagerly awaiting the revelation of God's children'. I have simplified this somewhat in my own translation, where, like most translators, I have made 'creation itself' to be the subject ('creation itself is on tiptoe'). Paul constructs his sentence with these two crunchy assonant words (*apokaradokia, apekdechetai*) at either end – and the central feature, *apokalypsin*, held between them. And this central feature is *the revealing, the unveiling, of God's children*. That is you and me. That, declares Paul, is what creation is waiting for.

Paul assumes, of course, that this will be the revelation of God, and of Jesus. But what counts here, because this is how God made the world from the beginning, is that creation is longing for *us* – us humans, us Jesus-followers, us spirit-temples – to be unveiled as the glorified, in other words the empowered, stewards of creation, called to restore creation to its proper purpose. Creation is, of course, waiting for its creator. But what it mostly wants is its proper steward, the wise human family in whom the creator's own spirit is at work. One day we, Jesus' followers, shall be revealed as exactly that. This, we note in passing, is exactly what the book of Revelation says about God's plan for his redeemed human creatures: we are rescued in order to become 'the royal priesthood'.[2]

Verses 20 and 21 then explain this: note the *gar* at the start, which I have translated as 'you see', a regular English way of signalling explanation. Paul here takes us back to Genesis 3; he

---

2 Rev. 1.6; 5.10; 20.6.

has actually had the whole creation story in mind throughout, as he did in the earlier chapters of Romans. This is where the programmatic statement of Romans 5.12–21 (the Adam-and-Messiah passage) comes into its own. Adam's sin meant not only that he and Eve were expelled from the garden, but that the earth itself would now produce thorns and thistles. Genesis 1 and 2, after all, described the launching of a *project*, not a static tableau. Creation as there described was supposed to be the start of something even greater. But that was to happen through the stewardship of the image-bearers. Their rebellion meant that the project was thwarted. It suffered from *mataiotēs*, the third Greek word in verse 20, meaning 'frustration' or 'futility'. Without wise, obedient humans to guide it, creation was going nowhere, and it knew it.

This was not the fault of creation itself. When, in verse 20, Paul says 'not of its own volition', he is ruling out any Platonic notion that the created order is *by its own very nature* futile and corrupt. Rather, God the creator has ordered it this way because his creation was designed to flourish under the authority of genuine God-reflecting humans, and until such are found it will stay frustrated. The creator is not going to erase the working principle of his original creation, the principle according to which his world would work properly through obedient humans. That, after all, had been (as we see with long Christian hindsight) a plan designed for God's own use, for his own second self to come as the ultimate wise and obedient human, and for his own spirit to reanimate other humans and equip them for their own consequent roles.

So creation was subjected to this futility, but always 'in hope'. The Greek phrase *eph' helpidi* at the end of verse 20 could go either with what comes before ('subjected in hope', that is, 'subjected with a purpose'), or with what comes after ('in the hope that . . .' – especially if, as in some manuscripts, the first word of verse 21 is *hoti*, 'that', rather than *dihoti*, 'because').[3] The difference is small. Both meanings are well within the larger point Paul is making: God's purpose, behind the present sad state of creation, was always looking forward to the ultimate redemption.

This brings us, then, to the glorious claim of verse 21 – but the claim is often misunderstood. Many translations make Paul say that the creation will *share* the 'glorious freedom of God's children' or something like that. But that string of genitives – the *eleutheria* of the *doxa* of the *tekna* of *theos*, 'the freedom of the glory of the children of God' – can't in fact be rendered by a simple phrase like this. The 'freedom' here is *creation's* freedom, as opposed to its slavery to decay; but the 'glory' here is the human authority *over* creation. Of course, we too will be free from sin and death, but that's not the point Paul is making. *Creation* will, he declares, be set free from its slavery to decay; and this will happen when *the Messiah's people* are glorified, raised from the dead and thereby given their always-intended authority over the world. *This is the glory that will be revealed upon us in verse 18. This is the revelation of God's children from verse 19.* The proper translation of verse 21 is therefore something like what I have offered: creation will in that new day 'enjoy the freedom that comes when God's children are glorified'.

Now, at last, we see the whole flow of thought. Verses 17 and 18: the final new creation, with us playing our glorious part, will be so spectacular that no present suffering can weigh against it. This is because, as in verses 19–21, the presently frustrated creation will be released from its slavery to decay when God's children are given their glorious sovereign stewardship. As for the suffering in question, Paul will go on to describe it in

---

3 The best manuscripts are more or less evenly divided on this point.

verses 22 to 27: the groaning of God's people in the midst of the groaning of creation, and the spirit groaning within us at its heart. He will then pull it all together in the last verses of the long central section of the chapter, with the Messiah himself as the truly human one, and ourselves conformed to his image.

Paul has thus described in verses 17 to 21, in language full of biblical resonance, the hope for all creation – the hope which a great many Christians to this day have simply ignored. For a full account, we need the other key passages, 1 Corinthians 15, 2 Corinthians 5 and Philippians 3, not to mention the hints in Acts (3.21 and elsewhere) and Revelation 21—22. But this passage is where that extraordinary sense of double glory – the glorious return of YHWH and the glorious rule of the true humans – comes together in Paul's christologically grounded inaugurated eschatology. Until we've got our heads around this (or perhaps we should say until it has taken root in our hearts and lives) we haven't got the measure of the chapter.

I hope it is clear just how relevant all this is to today's urgent concerns. There are serious debates just now about human responsibility in and for creation. Some, seeing the awful mess that humans have made of the world, are saying that we should back off, live simply and let nature put itself right. Others still insist that God is going to burn up the present world anyway and take us off to heaven, so that ecological concern is a distraction from the gospel. And others, including many in our own day, are saying that we humans have to do it all, to sort it all out. What role might a Pauline Christian have in all this?

Some might respond that perhaps indeed in God's new creation we will have this authority to set creation free; but we are not yet raised from the dead! The new heavens and new earth aren't here yet; so there's not much we can do at the moment, is there? When people say that to me, as they sometimes do, one of the possible answers goes like this. Suppose someone came to me for a pastoral visit, and said something like, 'You see, I have this problem with sin. I keep on sinning and I can't stop. But one day God will give me a moral makeover! So I don't need to worry about it now, do I?' The proper answer to that would be firmly but gently to confront such an enquirer with a Romans-based inaugurated eschatology. According to Romans 6 and 8, and for that matter Colossians 3, we are *already* raised with the Messiah, so we are supposed, in the power of the spirit, to anticipate the eventual resurrection in our present moral life and outward-facing responsibility in God's world. New creation *has* begun, with Jesus' resurrection and the gift of the spirit. That is our starting-point. No excuses.

So what then is the present task of the church? It begins in verses 22 to 27, which we'll examine in our next chapter. It is focused on lament – perhaps surprisingly for those who assume that Romans 8 is all about the joy of salvation. All else follows from that. As in the Psalms, the pathway to celebration regularly passes through the valley of shadows.

One final question, which people ask from time to time. The scientists tell us that, according to their observations of the way things currently are, the present creation will eventually either cool down or heat up. It will either expand indefinitely into the vast cold emptiness of space, or (with the reassertion of gravitational force) rush back together again. The big chill, or the big crunch! How can we then believe that God will renew and restore it?

The answer is that, in the present passage, God promises to do for the whole creation *what he did for Jesus at Easter*. Neither more nor less. Science will quite rightly tell you that when humans die, that's it. Science studies the normal, repeatable evidence within the old creation. That's its job. But the resurrection is the start of the new creation. And when we understand Easter the way Paul does – according to the scriptures, in fact! – we will see that it takes the same faith to believe in the eventual renewal of God's world as it takes to believe that God raised Jesus from the dead. 'Reckoning' that the present suffering cannot compare with the coming glory turns out to be the same Jesus-based act of faith that Paul urges in Romans 6, 'reckoning' that we are already dead to sin and alive to God in the Messiah. Learning to 'reckon' these things is basic to wise, God-reflecting human life.

6
Romans 8.22–7: The Groaning of the Spirit

²²Let me explain. We know that the entire creation is groaning together, and going through labour pains together, up until the present time. ²³Not only so: we too, we who have the first fruits of the spirit's life within us, are groaning within ourselves, as we eagerly await our adoption, the redemption of our body. ²⁴We were saved, you see, in hope. But hope isn't hope if you can see it! Who hopes for what they can see? ²⁵But if we hope for what we don't see, we wait for it eagerly – but also patiently. ²⁶In the same way, too, the spirit comes alongside and helps us in our weakness. We don't know what to pray for as we ought to; but that same spirit pleads on our behalf, with groanings too deep for words.

²²*oidamen gar hoti pasa hē ktisis systenazei kai synōdinei achri tou nyn.*

²³*ou monon de, alla kai autoi tēn aparchēn tou pneumatos echontes, hēmeis kai autoi en heautois stenazomen hyiothesian apekdechomenoi, tēn apolytrōsin tou sōmatos hēmōn.*
²⁴*tē gar elpidi esōthēmen. elpis de blepomenē ouk estin elpis. ho gar blepei tis elpizei?*

²⁵*ei de ho ou blepomen elpizomen, di' hypomenēs apekdechometha.*
²⁶*hōsautōs de kai to pneuma synantilambanetai tē astheneia hēmōn. to gar ti proseuxōmetha katho dei ouk oidamen, alla auto to pneuma hyperentyngchanei stenagmois alalētois.*

²⁷And the Searcher of Hearts knows what the spirit is thinking, because the spirit pleads for God's people according to God's will.

²⁷*ho de eraunōn tas kardias oiden ti to phronēma tou pneumatos, hoti kata theon entyngchanei hyper hagiōn.*

We come now to one of the strangest and perhaps darkest moments in the chapter and indeed the letter as a whole. Paul now takes us to a place which is not what many people would expect from their normal reading of Romans. Actually, Christian readers and even preachers often skip quickly over this bit, treating it as an odd blip as they speed on to verses 28 to 30, and the glorious finale from verse 31 onwards. But remember how Paul has set things up. He insisted in verses 17 and 18 that we get to the glory by passing through the valley of suffering. Well, verses 19 to 21 do indeed outline that coming glory, as we saw in our previous chapter. But he means something rather different from what we might have imagined. Now he speaks about the suffering, and again not in the way we'd expect.

The suffering here is deeply personal, even intimate. Paul isn't here simply talking about outward persecution, beatings or imprisonment, or indeed poverty, sickness, shipwreck or anything so tangible, though no doubt those all create the outward conditions for what he's saying here. Paul writes in this passage – with 2 Corinthians in recent memory, with all its extraordinary catalogue of personal trauma – about the deepest, most incomprehensible groanings that emerge from the innermost depths of our own being.

This isn't just about 'going through a rough time'. Nor is it simply 'something we occasionally have to put up with'. Paul is talking about our *vocation* not just to *get through* difficult times but **to stand in prayer where the world is in pain so that God's own spirit may be present, and intercede, right there.** This is one of the most revolutionary and innovative moments in the whole letter. Paul here fills out *both* his Trinitarian theology of new creation *and* his pastoral understanding of the depths of the Christian heart, and joins them together. God's spirit comes to dwell in the midst of his world, in the persons of Jesus' faithful followers; but that world is in great pain. The spirit *inhabits* that pain, and calls out to the father from its darkest depths, *by means of* God's people being in prayer, spirit-inspired prayer, at that place.

This painful vocation is at the heart of God's rescuing plan for the whole creation. Because this is so unexpected to so many readers, verses 26 and 27 have often been treated as a detached little statement, and a puzzling one at that, about praying when we don't know what to pray for, and the spirit groaning within us. What, people might ask, has *that* to do with the main theme of the chapter? The normal readings of Romans 8 would be thinking of the pathway to our own salvation, with this strange mention of prayer as at best an aside. But if we follow through what we've already said about the meaning of 'glory', with Psalm 8 in mind in terms of God's plan for humans to bring his wise order into the world, and with the promise in verse 22 that the glorification of human beings will be the key to God's rescue of his whole creation from its slavery to corruption, then this whole passage, verses 23 to 27, makes sense *as* a whole, with the two verses about prayer not as a footnote but as the climax. Verses 26 and 27, then, are not a strange add-on to a chapter about something else.

This makes sense if we think for a moment about how the chapter works rhetorically. Paul doesn't just toss extraneous ideas into the flow of a discourse about something else. He is building to a deliberate, sustained and indeed spectacular climax. The last thing he would do at such a point would be to add a strange and irrelevant little aside.

So how does it all work out? As we have said, God's plan is not to rescue humans *from* creation, to go and be with him somewhere else, but to come in person to dwell *with* his image-bearing creatures, so that together he and they may bring his rescuing, ordering wisdom to bear upon the world, 'on earth as in heaven'. This is the key to early Christology: God himself comes into his world as the truly human rescuer and ruler. In this passage we see that it is also the key to pneumatology, to understanding the holy spirit: God himself comes into his world, into the hearts and lives of puzzled and frightened believers who don't know what to pray for as they ought, so that precisely in their prayer of unknowing, their prayer from within the darkness of their own lives and of the world around them, God himself will be at work, interceding from within his creation. As we shall see in verse 28, this means that God is working *with* these praying-in-the-dark people for the wider good of his world. And in that verse, too, Paul speaks of these people as 'those who love him'. To speak of humans loving God is not, for Paul, primarily about people having wonderful mystical experiences of being caught up in a kind of heavenly bliss, though no doubt he would say that such things happen and it's wonderful when they do. When he speaks here of 'those who love God' he is referring to those who, precisely at the point where they are at the end of their mental, emotional and spiritual tether, find within themselves the deep sorrow of all the world, as it were concentrated into one place, and find at that moment that they are part of the dialogue of love between the father and the spirit. This, he says, is what we are called to do and be.

Just as the glory of Jesus was fully revealed on the cross, so the spirit-given glory of Jesus' followers is fully present at that moment. Like Jesus in Gethsemane, where he prayed the Abba-prayer that Paul invokes in verse 15, God's suffering people ask in perplexity whether there might not be another way. Like Jesus on the cross, God's people feel as though they have been forsaken entirely. At such points we are to discover that what we deeply want to say has already been said by Jesus himself, drawing on one of the great prayers in the scriptures.

This passage, then, is about the Christian *vocation*. (Paul seems to think this is true for all Christians; but how much more is it true for those called to minister in the church, called to organize and lead public worship, to be pastors and teachers, to shape communities within which this spirit-led intercession will take place.) This moment is the climax of what has been said about the spirit through the whole chapter. In verses 5 to 8, the spirit directs our mind; in verses 9 to 11, the indwelling spirit will raise us from the dead; in verses 15 and 16, the spirit assures us that we are God's children and leads us towards our inheritance, even as we pray the Abba-prayer. Now, in verses 22–7, in the midst of a world in pain, God's own spirit shares and bears that pain *through God's people sharing it themselves.*

Paul here seems to be radically applying the theology of the cross to the work of the spirit in the church. We might suppose – and the whole charismatic movement which has so transformed many churches in the last generation would bear this out – that being filled with the spirit means celebration, excitement, being empowered. That is indeed often the case. But the holy spirit is the spirit of the creator God, who grieves over his world gone wrong. The holy spirit is the spirit of Jesus who went to the cross to defeat the powers of evil by bearing our sin and death. This passage is, as I hinted just now, a kind of spirit-equivalent to Jesus' terrible cry, 'My God, my God, why did you abandon me?'

At this point we are near the heart of the early Christian answer to some of the deepest questions humans can ask. The philosophers, particularly following the Deism of the eighteenth century, have regularly asked a one-dimensional question which they have called 'the problem of evil'. How can we believe in an all-powerful and all-loving God in the face of the terrible evil and suffering in the world? Paul, faced with the same phenomena, gives a three-dimensional answer. Work it out: if you start off with a picture of God as the great celestial CEO, or even the heavenly puppet-master pulling the strings to make things happen, of course you're going to have problems. But if you start with the God of Abraham, Isaac and Jacob, the God who grieves over the pain of the world and the failings of his own people, the God who in the end reveals himself in and as the crucified Messiah, the God who then sends the spirit into the hearts of his people so that God himself may, in and through his people, stand at the heart of the pain of the world so that the world may be healed – why then the whole question looks very different.

These verses, I suggest, explain and contextualize the *present* work of **lament** which anticipates the *future promised* work of the redemption of all creation. The New Testament looks back to the great laments of scripture: to Jeremiah's lamentations, to the anguished prayers of Ezra 9, Nehemiah 9 and Daniel 9. Those laments – followed up by the centuries of prayerful, psalm-singing Judaeans between then and the coming of Jesus – lay the foundation, in humble worship and creational sorrow, for the eventual coming of Jesus. Simeon and Anna in Luke 1, and indeed Zechariah, Mary and Elizabeth too, are all part of that long lament, 'looking for the consolation of Israel', as Luke puts it. The two on the road to Emmaus say, 'We had hoped that he was the one to redeem Israel.' The centuries of prayer and especially of lament formed and moistened the soil into which the good seed was sown. I am suggesting that Paul, by echoing Israel's lament in this passage (Psalm 44 is echoed in verse 27, but the whole idea of groaning in slavery naturally sends the mind back to the children of Israel in Egypt), is placing the church in the present time in a similar position. We have hoped, and we go on hoping, that the spirit is the one through whom the world, creation itself, will be redeemed, given its freedom to be truly itself. Our calling is to go on with that hope even in the dark, even when hope seems dashed in war-torn and demolished cities of Syria and Ukraine, in the children's graveyard after yet another school shooting, in the horrors and terrors of a world that thought it was enlightened but turned out to be still in the dark. And in this passage, Paul is sketching the map of how this hope works, what it feels like, and what, theologically speaking, is actually going on.

So, if the 'glory' in verses 18 to 21 refers to the wise rule of God's image-bearing people over creation, the primary way that comes to expression in the present time is by prayer, particularly by lament. Particularly if you're a minister of the gospel, but also for every Christian sooner or later, there will be times when, as Paul says here, things will be so bad that you won't even know what to pray for. That does *not* mean you've gone off the rails somewhere (well, you might have done, but that would be a different issue). It could well mean that you are called to share, in the spirit, the agony of Jesus in Gethsemane and on the cross itself, as part of the ongoing, spirit-led application of God's strange work of taking the pain and sorrow of the world upon himself. Notice, by the way, that Jesus himself, at those moments, had the Psalms in mind. If the Psalms are not part of our bloodstream, how will we, and the people in our care, be Jesus-reflecting people of prayer and lament within the pain of the parish, of the city, of the world? I understand that some churches, eager to attract newcomers, have majored on happy, bouncy music. But without the biblical call to lament (which isn't the same thing as dreary music!) we are failing in our calling. In any case, there must be many potential newcomers who would at once appreciate being drawn into genuine lament.

Romans 8.22 to 27 thus goes from one extreme to the other: from the broad sweep of the whole created order in verse 22 to the most intimate and painful longings of the human heart in verses 26 and 27. And at that latter point, extraordinarily, even God the holy spirit has no words for what's going on, no words at least that we can understand. We who live at a time of groaning and perplexity about many issues in our global life – a pandemic, a climate crisis, a refugee crisis, various geopolitical crises whether in Afghanistan or eastern Europe or the South China Sea, and so on – well, it's good to know that there are moments when even the holy spirit seems to be lost for words.

I was struck by this some years ago, preparing for Pentecost in Durham Cathedral. In the Church of England, we have had many creative and innovative liturgies, and one of these new liturgies proposed, for the feast of Pentecost, a response that involved the congregation repeating the words, 'Alleluia! The Spirit of God fills the whole world.' This was obviously meant to sound cheerful: 'God is in everything, so let's not be gloomy dualists.' Look out at the world, the words seemed to say, and recognize the presence of God's spirit in anything and everything. Well, I don't like gloomy dualism either. But as Pentecost approached that year, I read the papers and watched the television news . . . and I found myself saying in my sermon that, if the spirit of God does indeed fill the whole world, then what the spirit is mostly doing right now is grieving. And groaning. The world was, and is, in a mess.

There is no room for easy-going optimism. If you want to avoid cosmic dualism – as of course you must if you are a biblical Christian – the road to take is not to some kind of monism, a form of soft Stoicism with the divine impulse simply present within whatever happens to be going on in the world. In a world that still groans in travail, the way to avoid cosmic dualism is to lament, and in patience to pray; perhaps to speak prophetic truth to power; and to be ready for any and all ways of bringing God's healing to his world, whether in the long or short term.[1]

This long introduction to our present passage is leading up to the double claim, first, that the ideas we find here in Romans 8.22–7 are unique in scripture, and second, that, so far from being an aside, this passage actually constitutes the very heart of the chapter and, as such, the heart of at least one major strand in the letter as a whole. We come to Romans 8 hoping, quite rightly, for assurance of salvation; but this chapter, while it does indeed provide that, focuses on *vocation*.

I am reminded of the wonderful scene in John 21 when Jesus interviews Peter, sounding him out after his triple denial. Three times he asks, 'Simon son of John, do you love me?' Even though Peter can't answer the question the way Jesus asks it – he uses a different word for 'love' – Jesus' response is not to say 'All right, you're forgiven' or 'Well, we'll draw a veil over what happened' or 'We'll let bygones be bygones', but to *commission him for his vocation*. Feed my lambs; tend my sheep; feed my sheep. Now, in Romans 8, I suggest that Paul does something similar. He begins the chapter with the word of 'no condemnation', and ends it by insisting that nothing can separate us

---

1 One should also note that the clause about God's spirit filling the whole world is taken from the Wisdom of Solomon 1.7, where the point is not celebration but warning to evildoers: God knows exactly what's going on!

from God's love. But the heart of the chapter, the verses now before us, have to do with the *vocation* of those who are held within that great assurance.

What, after all, is the church *for*? What are its ministers for? Well, many things – living the gospel, proclaiming the crucified and risen Jesus as Lord of the world. But to live and announce that message in and to the world, with the world in its current state, means engaging with the world's reality, its turmoil, its trouble, its tears. And we can't simply say 'Well, that's all right, because Jesus is the answer.' Nor can we say, 'Well, of course the world's a mess, because it doesn't know Jesus; but we're all right, heading for salvation somewhere else; we don't really belong here, we're just passing through.' Nor may we say, as some wanted to say when the COVID pandemic struck, 'It's all someone else's fault for being so wicked; God is punishing *those* people for the sins we've always known they were committing.' No: part of our primary calling as followers of Jesus is to lament: to stand in the place of pain in humility, sorrow and hope. That's what the children of Israel did in Egypt. It's what the Judaeans did for four hundred years before the Messiah came. It's what we are called to do as we stand in prayer at the heart of a world in pain.

This vocation will come for us whether we're ready or not. You see, this passage is all about being co-glorified with the Messiah – which sounds wonderful, until we recall that, for Jesus, glorification meant being betrayed, denied, vilified, whipped raw and hung up to die. This is again clearest in John's gospel, where the 'glorification' of Jesus occurs when Jesus is crucified. Conformed to the image of the son, Paul will say in verse 29. And, to say it again, standing at the place of pain isn't just something nasty to get through. It is *a vital part of the means by which* God is working out, in the present time, his glorious rescuing purposes for his world. Learning to lament is a non-negotiable part of becoming the people through whom God is accomplishing his saving plan for the whole creation. (This, again, is one of the reasons why the Psalms have always been central to daily Christian worship.) Of course, this can tip over into a martyr complex which brings its own variety of unhealth. The second-century church spotted that one early on: deliberately trying to get yourself killed isn't the point. We need to see the challenge coming and understand what's really going on.

Now all this so far is really by way of introduction. But now at last let's ask the three questions which as I've said we should always bring to a passage in Paul.

First, look at the beginning and ending of the paragraph. That's a bit artificial here because we've broken the single thread of verses 18 to 30 into three separate sections, 18–21 in our last chapter, 22–7 in this one, and 28–30 in the next one. So we are still within the overall sweep of suffering and glorification, as in the longer unit of Romans 8.18–30. But verses 22–7, our present concern, do have a clear theme of their own. There is one Greek root that occurs three times, here and only here in Romans. That is the clue.

The word in question is the word 'groaning': the verb *stenazō* in verses 22 and 23 and the cognate noun *stenagmos* in verse 26. This repetition tells us how to read the passage. First, the world is groaning in labour pains. Second, the Messiah's people are groaning as we await the resurrection. And then, climactically (not as a separate paragraph as in some translations, like the RSV and NRSV!), God's own spirit is groaning within us. We are caught up, vocationally, in the work that God is presently doing to bring about the redemption of creation. Our prayers, more specifically the anguished prayers that come when we are overwhelmed and don't know what to pray for – they are part of the vital means by which the triune God is doing and will do the work of liberating creation from its corruption and decay. That's what this passage is all about.

So if the first question is about the overall shape of the passage, our second question is to look at the little connecting words that hold things together. Paul begins verse 22 with *oidamen gar* – 'For' we know; I have translated that *gar* as 'let me explain'. This whole paragraph, in fact, is digging down beneath the grand statement of verses 19 to 21 to show 'what's really going on' 'right up to the present moment'. Paul emphasizes that the Christian's groaning is a special, focal part of the groaning of all creation. Then we have the two little verses about hope and patience, verses 24 and 25, which together explain why we are where we are. We were saved in and for hope (24a); this is explained by Paul's note about how hope works and why it produces patience:

> **24**For [*gar*] we were saved in hope; **but** [*alla*] it isn't hope if you can see it; **for** [*gar*] who hopes for what they can see? **25**But [*gar*] if we hope for what we don't see, this means patience.

That then brings us to the climax of the passage, which, to repeat, is certainly not an aside, as we can see from the start of verse 26: 'In the same way, too', *hōsautōs de*. The point Paul is making is new and perhaps unexpected, but the *hōsautōs* insists that it belongs exactly with what's just been said. The first half of verse 26 states the basic point, and the second half explains it with a *gar* which this time I've left untranslated. But then, as so often at the end of a train of thought, Paul rounds it off with a *de*, here in verse 27, as though to say, *but* notice that at the heart of this whole train of thought we find God himself, God the heart-searcher, God the father hearing and knowing the groaning of all creation and the inarticulate groaning of our hearts, because he, the father, knows the mind of the spirit which is groaning in those very places. Thus:

> ²⁶**In just the same way** [*hōsautōs de*] the spirit helps in our weakness; **for** [*gar*] we don't know how to pray as we ought, **but** [*alla*] that very spirit intercedes with inarticulate groanings. ²⁷**And, however** [*de*], the heart-searcher knows the spirit's mind, **because** [*hoti*] the spirit intercedes for God's people in accordance with God's will.

We need to pause and take in the extraordinary claim Paul is making. I have said before that when we look at the biblical sketch of Israel's coming Messiah, in the Psalms, in 2 Samuel, in Isaiah and elsewhere, we are being nudged to the realization that this is a vocation designed for God's own use. God creates the category of Messiahship, of the anointed king, so that he may himself come and *be* the anointed king of Israel, doing in person the work of judgment and mercy for which the ideal king would be equipped. Well, just as we can look back at the formation of that messianic portrait as a role designed for God's own use, so *the call to be people of lament at the place where the world is in pain is itself a vocation designed for God's own use, in the person of his spirit,* dwelling – and groaning! – in the hearts of God's people. The logic of these connecting words that tie together verses 22 to 27 makes this quite clear.

Our first question, then, has always been the overall shape of the passage. Our second question teases out the effect of the little connecting words by which Paul signals how he at least thinks the argument is held in place. Our third question is to examine the larger first-century context. Here, I suggest, there are two particular overtones that would strike the alert first-century listener.

The first is the image of creation as a woman in labour. I mentioned before the grandiose Roman imperial propaganda that displayed nature as a serene, fruitful matriarch, surrounded by the signs of peace and plenty. Paul too uses vivid female imagery, but for him it's creation rather than nature (that is, the world in relation to its creator rather than an independent being), and at each stage he depicts a woman groaning in labour pains, struggling to give birth. This evokes the biblical theme sometimes referred to, a bit vaguely, as the 'messianic woes'. It's a well-known biblical and Jewish theme, in which God's purposes will come about through, and even by means of, a time of intense suffering like that of a woman giving birth. You find this in Isaiah, Jeremiah, Hosea and elsewhere, and in second-Temple books such as *1 Enoch* and *4 Ezra*. Many Jews in Jesus' day clung to this hope: that sorrow and pain would increase but that, through it all, God's fresh, redeeming, restorative purpose would be fulfilled. Jesus picks up this theme in John 16, where he speaks of the woman in labour having sorrow but then her sorrow turning into joy. And now Paul declares that this is where we are. We are in the throes of labour pains.

The second larger context, to which I have already alluded, is the exodus. This might seem strange, since we've followed the exodus-story from Romans 6 (with the crossing of the Red Sea), through Romans 7 (arriving at Sinai), and now in Romans 8 being led to the promised inheritance. What are we doing back in Egypt again, with the Israelites 'groaning' in their slavery, as in Exodus 2? But the point is that, throughout Romans, and indeed throughout Christian experience in general, we are faced with the 'now and not yet' of salvation, as in verses 24 and 25. In the same way, as in verse 23, we are already 'children of God' but are simultaneously awaiting the resurrection as the ultimate moment of 'adoption'. This is the classic eschatological tension: we are *already* God's children, but this won't be apparent until the resurrection; we *have* escaped Egypt, but we are still groaning as we await full release from slavery.

So at last, with our overall survey in place, and our three questions asked and answered, we can plunge into the passage line by line.

Verse 22 offers a realistic appraisal of the present creation, as opposed to the bland optimism of imperial propaganda. Paul says 'we know'. The 'we' here can't simply be 'all human beings'. All humans are aware of earthquakes, epidemics and war. But only those inhabiting the biblical tradition are likely to understand these as the labour pains of a renewed creation, rather than the chance horrors of a random universe (for Epicureans), the blind power of the world's inner *logos* (for Stoics) or the flickering shadows of the insubstantial secondary world (for Platonists). So, paradoxically perhaps, though deeply biblically, this way of looking at the sufferings of the world is inherently positive: God's new world is waiting to be born! The fact that labour pains are simultaneously horrible and full of hope answers exactly to verse 18, with present sufferings unable to compete with coming glory.

Paul insists that this state of affairs is going on 'right up to the present'. Eschatology has been inaugurated. The new world has begun with Jesus and the spirit. But this doesn't diminish the ongoing pain and sorrow of the old world. Rather, it produces a highly uncomfortable tension. This is especially distressing for anyone who thought, as (alas) many have been taught, that becoming a Christian would be the gateway to a smooth, untroubled life . . .

So, with verse 22 as the basis, Paul moves quickly to the parallel truth about the church. What is happening in creation as a whole is mirrored in the experience of Jesus' followers. The phrase 'not only so' suggests that this too, as with the previous verse, is something that '"we" [ought to] know'. We ourselves are going through the labour pains, the messianic woes. We too, from one perspective, are still in Egypt, awaiting God's fresh word of sonship. How easy it would be for a Christian to think, well, of course the world is in a mess; people after all are sinful and deserve God's wrath; but we Christians are just fine, and anyway we'll be leaving this place before too long. No! The church is groaning at the heart of the groaning of creation. And that isn't an accident. It is where we are called to be. Standing in this place is our vocation, one key element in the present wise stewardship which, as redeemed humans, we are to exercise over creation.

This is accentuated, in verse 23, by the fact that we have 'the first fruits of the spirit's life within us'. Pentecost, fifty days after Passover, was the Jewish feast of the first-fruits. It was the welcome sign of the longer-term harvest. Paul frequently echoes this theme of 'first-fruits', indicating that the spirit is the 'down payment' in advance on the full promised inheritance.[2] In the spirit, we are already tasting God's new world. And that, of course, makes our ongoing life in the old world all the more painful.

That tension is then reflected in the initially surprising second half of the verse: we are still *eagerly awaiting* our 'full sonship'. Already in verses 15 and 16, the spirit has assured us of sonship as a present status, albeit with the coded warning that this will mean sharing Jesus' Abba-prayer, his Gethsemane-prayer. We now find ourselves in the in-between state, like the time in which Jesus himself, having been affirmed as God's son in his baptism, had to await his public vindication in the resurrection.[3] That interval was a time of fierce testing for Jesus, both in

---

2 E.g. Rom. 11.16; 1 Cor. 15.20. On 'down payment', *arrabōn*, see e.g. 2 Cor. 1.22; Eph. 1.14.
3 On Jesus' vindication as 'son' in the resurrection, see Rom. 1.3–4.

the desert and in his public career, and of course in his last days and hours. We too are waiting for resurrection: for vindication, yes, as Paul will say in 8.33–4, but here more particularly for 'the redemption of our body'. The word for 'redemption' here is *apolytrōsis*. This is a regular term, not just for someone purchasing the freedom of a slave. It is, more specifically, a reference to the exodus itself, as you might have guessed from the exodus-echoes that are awakened by the 'groaning' motif. God 'redeemed' his people from Egypt, declaring them thereby to be indeed his people. The resurrection of Jesus' people, the result of the spirit's work within them as in 8.9–11, will be our exodus, declaring us to be his people but also constituting our rescue from the slavery we have shared with the rest of creation (8.20–1).

Verse 23 thus places the church at the heart of the groaning of all creation. This is so, not *despite* the fact that we are the new-exodus people, but somehow *because* of it. As the people of the crucified Messiah, we are called – in the Messiah's spirit – to share the pain of the world.

We might ponder where precisely this vocation takes us. The world struggles with issues of authority; so do we. The world struggles with issues of sex and gender; so do we. The world is still in a mess over multi-culturalism and ethnic integration – and so are we. And so on. No doubt this is partly because the church is failing in its obedience. But at the same time this pain-within-pain, the pain of the church within, and mirroring, the pain of the world, doesn't surprise me. When Jesus breathed his spirit on his followers, he said, 'As the father sent me, so I send you.' And where had the father sent him? To the place where the world was in direst pain, so that he could take it upon himself. Our vocation, by the spirit, places us, right now, where the world is in pain, *so that, as Paul is about to say, we can be in prayer right there.*

Verses 24 and 25 then look back to the start of chapter 5. Living with 'hope that is not yet seen' constitutes a call to patience. Verse 24: salvation is given (past tense), but in and for hope. Some translations make the 'hope' here refer back to the coming resurrection: 'that's the hope for which we were saved', which may be pushing Paul's language further than he actually takes it, but which certainly expresses his thought. And again, we have that strong word *apekdechomai*, as in verses 19 and 23: we eagerly await it – but with patience. As we all know, getting the balance between eagerness and patience, in any context, is a tough call. But it is our call.

So to verses 26 and 27, the 'unutterable groanings'. Some have wondered whether Paul is referring here to speaking in tongues. But Paul elsewhere sees tongues as spirit-given *language*; I don't think he'd refer to that as *alalētos*, 'inarticulate'. Anyway, he is talking here about all Christians, but he knows that not all speak in tongues.[4] His point, rather, is to focus on the way the spirit enables us to fulfil our vocation as *intercessors at the heart of the groaning of creation*.

We are not good at this. We would much rather celebrate our own salvation. The 'weakness' here seems to be our failure to think sufficiently deeply into the real plight of the world, and hence our ignorance in knowing what to pray for. But at that point, he says, the spirit 'comes alongside to help': *synantilambanetai*, a double compound expressing the way the spirit acts *with* us (that's the *syn* bit) and *in our place* (that's the *anti* bit). This is the word Martha uses in Luke 10.40 when she wants Mary to 'come alongside and help with some of the work in the kitchen'. Paul is moulding the Greek language to say as best he can what he said in verses 14–16, that the spirit comes alongside our own spirit so that together they can do what's

---

4 1 Cor. 12.30.

needed. The spirit here works in us and with us, on our behalf and then through us.

So Paul now refers to the spirit's activity with the same vivid female metaphor he used for the groaning of the world and the church. The world is in labour pains; the church is in labour pains; and *the spirit is also going into labour*, the groaning labour pains of the new creation. Think of the *ruach Elohim*, the wind or spirit of God, brooding over the waters in Genesis 1.2. (Paul clearly has Genesis 1 in mind in Romans 8.) This is the ultimate seed of all hope: for the world in chaos, God's spirit is the agent, the source, of new life.

So what is the spirit doing with this groaning, with these labour pains? In that groaning the spirit is pleading for us. The word Paul uses here is *hyperentyngchanei*; it is possible (since it occurs nowhere else in surviving ancient Greek literature) that Paul has even made it up, to hold together the fact that the spirit is present and at work (*tyngchano*) within us (*en*) and on our behalf (*hyper*). At the very point where we find ourselves in pain and sorrow too deep for words, at the heart of creation's wordless pain – pandemics, climate crises, wars, violent crime and all the rest – in all this, God's own spirit is there, with powerful groans which, though wordless, form the ultimate language of intercession.

But how do we know that God's spirit will be there, doing this work? How do we know that God has not given up on his creation in disgust, as some Jewish thinkers speculated? Because *we will be there*, indwelt by that same spirit. *We are called to be people who stand at the place of pain – in the cancer ward, at the asylum-seeker's court hearing, by the graveyard full of memorials to small children or to families whose homes have been bombed in war – so as to be those within whose own painful perplexity the holy spirit will plead to the father on behalf of the whole creation.* Indwelt by God's spirit, we are to be right there in the chaos, so that God's new creation may finally emerge, this time with humans as its spirit-enabled agents.

This vocation is – to say the least – challenging. It is hard work. Fortunately, God has provided a prayer book to help us. It's called the book of Psalms. And that is where Paul goes now.

How do we know that this inarticulate groaning of the world, the church and the spirit is not in vain? God himself, God the father, says Paul in verse 27, searches all hearts. Nine verses later he quotes Psalm 44.22: 'for your sake we are killed all day long.' The previous verse of the psalm insists that God knows the secrets of our hearts. Paul, inhabiting this psalm, provides an example of God-given lament. And the picture that opens from this apparently unlikely place is a matchless image of the Trinity: the spirit calling to the father from the depth of the world's pain – and the church's pain! And God the father hearing and knowing what is going on, exactly as in Exodus 2.23–5, when God hears the groaning of his people in Egypt. And we who find ourselves caught up in this extraordinary communication of father and spirit are, says Paul in verse 29, *conformed to the image of the son.*

This is our own Gethsemane moment, our own 'why-did-you-abandon-me?' moment. It will come in one way or another as we follow Jesus, and specially as we minister to his people. Romans 8 is indeed about assurance, but it isn't just the assurance of salvation; it is the assurance that when we are in that dark place, sensing our own pain at the heart of the world's pain, this is not outside God's saving purposes, but is actually at their heart. This is why I insisted in early 2020 that the first proper response to the COVID pandemic was *lament.* Only when we hold back from knee-jerk reactions to the world's troubles and take the time to lament, to allow the spirit's wordless groanings to find a home within us, can we find a way forward.

Thus the glory to be revealed, the image-bearing authority exercised by God's people within the new creation (verses 18 to 21), is *anticipated in the present time* in the strange, dark work of prayer. We do not pray for the church and the world from a great height, as though we could look down on them from a safe and smug distance. We pray out of our own pain, whether of sickness or grief or injury or disappointment or opposition or apparent failure or depression. The God who *has* saved the world through Jesus and his death and resurrection *is saving* the world through the work of the spirit. And we are called to be the Tabernacle-people, the place where and the means by which the spirit undertakes this constant, often painful, frequently wordless work. The sign that the *divine* glory has come to dwell within us, in our midst, is that we are in this way exercising the *human* 'glory' of delegated 'authority' over the world. That is what prayer is about; and when the world is in a mess, prayer may well look and feel like what Paul says here. And all this is part of what Paul understands by 'loving God', being enfolded, taken up, within the Jesus-shaped love that constantly flows, in both directions, between the father and the spirit. That, indeed, is the vital link to the next verse (28), which we shall consider in our next chapter.

You see, faced with the world in chaos, and the church in a muddle, God doesn't just stand to one side and say, I wish you people could get your act together. The mystery of Trinitarian theology is the mystery of prayer, that God the spirit comes to that place of pain so that our griefs, sorrows and loves are taken up into the grief, sorrow and love of God. This is what it means, in verse 17, to suffer with the Messiah so that we may be glorified with him.

The famous hymn 'Come Down, O Love Divine' catches this sense of spirit-inspired wordless prayer. This hymn, the translation of a fourteenth-century Italian poem, ends with the confidence that God's work of healing is going ahead and that we are caught up within it, even if it is beyond human ability to describe it:

> And so the yearning strong,
> with which the soul will long,
> *shall far outpass the power of human telling;*
> for none can guess its grace,
> till she become the place,
> wherein the Holy Spirit makes his dwelling.[5]

And, we might add, wherein the holy spirit utters her groaning.

---

5 Translation by Richard Frederick Littledale, first published in 1867.

7
Romans 8.28–30: Justified and Glorified

²⁸We know, in fact, that God works all things together for good with those who love him, who are called according to his purpose. ²⁹Those he foreknew, you see, he also marked out in advance to be shaped according to the model of the image of his son, so that he might be the firstborn of a large family. ³⁰And those he marked out in advance, he also called; those he called, he also justified; those he justified, he also glorified.

²⁸*oidamen de hoti tois agapōsin ton theon panta synergei eis agathon, tois kata prothesin klētois ousin.*

²⁹*hoti hous proegnō, kai prohōrisen symmorphous tēs eikonos tou hyiou autou, eis to einai auton prōtotokon en pollois adelphois.*

³⁰*hous de prohōrisen, toutous kai ekalesen. kai hous ekalesen, toutous kai edikaiōsen. hous de edikaiōsen, toutous kai edoxasen.*

One of the frustrations of being an elderly exegete is to find the text refusing to say what you thought it said sixty years ago. I grew up with the King James Version of Romans 8.28 saying 'all things work together for good to them that love God'. As I look back now, I see that I understood that text to be saying that the multiple disparate elements of life would sort themselves out, under God's benevolent guiding, like a sort of automatic jigsaw puzzle. It might look chaotic, but a happy picture would emerge from it all.

Now there is a sense in which God's providence does indeed assure us of God's eventual victory over all the powers of evil. But the popular understanding of this verse will not stand up to close scrutiny, simply at the level of the meaning of the words, let alone of the overall sense of the passage.

Before we plunge into this detail, we should first follow our normal practice of asking the three introductory questions. The first (looking at the start and finish of the section) is less obvious than usual, because these three brief verses are really summing up the larger argument of the chapter so far, particularly verses 17 onwards. The emphatic 'those he justified, he also glorified' in verse 30 looks straight back to 'as long as we suffer with him so that we may also be glorified with him' in verse 17, with verse 21 ('. . . when God's children are glorified') as a marker on the way. But there may still be a sense in which these three verses, taken by themselves, make a small but important circle. Paul begins verse 28 (after the opening 'We know, in fact') with 'those who love God'. This, as we shall presently see, is a way of summing up the picture he's just painted, of believers being caught up in the agonized but loving Messiah-shaped interchange between the father and the spirit. And this, from one point of view, is what he means by 'glorification'. Those he describes are those in whom the spirit dwells, as the divine glory in the Temple; and they are simultaneously those who are standing in the truly human place of 'glory', in strange and paradoxical authority over God's world. We might actually have guessed this from the introductory paragraph Romans 5.1–5. 'Celebrating the hope of the glory of God' (5.2) is further explained by 'the love of God poured out in our hearts' (5.5). The small-scale circle of meaning between the start of 8.28 and the end of 8.30 is matched by the large-scale circle of meaning between 5.1–5 and 8.17–30.

The second opening question concerns the small linking words. The opening, *oidamen de hoti*, 'and we know that', indicates that what follows is a further, deeper interpretation of what has just been said; that's why in my translation I rendered it as 'We know, in fact'. The *de*, which is far more flexible than the 'but' that beginners in Greek are taught as its meaning, isn't introducing a contrary thought, but offering a different perspective, as with J. B. Phillips's 'Moreover'. All of this insists on the point that most exegetes and preachers miss: that verses 26–7 are not an 'aside' from the main argument, but take us to its very heart. And verses 28–30 now explain what that heart means in terms of the whole long-term divine plan.

Verse 29 begins with *hoti*, functioning now very similarly to the regular *gar*, 'for', or in my idiomatic translation, 'you see'. God's plan, you see (explains Paul), was to create a family of Messiah-shaped people through whom he would do what had to be done. This again looks back to verse 17, where the

Messiah's 'fellow heirs' suffer with him in order also to be glorified with him. The fact that verse 29 thus explains verse 28 – which in turn explains what was going on in verses 26 and 27 – indicates again that, as in John's gospel, the 'glory' is very closely tied to the Messiah's crucifixion and then to the outworking of that in the life, and the prayer, of his followers. That is how God's plan for the rescue of the whole creation is going ahead.

Verse 30 is then linked to this with another *de*, which again has the sense of 'moreover', as in the KJV. Thus, as verse 29 explained the overall plan of God, verse 30 describes how this plan has been put into effect. The four stages – foreordained, called, justified, glorified – are then linked with *kai* and *de*:

> **And** [*de*] those he marked out in advance, he also called; **and** [*kai*] those he called, he also justified; **and** [*de*] those he justified, he also glorified.

In English, this repetition of small words is often deemed unnecessary, with the juxtaposition of statements being sufficient to indicate their linkage. Hence, in my own translation, I have the opening 'and', but neither of the subsequent ones.

What echoes would arise in Paul's world of which we should take account? We can postpone our answer to that regular third question until we have dug a bit more deeply into the whole passage.

Returning, then, to the popularly misread verse 28, I have to give credit where credit is due to three friends whose work on Romans 8 has joggled me out of the comfortable assumptions of many years. Haley Jacob of Whitworth University on the one hand, and Sylvia Keesmaat and Brian Walsh of Toronto on the other, have argued strongly (and, I believe, rightly) that we should go, not with the popular translations, but with the old RSV: 'In everything God works for good with those who love him.' The verse doesn't say (in other words) that 'all things work together for good *to* those who love God', which appears to give God's people a kind of inside privilege of knowing that things will fall out the way they want them to. It means that God is the subject of the main verb: it is *God* who is 'working', rather than the 'all things'. And it means that God works not just *for* those who love him – as though they were simply the passive recipients of his ongoing benevolence – but that he works *with* those who love him.[1] He is affirming, in other words, that their present work and struggles, to which Paul has just referred, and which are themselves part of what's happening through the spirit's work in them, actively contribute in the present time to God's overall working out of his purposes. Paul is saying that we – 'those who love God', in the sense of those in whose hearts the seemingly inarticulate dialogue of the spirit and the father is going on – are God's co-workers. This fits with Paul's other uses of the verb, to which we shall come in a moment.

It is the verb, in fact, that provides the clue. The Greek *synergeō* means, literally, 'work with'. It's the word from which we get 'synergism' – which has had a bad press in theological discourse, to which I'll return presently, but there's no getting away from its literal meaning. In the traditional translation, this was understood in terms of 'everything working together', that is, the different bits of life's jigsaw coming together with one another, as it were automatically. But that is not quite what

---

1 The RSV ('in everything God works for good with those who love him') adds a footnote reference to the manuscript variation which, as in Nestle-Aland 27, omits 'God', either leaving it to be understood from the context that 'God' is the subject of 'works' or suggesting that 'everything' might then be the subject, as in the KJV and, indeed, in the NRSV. Jacob's work is published in *Conformed to the Image of His Son* (Downers Grove, IL: IVP Academic, 2018), pp. 245–51; that of Keesmaat and Walsh in their *Romans Disarmed* (Grand Rapids, MI: Brazos Press, 2019), pp. 375–9. Others have understood the spirit to be the subject of the verb, as in the NEB, which does at least see that *synergei* means 'co-operate with'.

the word means. When Paul uses *synergeō* elsewhere it means, as the Greek implies, two people or agencies *collaborating with* one another on a shared task, not various objects fitting together like the components of a mechanical clock.

The way the word works is that the person or people with whom the subject is collaborating are regularly placed in the dative case; so here, the Greek dative *tois agapōsin ton theon* tells us who it is that God is co-working with. God is collaborating *with those who love him*. The subject, to repeat, is 'God', not 'all things': God, implied here from the previous phrase ('those who love God'), works all things for good *with* those who love him. Thus, I was going to say, we are God's collaborators. That's what the verb means in the two other passages (see below) where Paul uses it. But actually he is here saying that God is *our* collaborator. God works with and through 'those who love him'.

That phrase 'those who love God' is a standard designation for Israel. It echoes the Shema prayer in Deuteronomy: Hear O Israel, YHWH our God is One God, and you shall *love* YHWH your God . . . Romans 8.28 thus looks back, in a long arc, to Romans 5.5, where the Messiah's people have had the love of God poured into their hearts through the holy spirit. For Paul, 'those who love God' becomes a kind of shorthand for 'all Jesus-followers', 'all those who are at last able to keep the Shema of Deuteronomy 6', and also a hint that love, their primary identity, must also be their primary characteristic. But in this passage, Paul appears to be picking up what he's just said in verse 27. The Greek puts 'with those who love God' as the first phrase in the verse: so, literally, the verse reads 'we know that *with those who love God* he collaborates for good'. So here, with a meaning we might not have guessed from Romans 5.5, we have in effect a definition of 'those who love God'. The phrase refers back directly to those in whose painful prayer the spirit is calling to the father, with the father knowing, understanding and acting.

At this point, some readers may be thinking it's all been getting too technical. They may regret the apparent loss of the familiar translation and meaning. So why can't we just leave verse 28 saying 'all things work together for good to those who love God'?

First, a general thematic point. Paul is reaching the central climax of this letter. The main theme of the letter has been God, God's righteousness, God's love, God's gospel. It would be rhetorically as well as theologically odd if here Paul had made 'all things' the main subject, rather than God himself, as though he were invoking a kind of Stoic pantheism.

More specifically, it is linguistically far more likely that God is the subject of the verb *synergei*. The sentence falls that way. Some have argued that the spirit might be the real subject, following the end of verse 27 where Paul has said that 'the spirit intercedes for the saints according to God's will'. But actually, the run of the Greek sentence is strongly in favour of God himself being the subject. God was in any case the main subject of verse 27 (the one who searches the hearts knows the mind of the spirit, because according to God he [the spirit] intercedes for the saints). Then in verse 28 itself, Paul places *tois agapōsin ton theon* up front so that it's easy to understand *theos*, God, as the subject of the following phrase *panta synergei*, 'works all things with' . . . with *panta* as the object. In the same way, as the verse goes on, we clearly have to understand *theos*, God, as the subject also of the implicit verbs in the rest of the verse ('called according to [his] purpose'). It is God who calls, whose purpose is thereby implemented. And when we move to verses 29 and 30, God is indisputably the main subject throughout. So the most natural reading is, 'We know that, with those who love God (that is, the ones God calls according to God's purpose), God works all things for good.' Several early manuscripts actually add the phrase *ho theos* after *synergei*, I assume to make it clear that this is how the verse ought to be read.

The final reason for this revisionist reading, to come back to where we began, is that the normal meaning of *synergeō* with the dative is 'work with': the *syn* ('with') in *synergeō* takes the dative of the person *with whom* the verb's subject is collaborating. And the dative here is *tois agapōsin ton theon*, 'those who love God'. That should settle the question.

If all this is so obvious, why hasn't it all been sorted out long ago? Well, protestant theologians have always, quite rightly, worried about **synergism**, that is, the idea that people get saved as the result of a combined effort, from God on the one hand and the believer on the other. In classic 'synergism', God does his bit, we do ours, and together we accomplish salvation. Not so, we hear in a thundering chorus from everyone from Martin Luther to John Piper: salvation is God's work from first to last! All we have to do is trust! Any suggestion that we *contribute* in any way, let alone *collaborate*, is strictly ruled out.

But the point is that here – as in the other places where he uses the word – Paul is not after all speaking about *how salvation is accomplished*. Assurance of salvation is indeed based, throughout Romans, on the sovereign love of God poured out in the death of his son. But this passage, Romans 8.18–30, is speaking about the *vocation* of the saved community, the calling to *implement* the already-*accomplished* work of Jesus the Messiah within and for the benefit of the wider world of all creation. The way this happens, as we saw in our previous chapter, is through the spirit calling Jesus' followers to be people of prayer at the heart of the pain of the world.

That fits closely with the two other passages where Paul uses the verb *synergeō*, namely 1 Corinthians 3.9 ('we are God's fellow workers') and 2 Corinthians 6.1 ('as we work together with God'). In 1 Corinthians 3.9, Paul is talking about the apostles being the ones with whom God goes into partnership to get things done. This is about vocation, not salvation. In 2 Corinthians 5.20—6.1, Paul talks about being 'ambassadors for the Messiah' so that God 'is making his appeal *through* us', with the result that, in 6.1, we are 'working together with him', *synergountos auto*. This again is not about how Paul got saved. It is about how God works with Paul, and how Paul works with God, for the wider work of the gospel.[2]

We saw in the previous chapter that God goes to work, in this period when all creation is groaning, *through* the spirit-led prayer life, particularly the lament, of God's people. We are thereby formed into the Messiah-pattern, the place where the healing love of God and the convulsive pains of the world come together, producing a depth of prayerful groaning that can't even attain articulate speech. That's what Paul has in mind in verse 28. 'Those who love God', after all, is not a miscellaneous designation for Christians, plucked out of thin air. It summarizes what's happening in verse 27. Those in whose hearts the spirit has produced that God-directed groaning, which is heard and known by God the heart-searcher, have become the *location of the triune love of God*. Thus Paul's point, tying together verses 27 and 28, is that the spirit-led God-lovers are assured that God is at work *with them*, and therefore *through* them. God's ultimate will – here simply 'the good' – is set forward by God's sovereign action, *taking up within itself* the active groaning of his image-bearing people.

So this is what it means that the God-lovers, the Jesus-followers, are 'called according to his purpose'. The gospel-shaped call of God to human beings is not, in this passage, a matter of

---

2 This fits with the real meaning – as opposed to the normally assumed meaning – of 2 Cor. 5.20–1: see *PFG*, pp. 20, 70, 558, 724, 881–4, 909, 951, 980, 1343 and 1494.

rescuing them from sin and death, though of course it has that effect as well. It is about being *called* for a *purpose*, a purpose that works not just *for* them but *through* them.

All this means that western Christians have some unlearning to do, as well as some fresh learning. Ever since the Middle Ages, the western church has been fixated on how to get to heaven and avoid hell, and how to be sure that one is on the right path. The result is that the church has read all its key texts as though this was what they 'must have been' talking about. But, as Israel's prophets would tell you (thinking for instance of Isaiah 40—55), salvation is not simply God's gift *to* his people, it is God's gift *through* his people – to the wider world.

Think how Paul himself uses the language of being 'called'. He describes his own 'call' on the Damascus road as being because God intended to 'reveal his son in me' (Gal. 1.16). This corresponds to his regular usage. When God reaches out with the gospel and *calls* someone, this is not simply a synonym for 'conversion', though in some senses and contexts it involves that too. It is God's call *for a purpose*, precisely as Paul says here.

So where, in Paul's biblically soaked mind, do we find this theme? Answer: Isaiah 40—55. God calls Israel, the Servant-people, *for a purpose*. God articulated that purpose from the start with the call of Abraham, *through whom* God would bless all nations. This was repeated in Exodus 19.5–6 with Israel's call to be the royal priesthood: God would, through them, reveal his glory to the world. Then, in the Isaianic Servant-songs, God addresses Israel as the Servant in whom he will be glorified (49.3) – 'glorified', as in Romans 8.30. God had promised in Isaiah 40.5 to reveal his glory to the world; but how was that to happen? The answer gradually emerges in the great poem of chapters 40—55: through the work, and supremely the suffering and death, of the Servant of the Lord.

At the same time, the Servant would be the personal, individual embodiment of *Israel* – the national vocation focused on to one person – and *also* the personal, individual embodiment of YHWH himself. He would be the one in whose calling, fate and vindication the nations would at last see 'the arm of YHWH' displayed in power.[3]

All this could be explored at more length in terms of the larger context in Isaiah, but that is outside our present purposes. It's enough for the moment to notice that, if we ask where in scripture the themes of Romans 8.28–30 come together – people being chosen, called, justified and glorified – the answer is obvious. Any Bible-aware first-century Jewish reader, hearing the climactic phrase 'those he justified, he also glorified', would think naturally of Isaiah 40—55, particularly passages such as 45.25. In the previous verses, YHWH has declared his own absolute uniqueness (45.21), insisting that every knee will bow to him (45.23), and that in him alone are to be found 'righteousness and glory' (45.24).[4] This leads up to 45.25, where we have, again more clearly in the Septuagint than in most English translations, the statement that *from* YHWH, and *in* God, all the seed of Israel *dikaiōthēsontai kai endoxasthēsontai*, 'shall be justified and shall be glorified'.

'Those he justified, he also glorified.' Paul knew Isaiah like the back of his hand. When he alludes to it as obviously as this, he must intend his readers to hear what he says in the same vein. God called Israel for a *purpose*; and in the Messiah and by the spirit he has fulfilled and is fulfilling that purpose. Just like the phrase 'those who love God', this clause is an Israel-designation; and in Isaiah, as in the scriptures more generally, Israel is called into being by YHWH for the larger purposes

---

3 See e.g. Isa. 40.10.

4 The LXX *dikaiosynē kai doxa* marks a change from the Hebrew which is normally translated 'righteousness and strength'.

already indicated in the promises to Abraham. Israel is to be the means of bringing God's rescue operation to humans and to the whole creation.

Some have objected to this idea. God, some will say, loves us just because he loves us, not because he wants to use us for a purpose. But biblically speaking that's a false either/or. God's loving purpose *for* Israel always involved God's loving purpose *through* Israel. Paul's own awareness that the son of God 'loved me and gave himself for me' is fully at one with Paul's equal awareness that God had *called* him to be the apostle to the nations; to be, in fact, the one who would make the Servant-vocation of Isaiah 40—55 a reality. Think again of Galatians 1.16: what happened on the road to Damascus was that God was revealing himself not just *to* Paul but *in* Paul – with the purpose that he might proclaim him among the nations. There has been quite a debate in the last generation as to whether Paul was 'converted' or 'called' – a debate fuelled not least by Jewish scholars who have wanted to stress that Paul did not, as it were, change from one religion to another. That is absolutely fair enough. Paul's own testimony was that he had always worshipped the one God of Israel, and what had changed was not that primary allegiance but his recognition that the crucified and risen Jesus was Israel's Messiah. The real change of meaning we need to consider is that, while so many Christian readers have seen the Damascus road as the moment when Paul was 'saved', Paul saw it primarily as the moment when he was *sent*.[5]

There is another possible objection. Surely, someone might say, 'the Servant' is Jesus himself, not his people? Well, Paul draws on the Servant-songs in various places, not just to talk about Jesus, but to speak both of himself as the apostle to

---

5   See too 2 Cor. 5.1—6.1; Phil. 3.12–16.

the gentiles and (as we shall see in verses 31–9) of the whole renewed, messianically shaped people of God. Paul clearly sees a fluidity between the Servant-Messiah and his people which modern western logic finds hard to grasp. Indeed, once you see the Servant-shaped theme of verses 18 to 27, and then the explicit evocation of the Servant in verses 32 to 35, we have a strong contextual argument for reading verses 28 to 30, held between those two passages, in the same Isaianic terms. This is about the call of God's people to be the ones *through whom* God reveals his glory to the world.

The upshot of verse 28, then, exactly in line with what we've seen in verses 18 to 27, is to do with God's overall purpose when he calls people to believe the gospel and follow Jesus. God's loving call of Jesus' followers, Jew and gentile alike, was not aimed at helping them to escape this world and go and live with him somewhere else. The purpose was so that, in rescuing them from sin and death, God would manifest his glory *through them*, not least through their suffering and prayer. God's purposes are going ahead, and he recruits – that is, he calls – human beings to share in those purposes, as Genesis 1 always indicated he would do.

This is where Paul's theme of assurance comes into its own. We need to think of the little Roman house-churches, squashed into someone's tenement attic or the small room behind a shop, anxious about other Jesus-followers in town who do some key things differently, fearful of the all-pervasive and socially coercive paganism, particularly the Caesar-worship that's become all the rage. At this point in Rome, a city of around a million people, there were perhaps a couple of hundred Jesus-followers. They were a tiny micro-minority. But already they were known as trouble-makers, as a dangerous, subversive, disruptive little clique. And Paul's doctrine of assurance was not simply that they would go to heaven when they died – though of course he believed that at death they would be 'with the Messiah', and that the spirit would then give them new bodily life in the final resurrection. His doctrine of assurance was to confirm that they, the Jesus-believing messianic people, were in fact the true people of the creator God, *and that God was being glorified and would be glorified through their suffering and prayerful witness, even in the present time.*

So here, as earlier, Paul is cashing out a bit more what he had said in 5.17, a verse often ignored. There he insists that those who receive the gift of *dikaiosynē*, God's covenant justice, or 'righteousness' in the old parlance, *will reign in life*. The NRSV translates 5.17 in terms of those who receive God's gift of right-eousness 'exercising dominion'. That somewhat heavy phrase translates the Greek *basileusousin*, from the noun *basileus* which means 'king'. What's being promised is royal authority – which of course, as always in the New Testament, means royal authority *as redefined by and around Jesus.*[6]

Of course, ruling or reigning on earth sounds a bit strange from the point of view of western theology, especially in the context of modern liberal democracy. We are trained implicitly to reject the idea of 'religious' people bossing everyone else around! But the idea of ruling or reigning makes perfect sense in first-century Jewish kingdom-of-God thinking. The Qumran sect believed that they would inherit 'all the glory of Adam'; in other words, when the great day dawned they would be running the whole world. Paul said in 1 Corinthians 6.3 that the Jesus-believers would one day have the task of judging angels! The book of Revelation says similar things: the slaugh-tered lamb has rescued people so that they can be the 'royal priesthood', reigning (the same word, *basileusousin*) on earth. What does this all mean? What happens when we release Paul

---

6 See e.g. Mark 10.35–45.

from the burden of trying to address sixteenth-century issues and let him speak into his own time – and, through that, into ours as well?

Part of our problem is that those who thought they spoke and acted for God in the sixteenth century, as in many other centuries, tried to implement that vocation in the usual worldly way, by force of arms. But, as Jesus insisted, God's kingdom goes forwards in the ways set out in the Sermon on the Mount, in peacemaking, in justice-bringing, in mourning over the world's ills, in meekness, purity of heart and so on. That's what 'ruling' looks like now. And it begins, in the present time, with the inarticulate and anguished prayer that Paul describes in Romans 8.26–7 – the prayer of those who are indwelt by the spirit, caught up in the love of God for his suffering world.

Thus Paul is assuring the Messiah-followers in Rome that they are in fact the people through whom the creator God will work out his purposes of new creation, and through whom this God *is already working them out*. How easy it was, some centuries later, for some in the church to imagine that this meant Jesus' followers holding ordinary worldly power, and for others to react by pushing the whole thing away to a distant 'heaven'. But the abuse doesn't take away the use. From the Sermon on the Mount onwards, Jesus' promises that the meek would inherit the earth, that the poor in spirit would inherit God's kingdom on earth as in heaven, meant what they said. Romans 8 is one of the most vivid applications of the same point. *God is working all things for good with and through those who love him, who are called according to his purpose.*

Of course, it doesn't look like that on the ground. What Jesus' followers mostly see is danger, suffering, wordless lament, tragic disunity. Paul is assuring them, and us, that God's purpose is going ahead precisely through this faithful and prayerful, if frequently uncomprehending, witness. Rescuing Romans 8.28

from the normal misunderstandings opens up the possibility of a whole new view of the church's present vocation.

Paul explains this in verse 29 through an explosive christological statement. God *knew* in advance, that is, he 'foreknew', the people he was going to shape so he could work through them in this way. This is a prophetic call, like God saying to Jeremiah, 'Before I formed you in the womb *I knew you*, and . . . I appointed you a prophet to the nations'. Paul alludes to that in Galatians 1 when describing his own 'call'.[7] Scripture speaks, in Amos and Hosea and elsewhere, of God having 'known' Israel from of old.[8] And this goes closely with Paul's next verb, *prohōrisen*, 'marked out in advance', referring to God sketching, ahead of time, how his purposes were to be worked out.

So this is not about 'predestination to salvation' – or indeed its opposite. Subsequent theological traditions have invented puzzles of which the first Christians were innocent. Paul is speaking, as Isaiah was speaking, of God's purposes to reveal his name and glory to the whole world. He uses similar language, to the same effect, in the great paean of praise in Ephesians 1, the purpose being that God's glory would be displayed before the watching and often hostile world. That is precisely the point made over and over again in Isaiah 40—55. Here in verse 29, the Messiah's people are to display before the world the truth *which is in Jesus himself*. They are – we are – to be 'conformed to the image of his son', or as I've translated it to bring out the flavour of *symmorphous tēs eikonos*, 'shaped according to the model' of his son.

This language at once conjures up the larger image-of-God theology which we find when Paul draws on Genesis 1, Psalm

7 Jer. 1.5; see Gal. 1.15.
8 Amos 3.2; Hos. 5.3, cf. 13.5, where the Hebrew (but not the LXX) says, 'It was I who *knew* you in the wilderness.'

8 and other passages, for instance in 2 Corinthians 4.4–6 or Colossians 1.15–20. As we have seen when looking at the 'sending of the son' in Romans 8.3, this carries the overtones of Davidic Messiahship. But now the Davidic promises have been democratized, as promised in Isaiah 55.3. The spirit has worked in people's hearts through the gospel, so that the unique role marked out in scripture for the king is now shared, again as foreseen in scripture, with all his people.

So, says Paul, Jesus is to be the 'firstborn among many brothers', the senior member of a larger family. In Exodus 4.22, Israel is God's firstborn. In Psalm 89.27, it's the Messiah who is the firstborn. In Colossians 1.18, it is Jesus himself. In other words, the spirit is given so that Jesus-believers may become Jesus-lookalikes, sharing his status as the people who inherit the promises; and the people doing the 'looking' are the hostile and puzzled unbelieving world. With this dense christological phrase, Paul is alluding, as in chapter 5 or Philippians 3.19–21, to Jesus both as Messiah and as the true Adam, echoing Psalm 8 where the 'image-bearing' vocation of Genesis 1 is cashed out in relation to the intended universal sovereignty of human beings over God's world. Jesus, the true human, is ruling the world in glory. His followers are called to be Jesus-reflectors in the world. And, as Paul says in 2 Corinthians 3.18, this means already being 'changed from glory to glory'. Glory does not mean 'going to heaven and shining like a light bulb'. It means regaining the proper human vocation and dignity, under God and over the world – a vocation and dignity now made possible by the indwelling of the spirit, like the divine presence in the Temple. Or even, we should say, *as* the divine presence in the Temple.

This brings us back to themes we have already mentioned. In this verse, Paul squashes together into one dense little sentence the deeply biblical idea that God from the beginning made his world in such a way that it would work as designed, moving towards its intended goal, *through obedient humans*. Christology is already implicit in Genesis 1 and Psalm 8. The biblical echoes of what Paul now says point to the belief that this God, having seen idolatry and injustice displace worship and stewardship, created his rescue project – the call of Abraham and his family to be the Servant-people through whom his glory would be displayed in all the world – in such a way that this, too, would be fulfilled *through the ultimate obedient human*. That is precisely what Paul says, albeit with tantalizing brevity, in Romans 5.

So now Paul sees God's earlier human-shaped and Messiah-shaped project focusing with laser-like precision on Jesus, Israel's representative Messiah. Paul already knows him to be the 'son of God' in the double sense, not just of Israel's king, the coming Messiah, but of the one sent *from* God, embodying (as we have seen already) *both* God's purpose for Israel *and* God's purpose for his own self. Paul does not here explain this amazing Christology. But if we are to feel the force of what he is summarizing, we need this combination of themes in mind.

Paul is here looking back, of course, to 8.3–4, where God sent the son in the *likeness* of sinful flesh and as a sin-offering. He is also echoing the letter's opening statement in 1.3–4. There he gives his initial definition of the gospel: the message about God's son (this letter is going to Rome, which already had a 'gospel' about a 'son of God'), the one descended from the seed of David according to the flesh and now marked out, publicly declared, as 'son of God' in power through his resurrection. In 1.4 the word Paul uses for his being 'marked out' is *horisthentos*, which is cognate with the *prohorizō*, 'marked out in advance', which he uses here in verse 29. Jesus' people are now marked out in their baptism (6.1–14) as 'resurrection-people', in advance of this becoming publicly visible. Their calling is to be like him, to share his sonship, his inheritance, his suffering, his glory. All this is *already* true of them. This is the basis of their *present vocation*. That is what this whole section of the chapter (verses 12–30) is all about.

This christological frame – the focus on Jesus as God's Messiah, and then the shaping of his people to be like him – holds the first eight chapters of Romans firmly together. Paul's argument is emphatically messianic, emphatically in that sense political, having to do with the present world and not just a distant heaven. It is emphatically a call to 'the obedience of faith'. It is, clearly and strongly, a call to be part of a new version of the human race itself, a company to whose coming rule the whole world is to be subject, a rule whose present manifestation, in paradoxical glory, would be, like the manifestation of Jesus himself, one of self-giving love, seen here in the spirit-filled work of lament and intercession. Suffering and glory, etched in the portraits of Jesus which four of Paul's contemporaries were to write, was already marking out the lookalike Messiah-people who were conformed to the image of the son, as they found themselves called to live within his extended family and to display the family likeness to the world.

As the letter moves forwards from here, Paul continues to shape it christologically. He gives a fresh summary statement, pointing to the particular argument he's going to put forward in chapters 9—11, at 9.5. He gives another summary, looking ahead to chapters 12—16 as a whole, at 12.5. The letter's real finale in 15.12, making a full circle with 1.1–5, has Paul quoting Isaiah 11.10, about the root of Jesse who rises to rule the nations, echoing the great chapter in which the Davidic Messiah presides over a world where the wolf lies down with the lamb with a little child leading them.[9] When we look

---

9 Isa. 11.1–10.

back across Romans with that amazing sweep of messianic thought – the gospel, the cross, the Messiah, the one body in the Messiah, and then the risen Messiah ruling God's world – it is remarkable to realize how Paul has distilled all of that down into a single powerful, pregnant phrase here in verse 29. *We who believe, we who love God, have been marked out to be shaped according to this pattern, this messianic reality, this glory-revealing family.* The more the world objects, mocks and threatens, the more it becomes apparent that the message is getting through. And that will take us into the last nine verses of the chapter.

But for the moment we are left with the great hammer-blows of verse 30. I have often likened these to the crashing chords at the end of Sibelius's fifth symphony.

> *Hous de **prohōrisen**, toutous kai **ekalesen**; kai hous **ekalesen**, toutous kai **edikaiōsen**; hous de **edikaiōsen**, toutous kai **edoxasen**.*
> Those he **marked out**, he also **called**; those he **called**, he also **justified**; those he **justified**, he also **glorified**.

This, the summing up of the whole letter so far – more especially of chapters 5—8, and more particularly still of 8.12 onwards! – has the strong feel of a QED, celebrating the divine sovereignty that undergirds Paul's thought in general and Romans in particular. There is, it appears, no stopping this God. Those who believe, having responded in faith to the 'call' which turns out to have been planned by God long ago, are declared to be 'in the right'. That does not *simply* mean that their sins are forgiven for ever, though they are. It means that they can hold their heads up, now in their rat-ridden apartments on the wrong side of Rome's polluted River Tiber, or in the slaves' quarters at the back of some great house, or camping out in a ditch somewhere, having been kicked out of a home or town. They can be assured that they are the true people of the one creator God; that this God is working his purposes out, that one day at the name of Jesus every knee shall bow. And as the spirit bears witness with their spirit that they are God's children, as the spirit groans within their own groaning, longing for their full adoption in the coming resurrection, they are summoned, as are we ourselves, to faithful patience.

I have suggested that this short passage, verses 28–30, is basically Servant-theology, focused on Jesus and then opening up to include all his people. Up to now in chapter 8, we have seen the mystery in which suffering seems to be not only something God's people will have to go through but something *as a result of which* God's purposes will come to birth. Of all the biblical roots for such an idea, Isaiah 40—55 stands out, not least because that's where Paul will go explicitly in verses 32 to 35. And, at the heart of our present passage, he speaks of being conformed to the image of the son, the representative of God's people, firstborn of a large family. All this says to me that Paul is thinking here of Isaiah 40—55, and especially the Servant-songs upon which he based his amazing Jesus-poem, likewise replete with Adamic references, in Philippians 2. That is why I am encouraged to read this otherwise difficult passage in the light of Isaiah, and to see the language that has commonly been taken to refer to 'predestination to salvation', generating well-known puzzles from Augustine to Calvin and beyond, in terms instead of the purposes of God *through* his people for the world. 'You are my servant, Israel, in whom I will be *glorified.*'

All this is anchored in the story of Jesus himself. Paul's doctrines are never simply theories with a loose base in an abstract Christology. They are about the living Jesus himself. At his baptism, the father declared him to be the beloved son, the Servant. This was repeated at the Transfiguration. Jesus was marked out, with heavy irony, in Caiaphas's words at the trial ('the Messiah, the son of the Blessed?'[10]), and in the title on the cross, where, as king of the Jews, Jesus fulfilled the role for which he, the eternal son, had been foreknown, foreordained from before the foundation of the world. Thus his baptism was the moment of his public *calling*; his resurrection was when God *justified* him, declaring that he really was his son; his elevation to global sovereignty, as in Daniel 7, installed him *gloriously* as world ruler from that day to this. (Of course, as in John, the glory shines all through; but this seems to be the way Paul tells the story.)

So everything Paul says about Jesus' followers, both the beleaguered little house-churches in Rome, and us today as we face a world in disarray and a church in puzzlement and sometimes in disobedience, as we face the fears and longings of our own hearts and our wider societies in a dangerous world – all that Paul says about us, he says because we are Jesus' people. It is 'in the Messiah', as explained here in Romans 8, that there is no condemnation. It is because of him that the spirit bears witness with our spirit that we are God's children, bringing us to the place where, in the yearning strong which shall far outpass the power of human telling, we find ourselves sharing the love that passes from spirit to father and back again by way of the son. Romans 8.28–30 provides a massive structural and logical conclusion to Paul's argument to this point. But far beyond structure and logic, these verses point us to the unbreakable, unshakeable reality of the triune God, whose love in creation and redemption has called us, justified us and glorified us. All that remains, in the final nine verses of the chapter, is for Paul to celebrate that love. And for us to join in that celebration.

---

10 Mark 14.61, echoing Peter's confession at Mark 8.29 and the heavenly voice at Jesus' baptism (1.11) and Transfiguration (9.7).

8
Romans 8.31–4: If God Is for Us

³¹What then shall we say to all this?

If God is for us, who is against us?

³²God, after all, did not spare his own son; he gave him up for us all!

How then will he not, with him, freely give all things to us?

³³Who will bring a charge against God's chosen ones? It is God who declares them in the right.

³⁴Who is going to condemn?

³¹*ti oun eroumen pros tauta? ei ho theos hyper hēmōn, tis kath' hēmōn?*

³²*hos ge tou idiou hyiou ouk epheisato, alla hyper hēmōn pantōn paredōken auton, pōs ouchi kai syn autō ta panta hēmin charisetai?*

³³*tis engkalesei kata eklektōn theou? theos ho dikaiōn.*

³⁴*tis ho katakrinōn?*

We come now to the final part of this amazing chapter and thus to the climactic conclusion of chapters 5—8, the second main section of Romans. In our present chapter, we will dive into these nine verses, first with an overview of verses 31–9 as a whole and then, more particularly, with the detail of verses 31 to 34. Then, in our final chapter, we will walk through the remaining five verses, enabling us to take a quick glance back at the chapter, and at where Paul's overall argument has now arrived.

These are, of course, some of the most famous verses Paul ever wrote. Just as 1 Corinthians 13 is often read at weddings, this passage is often read at funerals. *Nothing in all creation can separate us from God's love in Messiah, Jesus our Lord.* That is something you can cling on to as you find yourself hurtling round the sharp and dangerous bends of life. Not least the final one.

Once again, however, this passage is not actually about 'life after death', or even resurrection, though of course that remains the ultimate horizon. Nor, interestingly, is it about forgiveness of sins. Yes, Paul refers to Jesus' death on our behalf. He reaffirms God's justification of his believing people. But we should note that the list of potential threats in verses 35 and 38 does not include the sins that still cling to us, or the accusations or judgment which they might in principle incur. That has all been dealt with already. We find this hard to grasp, because, as I have said before, the western theological traditions have *moralized our anthropology*, so that the only question many Christians are interested in is how sinners get to heaven and how, in the meantime, they can avoid further sin. But Paul has already made it clear that those 'in the Messiah', indwelt by his spirit, will be raised from the dead. He has already made it clear that we are to live by the mindset of the spirit. That was the argument of verses 1–11. What has concerned him since then has been the *vocation* of God's people, particularly as they bear witness to Jesus in the dire circumstances they often face.

So when we look more closely we realize that Paul's task here is to *encourage* believers. Many of them will have belonged to little house-churches scattered about in Rome, often in the less salubrious parts of the city, or sometimes as servants or slaves in some great house, but in any case facing social stigma, ostracism, loss of jobs and livelihoods, hardship and poverty, and particularly head-on persecution, with the strong chance of violence and death either from vigilante action or from official state clamp-down. Paul's point, as with verse 37, is that *in* all these things we are 'more than conquerors', totally victorious. That phrase is dramatic. It means, not just winning a battle, but finding ourselves in complete control of the field.

Where does that place us today? Our world is increasingly hostile to genuine Christian faith, in the workplace, in social and cultural pressures, in public life, surrounded by sneering media and the whispering Twittersphere. Clergy today face angry come-back on issues that a generation ago wouldn't even have been thought of. New moralities are invented overnight and the church is expected to follow suit. When I read this passage, 'Who can be against us? Who will bring a charge against us? Who can condemn us?' I see in my mind's eye not only people outside the church, mocking us for being out of step with the times, but, sadly, some within the church, who will suddenly attack us for whatever reason – theological, practical, pastoral or political. Personality clashes easily clothe themselves in theological or liturgical dress. To clergy, I would say: make sure you always have this passage within easy and prayerful mental reach. You never know when the elder or deacon or churchwarden who you had thought was your closest ally will come round to tell you that they and the parish are furious about something you just did or said . . . And of course, this passage doesn't mean we'll never get anything wrong. We often will. But it assures us that, whether or not we deserve what comes to us, *God is for us and nothing can separate us from his love in Messiah Jesus*. This holds true for all members of the Messiah's family. But I suspect clergy and teachers, more than most, need to be regularly reminded of it.

So we revert to our normal opening question. What is the framework, the start and finish, of this final paragraph? The conclusion of the argument of the chapter, and of chapters 5—8 as a whole, is obviously that *God is for us*, verse 31b; and, verse 39, *nothing can separate us from his love* in Messiah Jesus.

The theme of God's 'love' appears quite suddenly in verse 35. It hasn't been mentioned since 5.6–11. But appearances here can be deceptive. When Paul speaks explicitly here of God's 'love', it's like a tune in a tone poem which, when at last it is stated in full, makes us realize that it's been woven into the music throughout. A similar thing happens with the christo-logical title 'son of God'; Paul mentions this only rarely, but when he does (as in verse 3 and now, in this passage, in verse 32) it's explosive. So it is with the theme of God's *love*. This is where we see how Paul has tied together the whole of chapters 5—8, looping back to 5.6–11 in a great arc. Love – God's love for us and our answering and spirit-inspired love for him – has been the subtext, the deep-level theme, all through.

I have already explained how Paul has used the narrative of Passover and exodus as the framework for chapters 6, 7 and 8, enabling the story of Jesus himself to stand out, as Jesus himself clearly intended, as embodying the ultimate Passover, the new exodus. Passover and exodus, as we know from Exodus 2.23–5, happened because of God's *faithfulness* to the promises he had made to Abraham. And when we think of *covenant faithfulness* we are thinking of 'love'. The stated theme of Romans is the revelation, in the gospel message of Jesus, of the *dikaiosynē theou*, the 'righteousness' of God; but, in the Psalms and Isaiah, that phrase denotes far more than the moralistic 'justice' that many have often imagined. It is equally about the covenant, which marks God's relationship with Israel. God's determination to put the world right ('justice') is of a piece with his determination to be faithful to the covenant with Israel. The 'justice' that is involved is God's firm intention to put all things right – which is anticipated when God puts sinful humans right through the gospel, as a sign, foretaste and even means of that ultimate cosmic putting-right. But behind all that is the covenant which expresses, in its focus on Israel and then decisively in Israel's Messiah, God's love for his world and his human creatures. It isn't, then, that God has a tidy mind and wants to get everything back in its proper place. Still less is it the case that God is simply a stern angry judge. It is that God *loves his world*, and especially his image-bearing creatures – loves so fully and thoroughly, in fact, that he cannot forever abide seeing his world in disarray and his human creatures ruining their own and others' lives. So in 5.6–11 Paul insists that the death of the Messiah is the outworking, and the supreme evidence, of God's sovereign love. The Messiah's cross declares that *God is for us*.

We should therefore never allow God's justice and love to be played off against each other. When Paul says, in 1 Corinthians 13, that 'the greatest of these is love', he is of course talking about the highest form of Christian virtue. But here in

Romans, he is saying the same thing, not just about human love, but about *God's* love. Romans towers above the other letters as a full-dress exposition of God's plan, his creation and new creation, his purposes and promises, focused on his covenant faithfulness and rooted and grounded in his love. And Romans 8 towers above the rest of the letter as the point where all this becomes explicit and is celebrated as such – in the teeth of all the evidence to the contrary, as the world does its best to throw us off course with all the things that can go wrong, not least human opposition to the gospel, perhaps even from within the church.

This should not surprise us. As we noted earlier, right after God had said to Jesus, you are my beloved son, he was driven out into the wilderness to be tempted by the devil. As soon as he came back to announce that God was now at last becoming king, all hell broke loose with shrieking demons in the synagogues, and Pharisees and Herodians plotting to kill him.

But, as in the gospel story, so in the story of those who are now shaped by the gospel: God's love is the anchor. *God is for us* – not something to be said casually or cheaply, certainly not a licence to go slack on our own faithfulness, but something on which we can rest when the storms are raging, to quieten our hearts when everything seems to be going wrong. That's what this passage is about.

These opening reflections have grown out of our observations on the framing of this passage and its place within chapters 5—8 as a whole. And, while we're looking at framing devices, we should notice how each part of the argument of these chapters ends with a christological summary: 5.11, 5.21, 6.11, 6.23, 7.25a and then gloriously here at 8.39.

So if that's the framework – the unconquerable love of God – how are these nine verses constructed? Our second question has normally been about the little connecting words, but here there is no sequence of *gar* and *de* as in most of the chapter. The only *gar* is in verse 38, 'I am persuaded, *you see*', explaining verses 35–7. The emphatic little Greek word *ge*, 'indeed', rare in Romans, joins verse 32 firmly to 31. Aside from that, most of the connections between phrases and sentences are made by implication. This is not accidental. Paul has completed the step-by-step argument that arrived at the great conclusion of verse 30. Now, to celebrate where he has got to, he switches from that careful argumentative style to a different rhetorical mode.

What he does instead is to weave together three ear-catching stylistic motifs. First, we have a string of rhetorical questions. Second, we have three biblical echoes or quotations, one from each section of the Hebrew canon (something Paul only does rarely; when he does this, it's certainly for special effect). Third, we have two lists of potential dangers, the first consisting of seven dangers and the second of ten. That, too, is the kind of thing that listeners in Paul's day would pick up and enjoy. What's more, all these rhetorical features interlock with one another. This is high-register writing. Many hearers in a Roman audience, aware of fine rhetoric, would appreciate this and see what Paul was doing.

The whole paragraph that consists of these last nine verses is tied together with the gospel narrative of God's action in Jesus. Here Paul, dramatically, tells the story of Jesus in miniature: God's son, not spared, crucified, risen, ascended and now interceding for his people at the father's right hand. Only here in all his writings does Paul offer such a complete summary of the Jesus-story. So if the rhetorical ploys (the three interlocking motifs I just mentioned) provide the striking *form* for the paragraph, Jesus himself provides the central *content*. There is a lesson there for all of us preachers and teachers.

So we begin at the beginning. 'What shall we say *to* this?' – not, as in the NRSV, what shall we say *about* this, as though Paul was simply going to offer a few comments on what he'd just said, but 'what do we *conclude*' from the line of thought in which, up to verse 30, Paul has displayed the triune work of God? That opening rhetorical question might lead us to expect a statement: 'We are safe for ever in God's love, QED.' That would be true; but Paul isn't going to be so flat-footed. *He wants his hearers to think it through*, to come up with the answers themselves. That's what the technique of rhetorical questions in verses 32–5 is designed to do, compelling the audience to think quickly as he then expands the obvious answers and moves rapidly to further questions.

Different interpreters and translations have had various theories about how precisely these rhetorical questions work (see Table 2).

We need to remember that the earliest manuscripts had no punctuation, or even breaks between words. So later scribes and editors have put these next verses together in slightly different ways. In particular, it's a matter of interpretation as to where we place the question marks. In my translation I have given what I (and many others) think best, but it's possible that Paul intended more question marks than I have suggested. For instance, you could read verse 33 as two questions, not one: Who will bring a charge? Will it be God, the one who declares us in the right? And similarly, verse 34: Who is going to condemn? Is it Messiah Jesus who died for us? That is indeed how verse 35 works: 'Who will separate us . . .? Will it be suffering and so on?' This becomes yet more complicated when we realize that verses 33 and 34 are linked, as in Isaiah 50.8: it is God who justifies, *and so* [understood], who is going to condemn?

It's impossible to be certain here. But I think the high probability is that Paul intended the questions to work in the way my

Table 2 Romans 8.31—4 in Various Bible Translations

	KJV	NIV	NJB	NRSV
v. 31	What shall we then say to these things? If God be for us, who can be against us?	What, then, shall we say in response to these things? If God is for us, who can be against us?	After saying this, what can we add? If God is for us, who can be against us?	What then are we to say about these things? If God is for us, who is against us?
v. 32	He that spared not his own Son, but delivered him up for us all, how shall he not with him also freely give us all things?	He who did not spare his own Son, but gave him up for us all – how will he not also, along with him, graciously give us all things?	Since he did not spare his own Son, but gave him up for the sake of all of us, then can we not expect that with him he will freely give us all his gifts?	He who did not withhold his own Son, but gave him up for all of us, will he not with him also give us everything else?
v. 33	Who shall lay any thing to the charge of God's elect? It is God that justifieth.	Who will bring any charge against those whom God has chosen? It is God who justifies.	Who can bring any accusation against those that God has chosen? When God grants saving justice	Who will bring any charge against God's elect? It is God who justifies.
v. 34	Who is he that condemneth? It is Christ that died, yea rather, that is risen again, who is even at the right hand of God, who also maketh intercession for us.	Who then is the one who condemns? No one. Christ Jesus who died – more than that, who was raised to life – is at the right hand of God and is also interceding for us.	who can condemn? Are we not sure that it is Christ Jesus, who died – yes and more, who was raised from the dead and is at God's right hand – and who is adding his plea for us?	Who is to condemn? It is Christ Jesus, who died, yes, who was raised, who is at the right hand of God, who indeed intercedes for us.

translation has laid them out. This allows the biblical allusions to resonate properly, and it enables Paul's main rhetorical tactic – the rhetorical questions with their implied answers – to form the backbone of his line of thought, until they themselves are overtaken in verse 35 by the question, and the answer, about the powerful and unbreakable love of God.

So to the majestic rhetorical question and answer in verse 31b and 32: *ei ho theos hyper hēmōn, tis kath' hēmōn?* If God is for us, who can be against us? A lot depends on the identity of the 'us'; you can't just pluck it out of the air and make it apply to anyone randomly, like the saying wrongly attributed to Voltaire, *Dieu pardonnera, c'est son métier* – 'God will pardon, that's his job' – hoping to shrug one's shoulders and leave it at that. No: the 'us' here is obviously the people described in the previous verses, those who in their suffering and hope, and their agonized, wordless prayer, are being 'conformed to the image of the son'; those who are *en Christō Iēsou* and hence know that there is 'no condemnation'. We must again state the obvious: just because God is 'for us', that doesn't mean we will never sin, or get speeding fines, or be turned down in job applications, or fall seriously ill, or have people misunderstand or misrepresent us. The rest of the passage makes that clear. The question 'who can be against us?' doesn't mean that nobody *will* ever oppose us, that nobody will ever stand firmly in our way, but that, when they do, we can know that, because God is for us, any such opposition will in the long run be negligible, however painful and frustrating it may be at the time.

The implicit answer to Paul's rhetorical question is, nobody, of course! And he backs this up with verse 32. He here calls to mind, and weaves into the text, an allusion to Genesis 22, where Abraham prepares to offer Isaac as a sacrifice. Abraham did not spare his only son; and now, remarkably enough, this can be said of God himself as well. So Paul, firmly basing himself on this astonishing act of divine self-giving love, assures his hearers, not that there won't be any opposition, but that 'all things' will be given to us. He isn't saying there won't be problems. He is holding out a stupendous promise that will far outshine any and all challenges.

By alluding to Genesis here, Paul introduces the first of three biblical allusions – from Torah, Prophets and Writings, in this case Genesis, Isaiah and the Psalms. Referring to all three sections of scripture in this way was a rabbinic rhetorical tactic, using a kind of three-legged scriptural stool to make the argument triply secure. Paul only does this at special moments. He uses it in the ultimate climax of Romans, 15.7–13; and in the climax of Galatians in 4.21–31.

What he is doing here is not mere proof-texting. Nor is it just decoration, introducing vaguely remembered canonical phraseology like a politician today dredging up half a line from Shakespeare to give a speech the appearance of intellectual respectability. It's a way of saying, as Paul's whole gospel is saying, that with this gospel we are living *kata tas graphas*, *in accordance with the scriptures*, not by random detached verses but within the flow of the mighty river of scripture, with its narrative, life and promise coming together in glorious dramatic fulfilment. So here we have Genesis 22; then, in verses 33 and 34, we have Isaiah 50, one of the Servant-songs, making explicit the Servant-shape of the earlier argument; and then in verse 36 we have Psalm 44, one of the classic 'suffering' psalms to which, again, Paul has already alluded. We need to examine these one by one.

The account in Genesis 22 of God commanding Abraham to sacrifice Isaac is, I think, one of the darkest moments in all scripture. The theme is frequently drawn on in Paul's Jewish world. Abraham obediently binds Isaac and places him on the altar; God intervenes at the last moment, with a ram as the sacrificial alternative. God then declares that because Abraham did not spare his beloved son (the LXX is almost identical to Paul's wording here, making it effectively certain that he intends the allusion), he would bless him enormously, with his seed inheriting the world and possessing the lands of their enemies. This scene was known to some later Jewish writers as 'the binding (*Aqedah*) of Isaac', and one explanation for the regular Jewish exploration of the theme is that it may have functioned as a post-Christian attempt to say, 'We have a sacrifice as good as yours.' But in the developing Jewish tradition, some rabbis linked the *Aqedah* together with other key moments: the creation of the world, the night of Passover, and the Day of Atonement. Well, Romans is about new creation, the ultimate Passover, and God's provision of atonement. We shouldn't be surprised that Genesis 22 comes in to complete the set.

Of course, for Paul, the near-sacrifice of Isaac wasn't atoning in the way some later Jewish teachers expounded it. But we recall that, at the climax of Romans 4, the earlier Abraham-chapter, Paul parallels Jesus and Isaac, with Isaac's birth set alongside Jesus' resurrection, both constituting God-given life out of death. He refers there to Jesus as having been 'handed over' to death, the same verb as here, *paradidōmi*. And in the same chapter, he mentions, almost casually, that the promise to Abraham was that he would 'inherit the world' (4.13), the promise which was dramatically restated in Genesis 22.15–18, amplifying the various earlier statements.[1] So my sense is that Paul here sees Genesis 22 as an oblique forward pointer to the fulfilment of the Abrahamic covenant in the death and resurrection of *God's* beloved son, not least in order to tie together the exposition of God's covenant faithfulness in

---

1 E.g. 12.1–3; 15.18–21; 17.4–6; 18.18.

chapters 1—4 with the exposition of the consequent security of God's covenant family in chapters 5—8.

The second half of verse 32 then makes more sense than we might have initially realized. A traditional western reading might have expected Paul to say that God, having not spared his own son but having given him up for us all, would then save us from our sins and bring us to heaven. But Paul instead speaks of God giving us all things with him (that is, with his son). As he said in verse 17, we are fellow heirs with the Messiah; and the focal point is then on the inheritance, which is the entire world, rescued and renewed. The promise we just mentioned, about Abraham inheriting the world, means that the promised land was itself a forward-looking signpost, as the messianic psalms indicate. Thus for instance, in Psalm 2, the promises to Abraham are focused sharply on the Messiah. He will be given the nations as his inheritance, and the uttermost parts of the world as his possession. Paul draws on that, as we have seen, in 8.17–27: the messianic *inheritance*, now to be shared with all the Messiah's people, is the whole creation, set free from its slavery to corruption. So when he says here that God 'will . . . freely give *all things* to us' this is quite specific. As in 1 Corinthians 3.21–3, 'all things are yours', because 'you belong to the Messiah and the Messiah belongs to God'. And in the typically paradoxical 2 Corinthians 6.10, the apostles 'have nothing yet possess everything'. What was darkly hinted at in Genesis has now come into the full light of the Messiah's new creation. The Messiah's people inherit the world, not in the way a Roman emperor would have imagined, through violent conquest, but in the healing, fruitful way promised in Isaiah and the Psalms and spelled out by Jesus himself in the Sermon on the Mount and elsewhere.

It is to Isaiah that Paul next goes, in verses 33 and 34. Verse 33 draws easily on Paul's earlier exposition of justification, concluding in 8.1–11 and referred to a moment ago in verse 30: those he called, he justified, that is, he declared them to be in the right. But if God has done that, then any charge raised against his people can be set aside (again, of course, without any implication that they are free to misbehave): who will bring a charge? The implied answer is, nobody, of course, because God is the justifier, declaring his people *already* to be in the right. We see here how rich Paul's justification-theology actually is: justification for him is not simply dealing with sin, but enabling his people to stand unafraid before the Pontius Pilates of the world. Paul quotes Isaiah 50: if Jesus is the ultimate Servant of the Lord, then his people are the Servant-people and can claim the Servant-promises. Isaiah's Servant faced accusation and violence and ultimately death. Go back to those passages when you face those things, says Paul, and claim the promises as your own.

Verse 34, still following Isaiah 50, is more complex again. It opens a sudden window on Paul's overall view of the risen and ascended Jesus and his continuing ministry on our behalf. Who is going to condemn? Condemning, of course, is one stage on beyond laying a charge, as in verse 33. Here, the charge has been laid and apparently proved, and sentence (condemnation) is about to be passed, as in the judgment scene in 2.1–16. But no: verse 1 of the present chapter declared that there was 'no condemnation' for the Messiah's people. Yes, God's final judgment will be just, without respect of persons. But those who belong to the Messiah already know the verdict, and they know that it has gone in their favour, because God raised Jesus from the dead, declaring that his death really had dealt with sins and that in him new creation had now been launched. In that light, all possible secondary condemnations for those 'in him' can be set aside as irrelevant.

So: who is going to condemn? As with the story in John 8.1–11 of Jesus and the men taken in hypocrisy (it's normally called 'the woman taken in adultery' but you see the point), Jesus asks the woman, 'Has nobody condemned you?' 'Nobody,' she replies in bemused astonishment. Jesus has stood in the way – and it's no accident that John 8 ends with people picking up stones to throw at Jesus instead. So, we ask again: who is to condemn? When we think about Jesus, we glimpse, with Paul in this passage, a theology of messianically achieved atonement that is larger, including more elements, than we normally imagine. The reason there is 'no condemnation' is, to be sure, because Jesus in his death has been the place where, and the means by which, sin has been condemned in the flesh. That's what Paul says in 8.3. But for Paul, as in Hebrews, 'atonement' isn't simply a matter of Jesus' death. In the Levitical sacrificial cult, as retrieved in Jesus' own day, the killing of the animal was not the central point. The central point was that the blood of the animal, released in death, was the God-given cleansing agent to rinse the Temple and its furniture clean from all traces of death and anything that goes with it, especially of course sin itself. And that is done so that the divine glory, the living presence of the living creator, may continue to abide with his people. So here, very similarly to Hebrews, and at this moment of climax for the whole letter so far, Paul sees not only Jesus' death but also his resurrection, his ascension and his continuing work of intercession as the fuller picture of atonement. The much earlier reference to Jesus' sacrificial blood in Romans 3.24–6 is not far away from his thought at this point. Jesus is the great high priest, providing with his shed blood the ultimate purification that enables God to dwell with his people. Jesus is himself the great sacrifice, the sin-offering, the guarantee of our union with God through his spirit. Jesus is the ultimate priestly intercessor.

This then gives us a rich and complex basis for complete assurance, especially when we feel ourselves under threat, and needing it most. This is assurance, not only for final salvation, but for every step of the way towards that goal. Yes, we are assured that the Messiah died for us. But we are also assured, and we are to tell ourselves this story again and again in case it slips out of view, that he 'much more' was raised from the dead. That 'much more' indicates that the cross only means what it means if Jesus was bodily raised. If he wasn't, as Paul says in 1 Corinthians 15.17, we are still in our sins. The defeat of death is the sign of the defeat of sin. The resurrection therefore carries its own kind of assurance. As in Romans 6, the Messiah and his baptized people stand already on resurrection ground. Having died to sin, we are not stuck in a theological no-man's land. We await final bodily resurrection, but we are already 'in the Messiah'. His resurrection is part of the truth about who we already are. That is why we already have the 'glory', even though it displays itself in paradoxical fashion.

And that is why, as here, the resurrection provides its own specific answer to the rhetorical question, 'Who is there to condemn?' The Messiah's people are to reply, with full confidence: 'What do you mean, condemnation? He has been raised from the dead, and we have already been raised from the dead in him.' But to make this even stronger, Paul moves on further, past the resurrection itself, to the present ongoing ministry of the ascended Jesus in the heavenly places. 'Who is going to condemn us?' asks the rhetorical question, and Jesus' people reply, 'How can there be any condemnation, when Messiah Jesus is standing at the father's right hand, interceding for us?'

I suspect that many Christians today give merely lip service to the fact of Jesus' ascension. Some may interpret it vaguely to mean that Jesus, having come from heaven, has gone back there again, and that we will follow him. I hope it's clear by now how inadequate and misleading this view would be. For others, the whole business of ascension remains a puzzle, because we know that Jesus wasn't a primitive spaceman heading off to some other place within our cosmos. But we do not have (because we have never been taught) a clear biblical metaphysic within which to understand the overlap of heaven and earth, and hence to envisage this part of the *purpose* of the ascension, namely that Jesus is there to intercede for us before the father.

To be clear: the point of the heaven/earth overlap is that, in the biblical world of ancient Israel and the Jewish world of Jesus and Paul, 'heaven' is not a long way away. Heaven and earth are meant to work together. It is only human idolatry and rebellion, colluding with the dark anti-creational powers, that have made it appear otherwise. So heaven is not detached from earth, as in some philosophies which many in the modern world have unthinkingly adopted or assumed. Heaven, as I've often said colloquially, is the CEO's office; it is the place from which 'earth' is run. That is Jesus' task right now, as he claimed in Matthew 28.18. There is already a wise obedient human being at the helm of the universe. That is what creation had always needed. We rejoice that it is already true in Jesus. The whole creation is on tiptoe waiting for it to become fully true in us as well. In the meantime, we anticipate that time in the lament and puzzled prayer of 8.26–7.

When Paul adds that Jesus is now at the father's right hand, this is one of several early Christian retrievals of that favourite early text, Psalm 110.1 ('YHWH said to my Lord, "Sit at my right hand until I make your enemies your footstool"'). According to Mark 14.62, Jesus himself combined this text with Daniel 7, where in the great apocalyptic denouement the 'one like a son of man' is raised up, brought to sit at the right hand of the Ancient of Days. Daniel's picture envisages the final triumph of

God's right-hand man against all the dark forces, the monsters from the deep. This is the fulfilment *both* of God's purpose for humanity – Daniel 7 is like a nightmare version of Genesis 1, with the human figure put in charge of the wild animals – *and* of God's purpose for the Messiah, *and* of God's purpose, if we can put it like this, for himself, for his own second self. Ever since creation, including the creation of humans in God's image, the divine purpose was always that the creator would come to dwell, to be at home, within his own world.

Paul has already spoken of Jesus as the true human, the last Adam, in chapter 5. There he insists (though it's dense and allusive) that, with the exaltation of Jesus, the victory of the kingdom has been won, a victory now to be shared with all Jesus' redeemed brothers and sisters. Once again, there comes into view the great arc of thought from chapter 5 to chapter 8; this is how the whole section works. Paul sets out the same theme, from a different point of view, in 1 Corinthians 15. This is hardly surprising, since that whole chapter, the full-dress exposition of resurrection, has to do with the first Adam and the last Adam. Paul weaves the theme, also, into his heaven-and-earth picture in Ephesians chapter 1.

Here, then, Jesus is God's right-hand man in heaven. He is there, in charge. Who shall condemn? asks the rhetorical question. No-one, Paul expects his hearers to reply – because Jesus, the Messiah, is the man at God's right hand. Jesus is the truly human being, doing what God always intended humans to do, that is, ruling the world as God's obedient agent and image-bearer. Those who know Jesus to be their older brother, as in verse 29, can and should rejoice at this. Our brother, the leading member of the new family, is there at God's right hand.

More particularly, to our delight and relief, he is *interceding on our behalf*. This is a wonderful encouragement, precisely at the moments when, whether in large matters or small, we find ourselves apparently under condemnation. (Again, this is not to say we will never get things horribly wrong, and need to be rebuked and restored to the right way.) Paul's question, 'Who is going to condemn?' is answered implicitly, No-one – because there is Jesus, standing at the father's right hand, saying 'Father, have mercy on this, my younger sister, my younger brother.' (In Psalm 110 and Daniel 7, and elsewhere in the New Testament, he is *sitting* at God's right hand. But, as in Stephen's vision in Acts 7.55–6, he is here *standing* to intercede.)

This picture of father and son is the reality that shows up the caricature in those mediaeval paintings where, tragically, you have a stern and angry father and a rather wet and feeble-looking son. No: as in verse 32, the father gave the son for this very purpose, and the son and the father are now working together. Jesus is the true, image-bearing human, reflecting the praises, prayers and urgent needs of his human family into the father's heart, and reflecting back to his people the rescuing and protective love of the father. He is not trying to persuade the father to act against his own nature or purpose. He is there to implement that nature and purpose, which was always self-giving love.

As we reflect on the significance of Jesus' ascension, I am impelled to put in at this point an aside about the present Christian liturgical calendar. Some readers, of course, may well not use any liturgical calendar, though I suspect most still take note at least of Christmas and Easter. But in many churches, including my own, the last Sunday in Advent, late in November, has been labelled as 'the feast of Christ the King'. This very modern innovation threatens to undermine the vital truth which Paul is here teaching, so it may be worth spelling out what's going on.

The idea of calling one particular Sunday 'the feast of Christ the King' was dreamed up by Pope Pius XI in 1925. For reasons that were obvious in Europe at the time, he wanted to get preachers and teachers to emphasize that loyalty to Jesus Christ came ahead of all other political and cultural allegiances. Now the day Pope Pius chose for this was the last Sunday in October. If you use a liturgical calendar, you will know that that is a nothing-in-particular time, a long way after Pentecost, let alone Easter, and a long way before Advent, let alone Christmas. But then Pope Paul VI, as recently as 1970, moved this newly invented so-called 'feast of Christ the King' to the last Sunday before Advent. And most non-Roman churches, including my own (where people interested in liturgy have often been eager to copy Rome), have meekly gone along with the proposal without noticing the effect it has had. Pope Pius's original idea for a feast of Christ the King did not originally form part of a *story*. It was just an extra theme to think about. But placing it where it now is strongly implies something about how the whole Christian story works. And the thing it implies completely undermines the truth of which Paul is speaking in this paragraph.

I have made this point in *Surprised by Hope* and elsewhere, but Romans 8 encourages me to emphasize two things in particular. First, *we already have a feast of Christ the King*. It's called Ascension Day. In liturgy, not least in the calendar, more is less. Adding something means taking it away from somewhere else. Having that extra day means that Ascension, by implication, will focus only on Jesus going away, not on his installation as God's right-hand man, ruling and inter-ceding. But second, putting this new 'feast' at the very end of the calendar, right before Advent begins, *gives the clear message that the installation of Jesus as the world's true Lord hasn't really happened yet*, rather than being *already* the case, as in Matthew 28. The church calendar is a wonderful gift in teaching the faith. If we pull it out of shape, we end up teaching something different. The kingdom *has* already been inaugurated. Jesus is already at God's right hand, reigning and interceding.

Having said all that, the most important thing about verses 33 and 34 is the way Paul retrieves and develops Isaiah 50. Isaiah 50.4–9 forms the third and penultimate Servant-song, in which the Servant, though complaining of ill-treatment, has learned to trust that God's will is going forwards. That is exactly the point Paul is making in this passage. 'YHWH helps me,' says the Servant, 'therefore I have not been disgraced; therefore I have set my face like flint, and I know that I shall not be put to shame.' (We recall that, in Romans 1.16, as part of his introductory statement for the whole letter, Paul had declared that he was 'not ashamed of the gospel', probably alluding to this very passage.) So then we come to Isaiah 50.8–9:

He who vindicates me is near.
Who will contend with me?
Let us stand up together.
Who are my adversaries?
Let them confront me.
It is the Sovereign God YHWH who helps me;
who will declare me guilty?
All of them will wear out like a garment;
the moth will eat them up.

This is a glorious passage, coming through suffering into a hard-won confidence and assurance. And that is exactly what's going on in Romans 8. Paul will have been well aware that this Isaiah-reference belonged closely with the Abraham-story to which he had just alluded in verse 32. In Isaiah 51.2, a mere four verses after the passage Paul is here quoting, God says, 'Look to Abraham your father, and to Sarah who bore you; for he was but one when I called him, but I blessed him and made him many.' That is exactly Paul's point. Things may look bleak, but think how God has always acted. 'YHWH will comfort Zion,' continues Isaiah in 51.3. 'He will comfort all her waste places, and will make her wilderness like Eden, her desert like the garden of YHWH.' There we find once more the extension of the 'promised land' theme: Abraham was promised the land to begin with, but the whole world in the end. 'Joy and gladness will be found in her; thanksgiving and the voice of song.'

Paul doesn't *quote* that last bit, Isaiah 51.3; he simply *does* it. At the end of this chapter of new creation, he celebrates the fact that the Abrahamic promise has been fulfilled through the suffering and vindicated Servant himself, and that the Servant-people, the Messiah's people, can therefore be confident of vindication. There is no condemnation for the Messiah's Servant-people, even though it will often feel as though that condemnation is precisely what's happening or about to happen. Our calling, when we find ourselves there, is to stand in humility and hope – there is no trace of arrogance in the confidence of Isaiah's Servant! – and to cling on to that opening statement of verse 31, rooted in the 'no condemnation' of 8.1: *If God is for us, who is against us?*

All this points to the final verses of the chapter and the section, to which we turn in the last chapter of the present book.

9
Romans 8.34–9: Nothing Can Separate Us from God's Love

³⁴It is the Messiah, Jesus, who has died, or rather has been raised;
who is at God's right hand, and who also prays on our behalf!
³⁵Who shall separate us from the Messiah's love?
Suffering, or hardship, or persecution, or famine, or nakedness, or danger, or sword?
³⁶As the Bible says,

> Because of you we are being killed all day long;
> we are regarded as sheep destined for slaughter.

³⁷No: in all these things we are completely victorious through the one who loved us.
³⁸I am persuaded, you see, that neither death nor life, nor angels nor rulers, nor the present, nor the future, nor powers,

³⁴*Christos Iēsous ho apothanōn, mallon de egertheis, hos kai estin en dexia tou theou, hos kai entyngchanei hyper hēmōn.*
³⁵*tis hēmas chōrisei apo tēs agapēs tou Christou? thlipsis ē stenochōria ē diōgmos ē limos ē gymnotēs ē kindynos ē machaira?*

³⁶*kathōs gegraptai hoti*

> *heneken sou thanatoumetha holēn tēn hēmeran,*
> *elogisthēmen hōs probata sphagēs.*

³⁷*all' en toutois pasin hypernikōmen dia tou agapēsantos hēmas.*
³⁸*pepeismai gar hoti oute thanatos oute zōē oute angeloi oute archai oute enestōta oute mellonta oute dynameis*

³⁹nor height, nor depth, nor any other creature will be able to separate us from the love of God in the Messiah Jesus our Lord.

³⁹oute hypsōma oute bathos oute tis ktisis hetera dynēsetai hēmas chōrisai apo tēs agapēs tou theou tēs en Christō Iēsou tō kyriō hēmōn.

Romans 8 ends on a note of wonderful confidence. Reflecting on this, I realized that confidence has long been the aim, not only of theologians, but also of philosophers and scientists. 'How can we *know*?' has been the question of so many. How do we get past misleading impressions and subjective fantasy to significant beliefs and then on to *true* beliefs?

Philosophers down the years have tried to find their way to that kind of epistemological confidence. 'I think, therefore I am,' claimed Descartes (*cogito, ergo sum*). Much subsequent western thought has tried to build on that, with (to say the least) mixed success. The late Bishop Lesslie Newbigin, with a glance at one of our major British supermarket chains, used to say that in our days Descartes' motto had degenerated into *Tesco, ergo sum*: 'I shop, therefore I am.' But Paul's answer, given loud and clear in these final verses of Romans 8, is altogether deeper: *amor, ergo sum*. I am loved, therefore I am.

I have argued elsewhere that the gospel urges upon us *an epistemology of love*. By 'love' here I mean, not simply a feeling, which tends to collapse the external world back into its own desires. I mean 'love' in the sense of the word *agapē* as the early Christians came to see it: love as the generous self-giving that reaches out with delight to affirm the reality of that which is known and loved. This is not the place to develop that further.[1] But when, in verse 38, Paul says 'I am persuaded', *pepeismai*,

---

1 See my *HE*, especially chs 3, 6 and 8.

he seems to be not only summing up the specific argument of chapters 5—8, and of Romans as a whole thus far, but also glancing out across the world of ancient intellectual life. He is saying to the philosophers, as much as to the political and religious establishments, *this is where you can stand.*

The love of which he speaks in this passage is the love of God the creator, anchored, of course, in Jesus. Paul lists in verse 35 the things that might go badly wrong for us, and in verses 38–9a the forces ranged against us. They would be quite enough to shake most people's confidence. But the gospel itself, the message about Jesus crucified, risen, ascended, interceding, holds us in place despite everything: God's love in the Messiah, Jesus our Lord.

That provides the obvious initial analysis of these last five verses: they start and end with God's love. 'Who shall separate us from the Messiah's love?' in verse 35 is answered by the expanded statement in verse 39: nothing in all creation will be able to separate us from the love of God in the Messiah, Jesus our Lord.

As in verses 31–4, Paul gets from the start to the finish of the paragraph, not by way of the kind of careful formal argument we saw earlier in the chapter, but by the rhetorical device of lists: the seven potential and actual threats in verse 35 and the ten larger powers in verses 38–9a. He places the first list on the map of biblical expectation by quoting from Psalm 44 in verse 36, then claiming that 'the one who loved us' (verse 37) enables us to be not just victorious over them but super-victorious. This is explained in verse 38, with the only *gar* ('for') in the passage, by Paul's conviction, based securely on the revelation of God's love in the Messiah, that no forces on earth or in heaven can separate us from that same love. The passage thus forms a clear whole, looking back once more to the opening of the whole section in Romans 5.1–5. Our first two regular exegetical questions (the start and finish of the passage, and the connections that link the verses together) are thus easily answered.

Our third regular question, the wider world within which Paul's hearers would receive this message, is also fairly clear. The question of confidence was vital for Paul's hearers in Rome – as it is, indeed, for many of Jesus' followers today. Paul's question here is not just whether God will look after his people after their deaths; of course he will. He has already affirmed that. Nor is the question simply about whether one can hold on to Jesus in faith when bad things are happening, though that was and is important too. The question included the more subtle problem, that people in Paul's culture, as also today, might well interpret the bad things that were happening to God's people as signs that God was angry with them, that they had done something wrong. As with Job's comforters, many in Paul's day, as in our own, assumed that if someone was in tune with God they wouldn't have any problems. Thus, if there were or are obvious catastrophes and problems, that must mean that the people concerned, or indeed the whole movement, had obviously gone off the rails.

The western world has looked this question in the face in recent years. The coronavirus pandemic raised the question in what, for many people, was a new way, though of course the challenge has been around in one form or another as long as there have been humans getting sick. Now the new geopolitical situation, whether focused on Russia and eastern Europe or China and its neighbours, has raised it again. Until fairly recently, western politicians and thinkers reckoned that the world was working fairly well, that liberal democracy was now obviously becoming a universal creed, so that things were more or less on track. (Too bad, of course, about Afghanistan, Yemen, Sudan, Syria and so on, not to mention North Korea,

Taiwan and other faraway places; but western arrogance had reduced those to less significance.) So how should we look out upon a world in a mess?

Serious thinkers in Paul's world must have been asking similar questions. Wars and rumours of wars continued. The still quite new Roman empire, in the century after Julius Caesar's assassination, put on a front of being not only impregnable but benevolent, bringing 'salvation', peace and prosperity to the world. But most people were not fooled by the rhetoric. The Jewish world had reasons for particular anxiety, especially after the emperor Gaius Caligula had nearly succeeded in having a huge statue of himself placed in the Jerusalem Temple. Similar things had happened before. Anti-Jewish riots were depressingly common, not least because the Jews had permission from Rome to absent themselves from the normal local cults, leading many people to suspect them of disloyalty to their communities or to blame them for bad things that happened, whether a fire, a flood or a defeat in war. Equally, many Jews, aware of Daniel's prophecy about the 490 years between the start of the Babylonian exile and the final heaven-sent vindication for God's people, were expecting that, even if things got very bad or dangerous, God would surely step in and act once and for all. For all these reasons, the two lists of dangers and hostile forces would represent real and present threats to Paul's hearers.

What happens, within such larger concerns, when the mess we can see in the wider world seems to be reflected or embodied in our own communities and personal lives? Paul had faced that challenge when some in Corinth were looking askance at his bizarre way of life, not least the many persecutions and dangers he had endured, and questioning whether God would allow a proper apostle to undergo that kind of thing. The second letter to the Corinthians provides a glorious, ironic rebuttal. Beatings, imprisonment, shipwreck and the like, Paul insisted, were actually the *defining marks* of genuine apostleship. Romans was written not long after 2 Corinthians, and Paul may have been only too aware that, within the vulnerable Christian groups in Rome, some might have suffered similarly, including perhaps the Jewish Christians who had been expelled under Claudius and had come back under Nero. Meanwhile other Christians, including those gentile Christians who had settled down after the Jews had departed, might themselves become 'Job's comforters' and regard the Jews in question as obviously under divine displeasure. (That is part of the situation that Paul addresses explicitly in chapter 11 and then again in chapters 14 and 15.)

So I suspect that in this passage Paul is not simply talking about 'assurance of final salvation' – the good news that not even death itself can break the powerful hold of God's love in Messiah Jesus. He is also addressing the issue of *penultimate* assurance – which is likewise part of the doctrine of justification. This is the assurance that every Christian group and individual must give to every other. We are to see one another's misfortunes and sorrows, not as signs of God's displeasure, and hence of our own superior virtue or spirituality, but rather as part of the calling to share in the 'messianic woes', in which – as in verses 26 and 27 – the spirit is calling out to the father from the heart of the pain and perplexity.

Of course, as I have said before, this doesn't mean that Christian communities and individuals are now incapable of making mistakes and going right off the rails. Sadly we may indeed fall into sin, make unwise decisions, embrace heresies. Sometimes that will produce outward disaster, though quite often it will actually result in an easier life. A worldly church no longer challenges its wider community. A compromised Christian may well have stepped off the steep ladder of vocation and settled for a gentler climb. But those who refuse to slide like that into the world's ways of thinking may well face real trouble of one sort or another.

Paul nails this point in verse 36 with his quotation of Psalm 44. That is one of the great psalms of complaint, following hard upon the double lament of Psalms 42 and 43. In Psalm 44, the psalmist celebrates God's great promises, but complains that they have not been coming true. Everything has gone wrong – despite the fact that God's suffering people have *not* been false to the covenant. They have not worshipped idols. They have remained faithful – *and yet* all these things have come upon them. So the psalmist concludes, dramatically, that all this is happening 'because of you': it is 'for your sake' (44.22). He doesn't suppose for a minute that God might no longer be in charge. He recognizes that there must be stranger, darker and deeper things going on than one would see on the surface.

Paul has already alluded to Psalm 44 in Romans 8.27, where he echoed the affirmation in Psalm 44.21 that God, who 'knows the secrets of the heart', is therefore well aware of his people's continuing loyalty. In that earlier passage, Paul had spoken of God as the heart-searcher who knows what the spirit is thinking when his people find their prayer consisting of inarticulate groanings within their own pain and that of the world. So, with Romans 8.17–27 already (as it were) on the table, Paul now quotes the next verse of the psalm to point to the belief that the severe troubles of God's people are somehow 'for God's sake'. As we have seen throughout verses 17–30, the point seems to be that those facing severe troubles are somehow sharing in the Messiah's present redemptive sufferings. This is a point to which we shall shortly return.

We must not allow this glorious, rhetorically charged paragraph to wash over us, as though Paul were simply saying, 'Everything's going to be all right, nothing else really matters.'

Of course in a way he *is* saying that. But he's saying it (to re-emphasize the point) in a world where misfortune and disaster would regularly be taken as an index of divine disfavour. No, he says; this is part of our vocation. It isn't just something we have to get through in order to arrive at our own salvation. As already in verses 18–30, we are called to bear, in the spirit, the pain of the world, to stand at that place so that God's spirit may be groaning right there. This, in other words, is part of our *salvific* ministry in and for the world. Paul is, as it were, *applying the unique fact of Jesus' crucifixion to the present suffering of Jesus' people as they stand in prayer, as in verses 26 and 27, at the heart of the suffering world.* He is hinting, as in Colossians 1.24, that, by sharing in the messianic woes, God's suffering people are part of the means by which the victorious death of Jesus is applied to the world. It isn't just that suffering and trouble can and will be overcome, ultimately in the resurrection within the whole new creation. The point is that, with the spirit's groaning within us, we are called to share in God's rescue plan for the whole world.

Let's remind ourselves of how the passage works. As I said in the previous chapter, the final five verses don't have many tell-tale connecting words. The *alla* at the start of verse 37 indicates that, contrary to what verse 35 might have implied, these troubles are not merely unpleasant things we have to get through, but actually the setting for a greater victory than we could have imagined – just as the Messiah's cross was not simply a ghastly event to be bravely borne, but actually his royal victory over all the powers. Yes, says verse 36, this is a deeply unpleasant place to be, *but – alla –* in all these things we are more than conquerors. That greater victory, in which all opposition is not just defeated but swept off the board, is then explained with the *gar* at the start of verse 38. Verse 37, the super-victory, may seem counter-intuitive. But it is based on the unbreakable love of God himself, of which Paul has become utterly persuaded.

That love is then, as we saw, the framework of these five verses. They open with verse 35, which highlights 'the Messiah's love'. They end in verse 39 with 'the love of God in the Messiah Jesus our Lord'. Verse 37 forms a kind of half-way marker between these two, with 'through the one who loved us' referring back, it seems, to verse 35. And with this, this major section of the letter, chapters 5—8, returns to where it began. In Romans 5.6–11, God's love is displayed in action in the death of Jesus, joining up with 5.1–5 where love for God has been poured out in our hearts by the spirit, generating, in the midst of suffering, the patience which produces the hope that does not disappoint. That is the great statement to which Paul has now at last worked his way back.

So, as part of Paul's heightening of rhetoric here, he offers two remarkable (though very Pauline!) lists. In verse 35, he lists seven bad things that might happen to you. Then in verses 38 and 39 he lists no fewer than ten power structures that might be ranged against you. That 'seven plus ten' indicates, within the assumptions of ancient rhetoric, a kind of completeness. These troubles and threats stand for anything and everything that the world, the flesh and the devil might throw at you.

Verses 31–9, in fact, draw together the whole scripture, all human experience, the whole hostile world, and the whole victorious gospel. The point is that none of these things – whether events, as in 35, or forces and powers as in 38 and 39 – can *separate* 'us' from God's Messiah-shaped love. Again, the 'us' here is those 'in the Messiah', the people in whose hearts the spirit witnesses that they are God's children, and groans with their pain at the world's dark depths. And Paul at last makes it explicit – for the first time since 5.6–10 – that this is all about *love*.

I suspect we don't sufficiently ponder what this means. Those who regularly preach, or listen to, 'normal' evangelistic addresses know very well that 'God so loved the world'. There is always a danger that we both take this for granted and reduce the 'love' to a general sense of benevolence. We need to rattle that cage a bit. One way of doing it is to look at two things that don't usually come across the radar of contemporary western Christianity.

First, many in Paul's day believed that the city of Rome had a secret name. Nobody was supposed to utter it, in case the city, its secret being revealed, might be exposed to hostile attack. That may sound like something out of 'Harry Potter'; but actually quite a bit of Harry Potter, not least the spells, is rooted in the classical world. There is good evidence that many not only assumed that Rome had a secret name but believed that the name in question was in fact 'Rome' backwards. Rome in Latin is *Roma*: so, spelled backwards, it is *Amor*. And *Amor* is the Latin for 'love'.

You see, the Romans believed (well, this is what they told themselves from time to time – how many actually believed it it's hard to know) that they were descended from Aeneas, who escaped from the sack of Troy, as in Virgil's epic, *The Aeneid*. And Aeneas was reputedly the son of Venus, the love-goddess. So it's quite possible that Paul, reaching the height of his theological rhetoric, writing to people fluent in both Latin and Greek, would want to reclaim Love, *agapē* in Greek, *Amor* in Latin, not as the secret name of the pagan city but as the deepest truth about the creator God. Remember the subversive way in which Paul opens the letter. He speaks of God's gospel, the 'good news' – and 'good news' was a word associated at the time with the achievements of Caesar Augustus, hailed as the son of the divine Julius, the *kyrios*, the Lord. But *this* good news is the real thing; and it has come about through the real 'son of God', Jesus, who through his resurrection has been marked out as son of God and lord of the whole world. And whereas the imperial rhetoric of the day spoke regularly about Caesar providing 'rescue', 'salvation', 'justice' and 'peace', Paul declares that in the gospel of Jesus God's genuine justice has been unveiled, bringing genuine salvation and resulting in genuine peace. It all fits. Here, at the climax of the first half of the letter, Paul homes in on the ultimate reality: not Rome, not *Amor* in Latin, but the unconquerable, unbreakable love of the one true God.

No wonder the rulers and authorities of Paul's day struck back in every way they could. That is the context for this final passage.

So the first thing to consider about Paul's highlighting of 'love' is the head-on clash with Roman ideology. But second, consider that, in verses 35 and 37, Paul speaks of the *Messiah's* love, 'the love of Christ' in regular translations. This is surprisingly rare. In 2 Corinthians 5 he says that 'the Messiah's love leaves us no choice, because, if one died for all, then all died'. In Galatians 2 he says that the son of God 'loved me and gave himself for me'. In Ephesians 3 he speaks of knowing the Messiah's love that surpasses knowledge. In Ephesians 5.2, the Messiah's self-giving love is the model for love in the community; in 5.25, more specifically, the love of husbands for wives. (There is one extra reference: in 2 Thessalonians 2.13 Paul speaks of the church as 'beloved by the Lord'.) That's it. It is considerably more common for Paul to refer to the love of God the father, the love that *sent* the son to die. And when he speaks of *grace* he speaks of 'the grace of the Lord Jesus', not of the Messiah. So why does Paul here speak of the *Messiah's* love, and then as it were weld that together with God's love in the last phrase ('the love of God in the Messiah Jesus')?

The specific idea of the Messiah's love does not come from Paul's scriptures, nor from the later Jewish texts known to us. You can search from Genesis to Malachi, and in the inter-testamental texts such as the Qumran scrolls or the *Psalms of Solomon*. You will find plenty about the Messiah and his coming work: he is tasked with defeating the pagans, building the Temple, establishing a reign of justice, wisdom and peace, and so on. But in all those texts, whether from the Psalms or Isaiah or anywhere else, there is nothing to suggest that if and when a Messiah turned up he would act out of *love*.

The closest might be passages such as Psalm 72, where the coming king will do justice for the poor and needy, though this doesn't mention 'love' as such. Isaiah's Servant will die a cruel but redemptive death, but the prophet doesn't say that the Servant was acting out of love. When the son of man is exalted to sit beside the Ancient of Days, he will rule over the monsters and destroy their deadly regimes, but Daniel never suggests that this would be the result of his love. But the Messiah's love is at the heart of today's passage, and hence at the rhetorical climax of the letter so far. Where does this idea come from?

The remarkable answer must be the great biblical theme of the love of YHWH himself, Israel's God, the creator. The idea of the Messiah's love, set within such a rich biblical context as here, must mean (as in 5.6–11) that the Messiah is the personal embodiment of Israel's God. YHWH loves his people; the Messiah clothes that love in human flesh and blood. That theme, of YHWH's love for his people, permeates many parts of the Old Testament. Think of Deuteronomy, where the reason for Israel's calling, protection and deliverance from slavery is not because Israel is larger, more numerous or stronger than other nations, but simply because God loves her. We then find it with the theme of Israel's judgment and rescue, not least in Hosea, but then in (as we might have guessed!) Isaiah 40—55.

That is where God's powerful love rescues Israel from Babylon. The theme is then repeated from several angles in some of the great psalms, where the *hesed* of God, his faithful, steadfast love, endures for ever. And in Deuteronomy, Isaiah and the Psalms, to speak of God's love is to speak about the *covenant*: God's unbreakable loyalty to his people, and his renewal of that covenant through the Messiah.

Now, as some readers may know, scholars have sometimes projected modern categories back on to Paul. Ever since the German philosopher Hegel, European thought has been divided between those who think that the world moves forwards by a steady evolution and those who think that the important events happen through sudden revolutions which break into that smooth narrative. So, projecting that nineteenth-century antithesis backwards – a ridiculous idea, really, but this is how it's happened – people have declared in the last generation or so that Paul's theology cannot be *both* 'covenantal' *and* 'apocalyptic', absurdly treating 'covenantal' as meaning 'evolutionary' and 'apocalyptic' as meaning 'revolutionary'. These modern categories have now joined others that scholars have used in analysing Paul, such as 'forensic' which means 'belonging to the law court'.[2] But in Romans 8 and many other places we have, in the same breath, the covenant with Israel, now focused on the Messiah, and at the same time we have the sudden in-breaking of God's powerful rescuing love in the new messianic exodus. After all, the original exodus itself, though it was a new event breaking in after generations of slavery, happened because God remembered his covenant with Abraham, Isaac and Jacob (Exodus 2.23–5). 'Apocalyptic' and 'covenant faithfulness' fit tightly together in ancient Israelite and Jewish thought, even if not in nineteenth-century philosophy. And one of the ways

---

2 On all this, see my *PRI*, chs 3, 4, 6, 7, and 8.

of saying all this in Paul's world was to speak, as he does in Romans 1.15–17, of the unveiling (in Greek, the *apokalypsis*) to the world of the *justice* of God. That is why I have sometimes translated his key term *dikaiosynē* not as 'righteousness', which has its own misleading history in relatively modern theology, but as 'covenant justice', which draws 'covenantal' and 'forensic' categories together in line with the Hebrew *tsedaqah* which often stands behind the Septuagint's use of *dikaiosynē*. As I've said before, we have to forget our modern categories, which usually reflect bits and pieces of post-Enlightenment philosophy. We have to stop giving nineteenth-century answers to sixteenth-century questions, and start giving twenty-first-century answers to first-century questions. We have to learn to think like first-century, Bible-soaked, Messiah-focused Jews. That, surprisingly to some, is the only firm foundation from which we can understand and address the new world of our own day.

So what exactly is this 'love' of which Paul speaks so passionately? People used to say that the word *agapē* referred to a special 'Christian' kind of love. Not so. The Septuagint uses the word for everything from God's love for Israel to Amnon's destructive lust for Tamar.[3] So why do the early Christians focus on *agapē* in the way they do, picking up the *theme* (rather than the linguistic phenomenon) of the Hebrew *hesed* in particular ('mercy', 'loving kindness', 'generosity' and so on)? They – John and Paul in particular – use the word to indicate the biblical theme of gratuitous divine love, God's faithfulness to his covenant, his determination to see the covenant purpose through for the sake of the world – and their strong sense that this purpose had been fulfilled in Jesus.

But – to say it again – biblical and Jewish thought never links this to the Messiah and his expected tasks. The closest

---

3 2 Sam. 13.1, 4, 15.

might be in Isaiah 40—55, where the prophet speaks of YHWH's powerful rescuing love and then speaks, in parallel, of 'the arm of YHWH' – which in chapter 53 seems to be identified with the Servant. This remains oblique, not explicit, but we could suggest that the Servant's suffering is displayed as the shocking, unanticipated display of divine love in action.

There are, however, three other converging answers as to why Paul speaks specifically about the *Messiah's* love.

First: early Christian thought began with reflection on the resurrection of the crucified Jesus. This appeared to Jesus' first followers as so obviously and overwhelmingly the inauguration of the long-awaited new exodus, the new creation, that they were bound to interpret the whole event, cross and resurrection together, as the revelation-in-action of the long-promised divine love. If this was the new exodus, it must be because Israel's God, the creator, had at last remembered his long-promised mercy. Or one could say that, if God's new creation had begun, sin must have been defeated, and so *this at last was what rescuing divine love looked like.* As Paul declares in 2 Corinthians 5, *in the Messiah God was reconciling the world to himself.* God had promised to act in reconciling love, and he had done so, and was doing so, in, as and through Jesus, Israel's Messiah. At the very heart of early Christology is the notion that God's plan for his own self, and God's scriptural blueprint for Israel's Messiah, converge into one in a way that was not apparent from contemporary Jewish readings of scripture but which became obvious in the light of Jesus. So the Messiah's own motivation for going to the cross could then appropriately, and explosively, be spoken of in terms of the Deuteronomic and Isaianic *hesed Adonai*, the loving kindness of YHWH himself. Scholars have sometimes noted that when Paul speaks of the church's relation to Jesus, that picture is modelled on Israel's relationship to YHWH in scripture.[4] This comes to a head in verse 35, where Paul transposes the biblical doctrine of YHWH's love into the newly revealed reality of the Messiah's love.

That theological answer to our question can be fleshed out with two more personal ones.

The second answer, then, is that Jesus' first followers did not separate his resurrection from their memory of him before his death. The gospels speak of Jesus looking with love at the rich young ruler; of Jesus touching the unclean, bringing healing and hope; of him weeping at Lazarus's tomb; and in general of what we might call a sovereign kindness in so much of what he did. His closest followers knew what sort of a person he was. When the resurrection revealed – as he had tried to hint at the Last Supper! – that his death was to be seen as the great rescuing act of new exodus, they naturally spoke of his crucifixion itself as the supreme act of love. 'He had always loved his own people in the world,' says John (13.1); 'now he loved them right through to the end.' This memory then coloured their interpretation of his death.

The third answer has to do with the church's *present awareness* of the person of Jesus himself. That strange presence, sometimes elusive, sometimes worryingly powerful and challenging, was always loving. His presence as the church told his story; his promised and experienced presence in the breaking of the bread; his mysterious presence which they met in their ministry to the poor; all these exuded the sense of his sovereign, self-giving loving friendship. The Jesus who was experienced as a man of love before his crucifixion was known personally as the loving Lord in the intimate prayerful life of his followers. Paul puts it all together: 'The son of God loved me and gave himself

---

4   E.g. C. Tilling, *Paul's Divine Christology*, 2nd edn (Grand Rapids, MI: Eerdmans, 2015 [2012]).

for me.' Memory and experience dovetail with the scriptural promises of YHWH's rescuing love, to produce – within twenty-five years of Jesus' death! – this remarkable theme of the Messiah's personal self-giving love.

Here we have, then, a radical innovation in Jewish messianic thinking. I am suggesting that the only explanation for it is that Jesus' first followers came to see him, as Messiah, as the human embodiment of Israel's God. God's love in Deuteronomic election, and then in Isaianic rescue, came together in Israel's Messiah. This passage, of course, is designed to give comfort and assurance; but underneath that is Paul's revolutionary theology of incarnation. When we join that up with the pneumatology earlier in Romans 8, the whole chapter offers itself as one of the greatest expositions of Trinitarian thought from any point of Christian history. Like all true Trinitarian theology it takes the form, not of cold theory, but of gratitude and allegiance, of faith, and hope, and answering love. It is a shout of praise, a song of joy.

So we can at last walk through these verses and see how they work. Paul lists in verse 35b the physical dangers and threats that he himself had met – or, in the case of the sword, was expecting to meet – and which his hearers might well be going to face soon, if they were not doing so already. Paul's repetition of the single-letter Greek word *ē*, which we normally translate as 'or', gives the list an extra audible punch which English translations, with a repeated 'or', can't easily catch: *thlipsis ē stenochōria ē diogmos ē limos ē gymnotēs ē kindynos ē machaira.* 'Suffering, or hardship, or persecution, or famine, or nakedness, or danger, or sword': that's quite a list, even in the less shrill English.

The first two items, 'suffering' and 'hardship', are broad terms. The first indicates physical pain, the second social and cultural challenges such as loss of job or home. Then there is persecution. Paul had experienced plenty of it, and he could now see it coming a mile off, heading for the community in Rome. Famine, the next item, happened in Paul's world from time to time, as in the mid 40s when Paul was in Antioch, or slightly later when he was writing to Corinth. We comfortable westerners have more or less never known real food shortages, though plenty of people in our world experience them all the time. All it takes is for something like a war to disrupt the normal supply lines, or for one or two vital harvests to fail. 'Nakedness', the next item on the list, is perhaps where one might end up after a shipwreck or public beating; that therefore probably goes with 'danger', as in 2 Corinthians 11 where Paul lists the multiple and often humiliating hazards of his remarkable travels. The Greek *machaira*, translated here as 'sword', refers to the short sword used for executions rather than the longer sword (the *xiphos*) used in military operations. Facing the 'sword' in this case means being killed, not randomly in battle but deliberately by the official executioner.

How then are such troubles to be interpreted? Many in Paul's day would have said, without hesitation, that they were signs that God, or the gods, were angry. You must have done something terribly wrong. People sometimes say that sort of thing today, citing the prophet Amos, and indeed Deuteronomy, to enable them to read off the sins that people must have committed from the bad things that are now happening to them. But Paul takes a different view. When in verse 36 he quotes Psalm 44.22 he is warding off and redirecting any suggestion that these troubles might be a sign of divine displeasure. On the contrary, declares the psalmist: 'All these things have come upon us, but we have *not* played you false or denied the covenant.' By this stage of Romans 8, we might have been tempted to treat the odd psalm-verse as a throwaway proof-text, but this is certainly not true here. As Paul indicated in verses 17 and 18, Israel, and now the followers of Jesus, are *sharing the sufferings of the Messiah*. The *heneken sou* in the verse he quotes here is vital: it is 'on your account'. It is 'because of you', says the psalmist boldly, with Paul now echoing him, that we find ourselves 'as sheep destined for slaughter'. Paul has chosen this text specifically because it insists that these sufferings, so far from being a sign of heaven-sent anger, are actually the outworking of the *purpose* which was sketched in 8.18–27.

What's more, this verse closely echoes the plight of the Servant as set out in the Septuagint of Isaiah. Psalm 44.22, quoted here, says that we have been accounted *hōs probata sphagēs*, 'as sheep of slaughter'. If we look across to Isaiah 53.7, we find the Servant being led like a lamb to the slaughter (*hōs probaton epi sphagēn*). The sufferings to which Paul has referred are therefore to be seen as *the messianic afflictions*. They are not just 'nasty things to get through'. As in 8.17–18, they are part of the redemptive vocations to be embraced, so that the love of the Messiah and the prayer of the spirit may be made known in the dark places of the earth. This is where the wounds of Jesus meet the wounds of the world. Easy-going preaching and teaching sometimes lull Christians into supposing that we can avoid being caught up in this, but it is what Jesus himself said would happen to those who decided to follow him.

Paul's use here of the word 'regarded', or as it's sometimes translated 'reckoned', to anyone who knows Romans, will resonate with Romans 4 and 6: 'reckoned as righteous' by faith, 'reckoned to have died and been raised' in baptism with the Messiah. Now those 'in the Messiah' are 'reckoned as sheep destined for slaughter'. Part of God's declaration in justification and in baptism includes the declaration that we will be sheep for slaughter.

But the darkness, the groaning, does not have the last word. Verse 37 begins, as we noted, with *alla*, 'but' – in other words, don't let all that stuff dominate your horizon! *In all these things* we are super-conquerors, *hypernikōmen*. In a military context, this word could describe a victory that was not just the usual kind, not just an ordinary victory, but one where the enemy has been completely wiped out. I suspect that Paul means, not just that the Christian can 'rise above it', but that through this participation in the Servant-work, in the messianic sufferings, we are called not just to 'come through all right in the end' but to be the means by which the pain and anger of the world may itself be exhausted and overcome. That is what our own darkness, struggles and inarticulate but prayerful groanings will have been all about. After all, Jesus didn't just conquer his sufferings by holding out and praying for his torturers. He conquered death itself by dying as his supreme act of love. We are called to be super-conquerors 'through the one who loved us'.

This way of putting it appears parallel to Philippians 4.13, 'I have strength for everything *en tō endynamounti me*, 'in the one who gives me power'. The Messiah's *power* in Philippi; the Messiah's *love* in Rome. Strength to cope as it's going on; love, ready to go prayerfully to the dark places, to bring God's light and healing right there.

The reason for this extraordinary analysis, and for this extraordinary confidence in how it works out, is given with the *gar* in verse 38, *pepeismai gar*, 'for I am persuaded'. As my American friends say, Paul has 'done the math'. He has figured it out. Having listed seven possible attacks or disasters in verse 35, he now lists ten sources from which such attacks might come; and he declares that none of them can come between the believer and the love of God in Messiah Jesus.

This list of ten is arranged mostly in pairs, with one odd one out, namely the word 'powers', which is then balanced by the final catch-all phrase, 'any other creature'. The first three pairs are 'death and life'; 'angels and rulers'; 'present and future'. Then Paul inserts 'powers', after which there is one more pair, 'height and depth', and then the final flourish, 'any other creature'. All together, this is the cosmic equivalent of saying 'north, south, east, west'. Paul is, as it were, covering the bases.

So what do these mean? 'Death and life' are the two basic states we might be in, and the mysterious powers of death and life that stand behind them. Angels and rulers are the actual powers of heaven and earth. Present and future are the two time zones we face; God has already dealt with the past on the cross, but the present is dangerous and the future is uncertain. 'Powers' might be any other forces left over after 'angels and rulers'. 'Height and depth' probably indicate the cosmic reach, the highest and lowest degrees that a star or planet can attain, from which they might exercise malign influence.

Part of Paul's point – and this seems to be indicated by 'any other creature' – is that these are indeed all *creatures*, part of the world *made by* God; whereas the gospel is about the incarnate love *of the creator himself*. It is of course possible that these elements of creation, in themselves or as they might be taken over and used by powers darker than themselves, might indeed try to separate us from the divine and messianic love, now or hereafter. That is part of the 'groaning of creation', the out-of-jointness of God's good creation which is part of the long entail of human idolatry and injustice (Romans 1.18). Romans 8, speaking in verses 19–25 of creation being rescued from its slavery to decay, contingent upon God's people being raised from the dead, provides the ultimate answer to that problem, and therefore also to any intermediate problems that might arise from the 'creatures' as they still are.

Paul has himself experienced the ways in which the powers of the present age try to separate us from God's love. We think particularly of the trouble he suffered at Ephesus, to which he alludes in 2 Corinthians 1. But if that's what these forces are trying to do, they will fail. Nothing can or will separate us from that love. We for whom human love routinely involves separation – for travel, work and ultimately in death itself – may find it hard to imagine a love that gives assurance of eternal unbreakability. But that is what the gospel provides.

We perhaps need to stress, as we draw together the threads of Paul's argument, that he is persuaded of all this, and we must be too, because of *the resurrection of the crucified son of God.* Some have tried to make everything depend on the cross. This was partly because an older liberalism didn't want to have the resurrection in the picture. It was also, I fear, because some preachers and teachers had a kind of tunnel-vision focus on a particular doctrine of atonement, for which the resurrection sometimes seemed barely necessary. But, as we've seen, it is the resurrection which declares that the cross was a victory – indeed, *the* victory. It is the resurrection in which the creator God declared publicly that the crucified and risen Jesus really was his son, Israel's Messiah and the world's lord.

That, after all, was where the letter had begun (1.3–5). It's good to think of that large sweep of thought as we arrive at the end of chapter 8, the half-way point for the epistle and the conclusion of its deepest argument. The letter's opening announces the gospel of God, disclosing at last (1.16–17) the covenant faithfulness of God, which is why the gospel is God's power for salvation. That then opens up the main argument of the letter. Humans have failed, through idolatry and injustice, in their vocation to be image-bearers, God-reflectors within creation (1.18—2.16). Israel, too, has failed, as the prophets continually pointed out (2.17–29), leaving all humankind in the dock with nothing to say in their own defence (3.10–20). But God remained faithful (3.1–9), coming in the person of the Messiah as the one faithful Israelite, to offer to God the obedience which was Israel's vocation but in which, as scripture had testified, Israel had failed. The result is the creation, through the gospel, of the single Jew-plus-gentile family of forgiven sinners, marked out by the faith that resonates with Jesus' own faithfulness. God has declared, on the basis of Jesus' death, that they are already in the right; their sins have been dealt with; they are part of the Abrahamic family (3.21—4.25).

Thus in 5—8, Paul can spread out the map of God's purposes. The two halves of chapter 5 (verses 1–11; 12–21) provide an advance overview of where his argument is heading. Chapters 6—8 retell the story of the exodus, in terms, now, of the new exodus accomplished by God through Jesus and the spirit. Chapter 8 comes back in full circle to the introduction in 5.1–11. Justification leads to glory, marking out the path of suffering and hope, sustained by the spirit-given love of God (5.1–5, pointing to 8.1–30); this is itself rooted in God's action of utter self-giving love in the Messiah (5.6–11, pointing to 8.31–9). That is where this first half of Romans now concludes.

The victorious covenant love of God is, then, far more than a religious feeling or a generalized 'sense of the transcendent', or any of the similar things that fuzzy-thinking preachers sometimes say. When Paul speaks of 'assurance', of 'being persuaded', he isn't suggesting that, in order to believe it, you have to shut one eye and ignore uncomfortable realities. It isn't that he has, as it were, talked himself into conviction, and is now going to pretend forever afterwards that everything is fine when it obviously isn't. His conviction, his persuasion, his assurance, all follow from the central 'good news' event of Easter itself. If God really did raise Jesus the Messiah from the dead . . . then everything follows.

I heard that point splendidly articulated in a surprising setting a few years ago. We began our journey through Romans 8 by thinking of Romans as a great city, and ourselves as the taxi-drivers needing to learn our way around it. One such real-life taxi-driver was taking me to catch a train in London. I had come from a church meeting and was still wearing my dog collar. The driver, a cheerful soul, looked at me, sized me up, and asked me about one of the contentious debates the church was having. Then he put his finger on the ultimate reality. 'What I always say,' he said, 'is this: *If God raised Jesus Christ from the dead, then everything else is just rock 'n' roll – i'n'it?'* That is Paul's doctrine of assurance in a nutshell. *Nothing else in all creation can separate us from God's love in the Messiah, Jesus our Lord.*

Appendix 1

Roman-Inaugurated Eschatology: The Return of the Golden Age (the Age of Saturn)

Virgil, *Eclogue* 4.11–41 (p. 51)

But for you, child, the earth untilled will pour forth its first pretty gifts . . . unbidden it will pour forth for you a cradle of smiling flowers. Unbidden, the goats will bring home their udders swollen with milk, and the cattle will not fear huge lions. The serpent, too, will perish, and perish will the plant that hides its poison . . . Earth will not suffer the harrow, nor the vine the pruning-hook; the sturdy ploughman, too, will now loose his oxen from the yoke.

Virgil, *Aeneid* 6.789–94 (p. 589)

And this in truth is he whom you so often hear promised you, Augustus Caesar, son of a god, who will again establish a Golden Age in Latium amid fields once ruled by Saturn. He will advance his empire . . . to a land which lies beyond our stars, beyond the path of year and sun.

Calpurnius Siculus, *Eclogue* 1.33–99

Rejoice, O my people . . . The golden age of untroubled peace is born again . . . the happy times are ruled by a youth [i.e. Nero] who won the victory while still in his mother's arms. When he shall himself reign as a god . . . Peace will appear . . . and mercy has broken in pieces the weapons of madness. Full peace will come upon us, a peace that shall bring back a second reign of Saturn.

Sources

Minor Latin Poets, vol. 1, trans. by J. W. Duff and A. M. Duff, Loeb Classical Library (Cambridge, MA: Harvard University Press, 1968)

Virgil, *Eclogues; Georgics; Aeneid I–VI*, trans. by H. R. Fairclough, rev. by G. P. Goold, Loeb Classical Library (Cambridge, MA: Harvard University Press, 1999)

Appendix 2
Hebrew Eschatology: The Messianic Age and/or the Coming of God's Glory

Isaiah 11.1–10

There shall come out a shoot from the stock of Jesse, and a branch shall grow out of his roots. The spirit of YHWH shall rest on him . . . the wolf shall live with the lamb, the leopard shall lie down with the kid, the calf and the lion and the fatling together . . . They will not hurt or destroy on all my holy mountain; for the earth will be full of the knowledge of YHWH as the waters cover the sea. On that day the root of Jesse shall stand as a signal to the peoples [LXX *ho anistamenos archein ethnōn*, as in Romans 15.12]; the nations shall enquire of him, and **his dwelling shall be glory** [MT *kabod*; LXX *timē*].

Isaiah 35.1–6

The wilderness and the dry land shall be glad . . . they shall see **the glory of YHWH**, the majesty of our God. Strengthen the weak hands, and make firm the feeble knees. Say to those who are of a fearful heart, Be strong, do not fear! **Here is your God.** He will come with vengeance, with terrible recompense. He will come and save you. Then shall the eyes of the blind be opened.

Isaiah 40.4–5, 10

Every valley shall be lifted up, and every mountain and hill be made low . . . Then **the glory of YHWH** shall be revealed, and all people shall see it together, for the mouth of YHWH has spoken . . . See, the Lord YHWH comes with might, and his arm rules for him; his reward is with him, and his recompense before him.

Isaiah 60.1–3, 19

Arise, shine, for your light has come, and **the glory of YHWH** has risen upon you. For darkness shall cover the earth, and thick darkness the peoples; but YHWH will arise upon you, and **his glory will appear over you.** Nations shall come to your light, and kings to the brightness of your dawn . . . The sun shall no longer be your light by day, nor for brightness shall the moon give light to you by night; but YHWH will be your everlasting light, and **your God will be your glory.**

[See too e.g. Psalms 96; 98; Isaiah 2.2–4; 55.1–13; Micah 4.1–5 (the renewal of creation); Psalm 72 (renewal of world under the true, justice-bringing king); Ezekiel 43 (the divine **glory** returns to the temple).]

Psalm 8.1, 4–6

O YHWH, our Sovereign, how majestic is your name in all the earth! . . . What are human beings that you are mindful of them, 'the son of man' that you care for him? You have made them a little lower than God [or: angels], and crowned them with **glory** and honour [LXX *doxa kai timē*]. You have given them dominion over the works of your hands; you have put all things under their feet.

[See further 1 Corinthians 15.27; Ephesians 1.22; Philippians 3.21; closely linked by Paul with Psalm 110.1; Daniel 7.27.]

Bibliography

1 Works Mentioned in the Text

P. Brown, *The Ransom of the Soul: Afterlife and Wealth in Early Western Christianity* (Cambridge, MA: Harvard University Press, 2015)

H. G. Jacob, *Conformed to the Image of His Son* (Downers Grove, IL: IVP Academic, 2018)

S. Keesmaat and B. Walsh, *Romans Disarmed* (Grand Rapids, MI: Brazos Press, 2019)

C. Kugler, *Paul and the Image of God* (Lanham, MD: Lexington Books/Fortress Academic, 2020)

C. C. Newman, *Paul's Glory-Christology: Tradition and Rhetoric* (Leiden: Brill, 1992)

C. Tilling, *Paul's Divine Christology*, 2nd edn (Grand Rapids, MI: Eerdmans, 2015 [2012])

2 Relevant Works by N. T. Wright

2021 *Galatians*, Christian Formation Commentaries (Grand Rapids, MI: Eerdmans)

2020 *Interpreting Paul: Essays on the Apostle and His Letters* (London: SPCK; Grand Rapids, MI: Zondervan)

2019 *History and Eschatology: Jesus and the Promise of Natural Theology* (*HE*), Gifford Lectures 2018 (Waco, TX: Baylor University Press; London: SPCK)

2018 *Paul: A Biography* (San Francisco, CA: HarperOne; London: SPCK)

2016 *The Day the Revolution Began: Reconsidering the Meaning of Jesus' Crucifixion* (*DRB*) (San Francisco, CA: HarperOne; London: SPCK)

Bibliography

2015 *Paul and His Recent Interpreters* (*PRI*) (London: SPCK; Minneapolis, MN: Fortress)

2013 *Paul and the Faithfulness of God* (*PFG*), Christian Origins and the Question of God 4 (London: SPCK; Minneapolis, MN: Fortress)

2013 *Pauline Perspectives* (London: SPCK; Minneapolis, MN: Fortress)

2007 *Surprised by Hope* (*SH*) (London: SPCK; San Francisco, CA: HarperOne [US edn, 2008, subtitle *Rethinking Heaven, Resurrection and the Mission of the Church*])

2005 *Paul: Fresh Perspectives* (London: SPCK; Minneapolis, MN: Fortress [US edn, title *Paul in Fresh Perspective*])

2004 *Paul for Everyone: Romans*, 2 vols (London: SPCK; Louisville, KY: Westminster John Knox)

2003 *The Resurrection of the Son of God* (*RSG*), Christian Origins and the Question of God 3 (London: SPCK; Minneapolis, MN: Fortress)

2002 'Romans', in the *New Interpreter's Bible*, ed. by L. E. Keck et al. (Nashville, TN: Abingdon), vol. X, pp. 393–770

1991 *The Climax of the Covenant: Christ and the Law in Pauline Theology* (*CC*) (Edinburgh: T&T Clark; Minneapolis, MN: Fortress [US edn, 1992])

Index of Ancient Sources and Biblical References

Note: References to Romans 8 have not been included.

Index of Ancient Sources and Biblical References

49.3 *163*
50 *186, 189, 196*
50.4–9 *196*
50.8 *183*
51.2 *196*
51.3 *197*
52 *19, 77, 122*
53 *19, 212*
53.7 *216*
54 *19*
54.10 *73*
55 *19*
55.1–13 *226*
55.3 *170*
60.1–3 *226*
60.19 *226*
63.7–14 *99*

Jeremiah
1.5 *169*

Ezekiel
34.25 *73*
37.26 *73*
40.1 *40*
43 *226*

Daniel
7 *120, 122, 175,
  192, 193, 194*
7.27 *226*
9 *40, 137*
9.24 *118*

Hosea
5.3 *169*
13.5 *169*

Amos
3.2 *169*

Micah
4.1–5 *226*

Habakkuk
2 *98*

Haggai
2.5 *99*

Malachi
2.5 *73* ·

DEUTEROCANONICAL
  BOOKS

**Wisdom of
  Solomon**
1.7 *140*
9 *54*

OLD TESTAMENT
PSEUDEPIGRAPHA

1 Enoch *145*

4 Ezra *145*

DEAD SEA SCROLLS

Dead Sea Scrolls
  99, 122

NEW TESTAMENT

Matthew
23.21 *76*
26.36–46 *101*
26.39 *106*
28 *124, 195*
28.18 *192*

Mark
1.11 *175*
7.17–23 *103*
8 *101*
8.29 *175*
9.7 *175*
10 *46*
10.35–45 *167*
14.32–42 *101*
14.36 *106*
14.61 *175*
14.62 *192*

Luke
1 *137*
10.40 *149*
15 *84*
23.46 *82*
24 *43, 71, 101*

John
3.8 *1*
3.16 *29*
7.39 *49, 65*
8.1–11 *190*
12.31–2 *65*
13.1 *213*
16 *145*
16.33 *65*
19.30 *82*
20.22 *49, 65*
21 *140*

Acts
1—2 *77*
3.17 *60*
3.21 *128*
7.55–6 *194*
7.59 *82*

Romans
1—4 *13, 188*
1—8 *22*
1.1–5 *172*
1.2 *6*
1.3 *54*
1.3–4 *147, 171*
1.3–5 *16, 219*
1.4 *55*
1.15–17 *211*
1.16 *196*
1.16–17 *13, 81,
  219*
1.17 *80*
1.18 *218*
1.18—2.16 *219*
1.32 *60*
2 *11*
2—5 *56*
2.1–16 *189*
2.7 *15*
2.7–10 *25*
2.10 *15, 122*
2.17–29 *219*
2.25–9 *81*
3 *2*
3.1–9 *219*
3.10–20 *219*
3.21—4.25 *21, 220*
3.23 *2*
3.24–6 *190*
3.25 *59*
3.31 *42*
4 *82, 187, 216*
4.13 *16, 21, 65,
  94, 187*
4.19–22 *66*
4.24 *82*
5 *15, 54–5, 58,
  121, 149, 170,
  171, 193*

Index of Ancient Sources and Biblical References